WINNING THE BATTLE, LOSING THE WAR

Winning the Battle, Losing the War:

Addressing the Drivers Fueling Armed Non-State Actors and Extremist Groups

Charles Lister, Paul Salem, eds.

 Middle East Institute

THE MIDDLE EAST INSTITUTE
1763 N STREET NW
WASHINGTON, D.C. 20036

Follow MEI:

 @MiddleEastInst

 /MiddleEastInstitute

Cover photo: A fighter of the militant group Hayat Tahrir al-Sham holds his weapon at the front lines of the armed opposition overlooking the Syrian government-held city of Aleppo. (*Photo by Anas Alkharboutli/ picture alliance via Getty Images*)

CONTENTS

INTRODUCTION   x
CHARLES LISTER AND PAUL SALEM

1. THE RISE OF VIOLENT TRANSNATIONAL MOVEMENTS IN THE MIDDLE EAST: 1
HISTORICAL CONTEXT, DYNAMIC DRIVERS, AND POLICY TAKEAWAYS
PAUL SALEM

2. AL-QAEDA VERSUS ISIS: 22
COMPETING JIHADIST BRANDS IN THE MIDDLE EAST
CHARLES LISTER

3. JIHADIST PROPAGANDA, OFFLINE: 42
STRATEGIC COMMUNICATIONS IN MODERN WARFARE
CHARLIE WINTER, HAID HAID

4. THE PRIMACY OF PRAXIS: 56
CLERICAL AUTHORITY IN THE SYRIAN CONFLICT
SHIRAZ MAHER

5. OUT OF THE DESERT: 70
ISIS's STRATEGY FOR A LONG WAR
HASSAN HASSAN

6. CONTEMPORARY JIHADI MILITANCY IN YEMEN: 90
HOW IS THE THREAT EVOLVING?
ELISABETH KENDALL

7. LIBYA's TERRORISM CHALLENGE: 114
ASSESSING THE SALAFI-JIHADI THREAT
LYDIA SIZER

8. IRAN'S USE OF SHI'I MILITANT PROXIES: 138
IDEOLOGICAL AND PRACTICAL EXPEDIENCY
VERSUS UNCERTAIN SUSTAINABILITY
ALEX VATANKA

9. HEZBOLLAH'S EVOLUTION: 159
FROM LEBANESE MILITIA TO REGIONAL PLAYER
NICHOLAS BLANFORD

10. IRAQ's FIFTH COLUMN: 180
IRAN's PROXY NETWORK
NICHOLAS A. HERAS

11. THE FATEMIYOUN DIVISION: 194
AFGHAN FIGHTERS IN THE SYRIAN CIVIL WAR
TOBIAS SCHNEIDER

12. TERRORISM AND HUMAN RIGHTS: 207
THE PERSPECTIVE OF INTERNATIONAL LAW
DAVID P. STEWART

13. POSTSCRIPT   228
CHARLES LISTER, PAUL SALEM

CONTRIBUTORS

PAUL SALEM
Paul Salem is the president of the Middle East Institute.

CHARLES LISTER
Charles Lister is a senior fellow at the Middle East Institute and the director of its Countering Terrorism and Extremism Program.

CHARLIE WINTER
Charlie Winter is a senior research fellow at the International Centre for the Study of Radicalisation at King's College London.

HAID HAID
Haid Haid is a Syrian columnist and a research fellow at the International Centre for the Study of Radicalisation at King's College London.

SHIRAZ MAHER
Dr. Shiraz Maher is Director of the International Centre for the Study of Radicalisation at King's College London.

HASSAN HASSAN
Hassan Hassan is a senior fellow at the Tahrir Institute for Middle East Policy.

ELISABETH KENDALL
Elisabeth Kendall is a senior research fellow in Arabic and Islamic Studies at Pembroke College, Oxford University.

LYDIA SIZER
Lydia Sizer is an independent consultant covering North Africa and the Gulf.

ALEX VATANKA
Alex Vatanka is a senior fellow at the Middle East Institute.

NICHOLAS BLANFORD
Nicholas Blanford has been a correspondent for *The Christian Science Monitor* since 2002.

NICHOLAS A. HERAS
Nicholas A. Heras is a fellow at the Center for a New American Security and a resident in the Middle East Security Program. He is also a senior analyst at the Jamestown Foundation.

Tobias Schneider

Tobias Schneider is a research fellow at the Global Public Policy Institute in Berlin and an editor of the weekly policy newsletter "Syria in Context."

David P. Stewart

David P. Stewart is a professor from practice at Georgetown University Law Center. He also directs the Center on Transnational Business and the Law and co-directs the Global Law Scholars Program.

ACKNOWLEDGEMENTS

The production of this book and its contents was a collaborative effort, benefiting from the hard work of many within and outside the Middle East Institute. We would first like to thank Alistair Taylor, editorial director at MEI, for his exceptional work pulling together research papers and turning them into polished chapters for this book. Sincere thanks must also be directed to Antoun Issa, Lillian Judge, Emily Mulder, and Alika Zangieva who spent considerable time editing content for publication. We also want to thank MEI interns Lina Rafaat, Evan McKay, and Kelly Baker, who provided invaluable research support during what has been more than two years of work.

We also express our sincere gratitude to all the contributing authors whose scholarship and subject-matter expertise underpins the real value of this volume, and who made the project a truly rewarding experience.

And finally, MEI would like to thank the Carnegie Corporation of New York whose generous support made this work possible.

This book is dedicated to the many victims of violent extremism, and to those who continue to stand against the threat and will continue to do so, until a more peaceful reality is established.

INTRODUCTION

CHARLES LISTER AND PAUL SALEM

It is not easy to situate a new volume on extremism and terrorism amid the sea of publications that already inundate the reader. Indeed, before the events of September 11, 2001, the body of research on the dynamics and drivers of extremist and terrorist groups was quite limited. Today "there is more information on terrorism in print than even the most dedicated and eager scholar could read in an entire lifetime." And the field remains very interdisciplinary, attracting contributions from political scientists, psychologists, security experts, area specialists, counter terrorism combatants, and even former terrorists themselves. A core of researchers like Bruce Hoffman, Brian Jenkins, Martha Crenshaw, Andrew Silke, David Rapoport, Paul Wilkinson, and others "have provided a steadfast presence within terrorism studies that is dedicated to the empirical and nonpartisan pursuit of data-driven findings."

The present volume limits itself to examining a particular set of violent transnational movements in today's Middle East. In particular, it focuses on the armed Islamist groups, both Sunni and Shi'i, that have come to dominate much of the landscape of the Middle East; it leaves for another volume valuable research that could be done on non-Islamist violent movements like the Kurdistan Workers' Party (PKK) and other ethnic, nationalist, and tribal armed groups. Among the armed Islamist groups, some of them are widely considered, by broad international consensus, to be terrorist groups, like ISIS and al-Qaeda; the categorization of others, like Hezbollah and a plethora of other Shi'i and Sunni militias, depends on what side of political and sectarian divides the categorizer stands.

This partly reflects the problem with the definition of terrorism and the concept of "terrorist group" itself. While some lone wolves might be attracted to terrorism as a nihilistic orgy of violence that can be a suicidal end in itself, most organized groups use terrorism quite purposefully as a means to achieve particular political ends. The Irish Republican Army used terrorism to drive out British rule, the Tamil Tigers sought Tamil independence, the Zionist Irgun movement sought to create a Jewish state, the Palestinian Fatah movement sought to create a Palestinian one, the PKK seeks Kurdish independence, Hezbollah seeks to counter Israel and maintain a strong Iranian alliance system in the Levant, and even al-Qaeda and ISIS have fairly well defined political goals, even if most people disagree with both their goals and their methods.

Indeed, the predominant problem in the Middle East is not that of lone wolves or small sleeper cells, as it is in the West, although those too exist in the Middle East. Rather, it is that entire swathes of territory have been taken over by radical armed actors that are not representing a small group of marginalized and alienated individuals, but rather drawing in tens of thousands to fight out some of the major political issues relating to the nature of the nation and the state, the role of religion, the presence of foreign forces, and the outcomes of civil wars. Armed non-state actors are not the rarity that they are in other regions of the world; in many parts of the Middle East, they have become a main form of political and security organization.

In this volume we bring together a distinguished group of experts to examine the drivers and dynamics that have given rise to this wide array of religious and sectarian-based armed and violent transnational movements. The volume begins with a historical and analytical overview, and then proceeds to examine the Sunni Salafist groups in one set of chapters, followed by examination of the Shi'i groups in another set. The volume ends with a chapter examining the international and human rights elements of the topic at hand, and a final chapter harvesting policy recommendations from the preceding work.

In the first chapter, entitled "The Rise of Violent Transnational Movements in the Middle East: Historical Context, Dynamic Drivers, and Policy Takeaways," Paul Salem explores the underlying conditions that have given rise to the prevalence of terrorist insurgencies across the region. Salem argues that violent transnational movements flourish within failing and broken states and that a web of political, socio-economic, and cultural contradictions across the modern Arab world have given rise to a "breeding ground" for radical movements. At its core, Salem's chapter suggests that many national governments have failed to convince populations of their legitimacy and have struggled to sustain any socio-political contract with the citizens, thus leaving them disenfranchised and vulnerable to alternative, often extremist narratives.

In the second chapter, Charles Lister explores the increasing prevalence and consequences of intra-jihadi competition. In his paper, entitled "Al-Qaeda Versus ISIS: Competing Jihadist Brands in the Middle East," Lister posits that rather than being a threat, the eruption of pro-democracy protests across the region in 2010 and 2011 presented the likes of al-Qaeda and ISIS with an invaluable opportunity for growth. Despite sharing the same ultimate objective though, the two jihadi movements adopted markedly different strategies in exploiting the so-called Arab Spring and in so doing, they became equally engaged in a state of competition to better the other's success and to differentiate from the other's actions and image. While al-Qaeda sought to ingratiate themselves with local populations by softening some of its traditionally hardest traits, ISIS escalated its violence and sought to spectacularly change the status quo in a rapid and chaotic fashion. Lister claims that both strategies presented short- and long-term advantages and disadvantages, with neither necessarily triumphing over the other. So long as the Middle East remains in a state of tension and conflict, both groups would remain ever-present threats.

In the third chapter, entitled "Jihadist Propaganda, Offline: Strategic Communications in Modern Warfare," co-authors Charlie Winter and Haid Haid compare and contrast the in-theater outreach strategies of ISIS and Hayat Tahrir al-Sham (HTS) in Syria. By using a qualitative mixed-methods approach, incorporating semi-structured interviews with activists and journalists operating inside Syria and in-depth longitudinal content analysis, Winter and Haid demonstrate that insurgency strategic communications have rarely posed as great a threat to local, regional, and international security as they do today in Syria. Despite ISIS and HTS maintaining markedly similar ideological foundations, they display substantial tactical and strategic disparities in their respective approaches toward public diplomacy. By determining those disparities, Winter and Haid write, one gains a more accurate understanding of what drives the enmity between the two groups and how they present differing challenges and threats.

In the fourth chapter, entitled "The Primacy of Praxis: Competing Claims of Authority in the Syrian Crisis," Shiraz Maher analyzes how the war in Syria has experienced multiple overlapping phases of religious ideological influence. Maher argues that the early period of the Syrian crisis saw local, indigenous Syrian clerics imposing strict military law codes upon the fledgling armed opposition, frequently codifying their rules of engagement. With time, however, these clerics often found themselves exiled, thus degrading their influence with actors on the ground, who over time turned to more conservative Salafist clerics based in the Gulf, contributing to an internationalization of the conflict. That second phase, Maher argues, paved the path toward the third, in which transnational and often millenarian jihadist movements like ISIS and al-Qaeda exploited Syria for their more extreme, global causes. At its core, Maher's paper seeks to explain how clerical authority in the context of Syria's crisis has been derived from praxis — or action — rather than through "theoretical abstraction" and theology.

In the fifth chapter, Hassan Hassan looks at the future prospects of ISIS following its territorial defeat at the hands of the U.S.-led global coalition in Syria and Iraq. In his paper entitled "Out of the Desert: ISIS's Strategy for a Long War," Hassan underlines that far from being defeated, ISIS planned in advance for its territorial losses and the group will remain a potent "post-caliphate" force within the "soft underbelly" desert region spanning between eastern Syria and western Iraq. Rural insurgency, Hassan argues is at least as important as urban warfare for ISIS, which looks set to focus on a three-part formula for long-term survival: Operating within the "*Sahraa,*" or desert; confronting the "*Sahwat,*" or Sunni opponents; and undertaking "*Sawlat,*" or hit-and-run operations. Far from being an organic or unpredictable strategy, Hassan reveals how ISIS itself has advertised its strategy for survival in public since at least May 2017 and that even older historical ISIS documents from 2009 reveal a close consistency with contemporary ISIS strategic thinking.

In the sixth chapter, Dr. Elisabeth Kendall gives a detailed look at "Contemporary Jihadi Militancy in Yemen: How is the Threat Evolving?" Having suffered from intense conflict, chaos, and state breakdown, Yemen has seen a revived threat from al-Qaeda in the Arabian Peninsula (AQAP) and the emergence of a new terrorist threat from ISIS in Yemen (ISY). While ISY has not controlled territory, it has sought to use selective, brutal violence to assert its presence, while conversely, AQAP has governed over territory and populations and in so doing, has refined its strategy to encompass more effective methods of local engagement. The paper analyzes the individual factors that have fed the emergence of both groups in Yemen and makes use of on-the-ground fieldwork and multiple sources of data to examine the challenges and pressures that have, in Dr. Kendall's estimation, catalyzed both groups' declines in fortune.

In the seventh, chapter, entitled "Libya's Terrorism Challenge: Assessing the Salafi-Jihadi Threat," Lydia Sizer reviews the state of jihadist groups linked to al-Qaeda and ISIS across Libya, framing their active presence there as being the result of many factors, but most particularly a rife security vacuum. Historically, Sizer notes, push factors in Libya such as declining standards of living, the marginalization of minorities and a frequently pervasive sense of victimhood among portions of the population have all provided the foundations for a durable jihadist presence and threat. Added to that are pull factors, such as the offer of status, income, and services that jihadist groups have typically offered to prospective recruits and civilian communities. Although al-Qaeda-linked groups and ISIS hold differing objectives in Libya, Sizer also notes that they both focus on achieving some extent of territorial control and influence, and at times, they have even collaborated. So long as Libya remains riven by civil unrest and internal political strife, Salafi-jihadi movements will continue to exist and pose internal and external threats.

The eighth chapter shifts to looking at the Shi'i armed movements in the region. In this chapter, Alex Vatanka provides a detailed analysis of "Iran's Use of Shi'i Militant Proxies: Ideological and Practical Expediency Versus Uncertain Sustainability." According to Vatanka, Iran has built up armed, radical, and often sectarian non-state groups across the Middle East since its 1979 revolution. The groups, collectively framed as individual components of Iran's region-wide "proxy model," have pursued locally-specific objectives within the broader strategic framework of Iranian revolutionary foreign policy. By comparing regional conflicts past and present that have been shaped in part by Iranian proxies, Vatanka argues that this "proxy model" became particularly prevalent following the 2003 U.S.-led invasion of Iraq and that in more recent years, the conflicts in Syria and Iraq have seen non-state proxies become the "primary tool" of Iranian regional interests.

The ninth chapter of this volume was written by Nicholas Blanford, who explores "Hezbollah's Evolution: From Lebanese Militia to Regional Player." Having started out as a Shi'a militia specific to Lebanese political dynamics, Hezbollah has changed substantially over the past decade, Blanford argues, expanding its influence throughout Lebanon and substantial swathes of the Middle East. The movement now commands tens of thousands of well-trained fighters and dominates the Lebanese political system, having enjoyed particular benefit from its intervention in defense of President Bashar al-Assad in Syria and its assistance to Iran-backed efforts to combat ISIS in Iraq. Hezbollah's heightened status and its role in Syria have increased the risk of conflict with Israel, but the two actors maintain a state of mutual deterrence that may ensure conflict remains abated for now, Blanford asserts. Though the United States has positioned itself in an increasingly adversarial position toward Iran and its partners like Hezbollah, Blanford suggests that options to push back on Hezbollah are minimal.

The tenth chapter, written by Nicholas A. Heras and entitled, "Iraq's Fifth Column: Iran's Proxy Network," provides a deep-dive into Iran's attempts to build, foster, and control a nexus of Shi'a militias in Iraq, under the guise of the Popular Mobilization Units (PMUs). Run by Iran's Islamic Revolutionary Guard Corps (IRGC), this strategy, Heras claims, has resulted in Tehran exerting control over 40 of an estimated 67 PMU militias across Iraq, most prominently including the Badr Organization, Asa'ib Ahl al-Haq, and Kataib Hezbollah. The emergence of the PMUs as an anti-ISIS umbrella force in 2014 may have been a relatively recent development, but Iran's proxy strategy is far more deeply established, and many of the PMU's most influential figures were part of Iran's regional Islamic Resistance in the 1980s and 1990s, Heras argues. As ISIS is weakened, however, internal political differences within the PMU umbrella will emerge more clearly, Heras reminds us, and that interaction with Iraqi domestic politics will shape the extent to which PMU groups, and Iran's influence, transition from the military to the mass political realm.

The eleventh chapter, by Tobias Schneider, conducts an in-depth analysis of "The Fatemiyoun Division: Afghan Fighters in the Syrian Civil War." Though it has made its name as a Shi'a militia fighting in support of the Bashar al-Assad regime in Syria since 2012, Schneider reveals how the Fatemiyoun's roots can be traced back to the days of the Soviet occupation of Afghanistan (1979-1989) and then to the Iran-Iraq war (1980-1988), as Shi'a Muslim Afghan members of the Hazara ethnic minority volunteered to fight in defense of the revolutionary Iranian state and its activist regional foreign policy. Since its dramatic growth in Syria, the Fatemiyoun Division, according to Schneider, became "a fixture" of the Syrian battlefield, operating directly under Iranian leadership and holding frontlines on many of the war's most dangerous fronts. With the nature of the crisis in Syria shifting and the regime consolidating an inevitable victory, Schneider argues that the Fatemiyoun look set to translate military victories into the "cultural, ideological, and social front," both inside Syria and beyond.

In the penultimate chapter of the series, Professor David Stewart examines international law as a frame through which to comprehensively explore the relationship between terrorism and human rights. Entitled "Terrorism and Human Rights: The Perspective of International Law," Stewart's paper reviews the long-standing issues surrounding the definitions of "terrorism" and "human rights," making clear that despite many years of effort, no internationally-shared definition of terrorism exists. Stewart also posits that terrorism by itself appears to be both a cause and product of human rights violations, and that many such human rights violations can themselves be the result of actions labelled as "counter-terrorism." As a result, Stewart argues, the international legal system remains incomplete and often inconsistent and that repressive counter-terror action is demonstrably counter-productive.

In the concluding chapter, Lister and Salem draw from the preceding chapters to put forward a number of policy ideas and recommendations that would serve to counter these groups and address the conditions and drivers that sustain them.

Before concluding, we would like to thank the Carnegie Corporation of New York for its generous support to this research project; the team of authors who cooperated in this project; and the excellent team of editors and interns at the

Middle East Institute who helped shepherd this project every step of the way. The problem of violent transnational movements and terrorism will be with us for some time to come, both in the Middle East and globally. We hope that this volume makes a contribution to the growing body of knowledge about this scourge of our time, and contributes to policies that will help reduce its footprint, and eventually make it a thing of the past.

CHAPTER ONE

THE RISE OF VIOLENT TRANSNATIONAL MOVEMENTS IN THE MIDDLE EAST:

HISTORICAL CONTEXT, DYNAMIC DRIVERS, AND POLICY TAKEAWAYS

PAUL SALEM

INTRODUCTION[1]

Violent transnational movements (V.T.M.s) are not unique to the Middle East nor to this epoch in history, but it is fair to say that the contemporary Middle East hosts an exceptionally high concentration.[2] This essay will examine some of the historical dynamics and systemic conditions that have brought us to the point we are at today, and suggest a way forward. The complex conditions that enable and encourage the rise of V.T.M.s vary, both in levels and sectors. This includes the meta-level of international and regional order or disorder, the macro-level of states and their health or breakdown, the meso-level of subnational communities, and the micro-level of the individual.[3] Factors that enable or encourage V.T.M.s typically include an array of political, socio-economic, and ideological or cultural factors. Some are "push" factors that render individuals or groups susceptible to V.T.M. recruitment, others are pull factors that turn that susceptibility into a radicalized and mobilized reality.[4] While a wide range of pull and push factors, at various levels and from various sectors, can be identified as contributing to this phenomenon, no constellation of factors works in the same way across different contexts. What might produce a powerful V.T.M. in one place and time, might not in another context. Understanding the rise and fall of V.T.M.s remains more of an approximate practical art than a fixed science.

This chapter will be divided into three sections. In the first, I will examine key turning points in contemporary Middle Eastern history that might help explain why the rise of V.T.M.s has become so prevalent in this part of the world. In the second section, I will engage with the general literature about the factors and drivers that explain the rise of V.T.M.s, and look for particular angles and insights that might enable a keener understanding of this phenomenon in the Arab world. In the final section, I will suggest broad policy outlines that are consistent with the findings of the preceding two sections.

A NOTE ON THE TERMS AND CONCEPTS

This study examines the rise of V.T.M.s. By describing them as movements, we are acknowledging that these groups, radical as they are, define themselves as movements with fairly clearly defined political or ideological goals. Organized violence, war, civil war, even terrorism, is the continuation of politics by other means. Understanding the political logic and context of these movements is key to understanding how to weaken and defeat them. The transnational aspect of the largest and most dangerous of these groups indicates their complex relationship with the vulnerabilities and failures of the modern nation-state system in the Arab world. Some V.T.M.s contest the definition of a nation and the borders that make them, while others accept borders, but contest political orders — i.e. the nature and identity of the state, with some actors seeking to ethnically cleanse the space within their defined borders to conform to their desired order. All are at war with some aspect of the nation-state system that has precariously persisted over the past decades. The transnational label also implies, of course, that they are non-state actors; even if some are backed by states, and others claim to be states.

The descriptor "violent" indicates, first of all, that these are armed non-state actors violating the state's monopoly on the use of force. But it also suggests a more ambiguous implication: That they are excessive or particularly wanton in their use of force. All armed non-state actors instrumentalize violence in some manner. Some use it in a limited tactical way, while others use violence, and spectacular, deliberately excessive violence, as a strategy. But for none of the groups is violence an end in itself. It is a means — whether used extravagantly or parsimoniously — to achieve the broader political or socio-religious goal in pursuit.[5]

And this brings us to the analytically troublesome category of terrorist groups. No members of so-designated groups define themselves as "terrorists," and hence it is difficult to gain much analytical advantage from trying to understand these groups in these terms. Each is a distinct movement with fairly distinct political (in the broad sense) goals. Use of large-scale violence against civilians — in other words, terrorism — is one of the tools at their disposal, not an identity or an end in itself. In addition, while there is broad international agreement about some V.T.M.s being designated as terrorist groups — e.g. ISIS and al-Qaeda — there is significant disagreement about other V.T.M.s: Hezbollah or the Kurdistan Workers' Party (P.K.K.), for example.

Historical Contextualization of Enabling Conditions

As Bruce Hoffman writes in his seminal *Inside Terrorism*, it is important to understand the growth of terrorist groups and V.T.M.s within their historical context.[6] Hoffman does so in regard to the emergence of terrorism as a tool of politics from ancient times, through the French Revolution's La Terreur, the Anarchists that helped unleash World War I, all the way to the contemporary struggle with Islamic, neo-Nazi white supremacist, and other violent movements. Raymond Hinnebusch, in his study of the international politics of terrorism, also warns against the dangers of an ahistorical approach.[7] In the first part of this essay, I will examine various contributing factors to the rise of V.T.M.s in the Middle East within a historical lens. This is to gain a deeper understanding of the particular conditions and drivers that led to the emergence of these movements, and to appreciate the complexity of finding long-term responses to them.

Low Nation-State Legitimacy

The problem of V.T.M.s is posed primarily in contrast to a presumed Westphalian state system ideal: Sovereignty is to be concentrated in discreet nation-states, and violence is to be monopolized by the state, while transnational mobilization or use of force is to be forsworn.[8] The problem of low nation-state legitimacy started early in the Arab world, and the state system setup after the collapse of the Ottoman Empire in World War I came under attack in the ensuing decades from four separate ideological directions. Islamists decried the division of the *Umma*, the abolishing of the caliphate, and the establishment of states on a geographic, linguistic or ethnic basis. Arab nationalists welcomed the collapse of the old Islamic order, but decried the division of the Arab world into what they perceived as illegitimate mini-states, and fought for a united Arab nation. Anti-colonialists saw the illegitimacy of the new states in their subservience to colonial masters, and fought to overthrow them for that reason. Leftists and communists saw the new states as entrenching local landowner and capitalist elites in league with first world capitalism against the interests of the peasant and working classes.

State elites fought back with various attempts to boost state legitimacy. Some appealed to an ancient past — e.g. pharaonic in the case of Egypt, Phoenician in the case of Lebanon — to claim a nationalist basis for statehood. Appeal was also made to the trappings of constitutional monarchy, for example in Egypt, Iraq, and Jordan, in which local elites inherited a British model that marries the pomp and circumstance of monarchy with the electoral, parliamentary, and prime ministerial institutions of Westminster-style government. Lebanon, Syria, and Tunisia inherited a more straightforward republican model from the French whose legitimacy was tied directly to elections and democratic institutions.[9] Other countries, to varying degrees, used a combination of monarchy and religion as legitimating factors, with a wide variation between Morocco in the west, the Wahhabi-Saud alliance in the heart of the Arabian Peninsula, and various local tribal arrangements in the small Arab Gulf States.

But the Arab countries never arrived at one broad collective legitimizing principle. Egypt under Gamal Abd al-Nasser, and with the support of a wide array of Arab nationalists and leftists, sought to create a unified, or at least united, Arab order led by Egypt with anti-colonialist, Arab nationalist, and socialist principles as its overarching legitimizing narrative. This attempt was thwarted by conservative powers such as Saudi Arabia, and the Egyptian defeat in war with Israel in 1967.[10] The defeat undermined the idea of the Arab nation as capable of unified action and undermined the idea of the state as able to achieve national goals. The repercussions of the 1967 defeat gave legitimacy to armed non-state actors like the Palestine Liberation Organization (P.L.O.). It also undermined the secular Arab nationalist narrative in favor of the Islamist narrative that began to gain ground after 1967. Arab state legitimacy generally declined over the 1970s and 1980s as the sheen of anti-colonial victories won after World War II and the promise of state-led progress gave way to the realities of entrenched authoritarian systems and sluggish economic growth. Some authoritarian systems, like Hosni Mubarak's Egypt, made a few concessions to façade democracy to shore up their legitimacy, while other regimes like Saddam's Iraq or Bashar al-Assad's Syria doubled down on repression.

One can say that for a moment very early in the Arab uprisings in 2011, there was a glimmer of promise, or an illusion, that perhaps a pro-democracy movement might transform the region and become the new legitimizing principle, as it had swept Eastern Europe after the Cold War, or Latin America in previous decades. But that illusion soon faded, to be followed by a counter-illusion among Islamists that perhaps the Muslim Brotherhood would sweep elections in several key Arab countries, and with support from a then rising

Turkey, and Qatar, could bring about a new Muslim Brotherhood-dominated Islamist regional order.[11] This illusion also soon ran aground.

The Arab state system, in other words, has never had, in its century-long modern history, a consistent overarching legitimizing principle. Nor is there one today, with the new logic being that it is better to have authoritarian government than chaotic state collapse and civil war, which some attempts at democratization have wrought in the region.

The low levels of ideological legitimacy were compounded by generally poor performance on several key governance indicators. Public services declined as public resources failed to keep up with ballooning populations amid slow economic growth. As legitimacy declined, the levels of repression increased. Entrenched elites and economic liberalization led to growing economic inequalities and highly visible levels of corruption. And political party systems, in several countries, degenerated into family dynasties, further eroding legitimacy.[12]

The chronic low level of ideological legitimacy for many of the modern nation-states of the region has been one of the factors enabling the rise of V.T.M.s that partially try to exploit the ideological spaces or voids left by existing states.

ROOTS OF LEGITIMACY FOR ARMED NON-STATE ACTORS

Alongside this trend of low levels of state legitimacy has grown a persistent side trend that legitimizes armed non-state actors. This trend has roots back in the armed Arab revolt against the Ottomans in World War I, and the various armed revolts against European rule in Syria, Libya, Sudan, Algeria, and elsewhere both before and after World War II. It found particular purchase after 1967 with the overwhelming public support of the P.L.O. in the armed struggle for the liberation of Palestine from Israeli occupation; that support soon later included the Palestinian movement's Islamist wing, Hamas.

The second broadly legitimized armed non-state actor movement was that of Hezbollah (before 2011). Hezbollah received widespread support in Arab public opinion for its fight against Israeli occupation of south Lebanon until the Israeli withdrawal in 2000, and then again in fighting Israel to a draw in 2006. The Lebanese state had not been able to protect or liberate south Lebanon, nor had any Arab state army fought the Israeli army to a draw before. Arab publics also looked approvingly at the fight of armed jihadi groups, which included many Arab volunteers, against the Soviet invasion of Afghanistan in 1979.

Further afield, Arab publics looked admiringly at the armed resistance of the Vietnamese against American power, and at the exploits of Fidel Castro and Che Guevara in South America. As states declined in legitimacy, armed non-state actors still had the potential to inspire. It is into this space that al-Qaeda exploded in 2001, violently poking the American imperium in the eye, to be followed later by ISIS in Iraq and Syria, which challenged the repressive rule of the Iran-backed Nouri Maliki and Bashar al-Assad respectively. As states have struggled to maintain their legitimacy, and some states have become a primary enemy of a significant portion of their own people (e.g. Assad's Syrian regime), armed non-state actors have found ways to retain and grow their legitimacy.

The widely popular struggle of many armed non-state actors in the region over the past century has created the broad space for various kinds of V.T.M.s to try to exploit that popular openness to armed non-state actors.

THE TRAJECTORY OF IDEOLOGICAL EVOLUTION: FROM NASSER TO THE ISLAMIC STATE

The radicalization of Islamist political thought is, in some ways, a rather recent ideological phenomenon. In the first two-thirds of the 20th century, it was nationalist or leftist ideological movements that were the more radical, calling for armed confrontation or armed rebellion — and in some cases, like the Algerian National Liberation Front (F.L.N.) or the P.L.O., using violence against civilians — as part of the nationalist or leftist struggle. Most Islamists still represented a more conservative bent of mind. Indeed, most of the vibrant ideological movements of the first two-thirds of the 20th century were reactions against, and attempts to move beyond, the conservative Islamic order and worldview that had prevailed under the Ottomans for five centuries. The liberal, local-nationalist, Arab-nationalist, and various leftist ideological strands were the most prominent among these trends. It is the decline of these various ideological movements, and the radicalization and resurgence of certain Islamist movements, that led to the ideological environment that we find ourselves in today.[13] The liberal experiment prevailed during the interwar period,[14] but collapsed after World War II. Arab states led by liberal elites were shunned by wide publics, as they appeared powerless to stop or reverse the establishment of the state of Israel over historic Palestine, and were seen as in compromising cahoots with Western colonial powers. The Arab nationalist leftist wave of military and one-party-led coups swept many Arab countries in the 1950s and 1960s and had a heyday for a while. But nationalist and socialist enthusiasms flagged after the humiliating defeat of 1967 and after initial economic development gave way to stagnation, income inequality, and growing unemployment or underemployment in the 1970s.[15] As the promises of democracy, nationalism, and socialism frayed, the call of "Islam is the way," gained renewed appeal.

The Muslim Brotherhood was formed in Egypt in 1928 as a "modern" political party, but one intent on resisting the secularizing tide, bringing back the caliphate — but not on Turkish terms — and restoring the Islamic order in state and society. They were partners with the Free Officers in overthrowing the Egyptian monarchy in 1952, but Nasser soon turned against them, as he led Egypt in a staunchly Arab nationalist, secular, and state socialist direction. The Muslim Brotherhood did espouse views that were considered radical by their opponents, and developed an armed wing as part of their struggle, but their main strategy was to build their powerbase through grassroots proselytizing and service-provision to try win over a majority of the population and then ride that popularity to power.[16]

The ideological bifurcation occurred in the 1960s, at the hands of Sayyed Qutb, a Muslim Brotherhood leader jailed by Nasser and later executed. In place of the proselytizing and gradualist approach of the mainstream Brotherhood, Qutb announced that Islamists — like the prophet before his flight (*hijra*) from Medina — are in a state of war, or *jihad*, not only with the government, but also with the general population that had abandoned Islam. Although Qutb remains revered in the Brotherhood, this ideological bifurcation was not adopted by the mainstream Brotherhood movement. It did, however, lead to a number of hyper-militant offshoots — e.g. the Islamic Jihad that assassinated Egyptian President Anwar Sadat — and most importantly provided one of the ideological pathways that led to the emergence of al-Qaeda and later ISIS.[17]

The early months of the Arab Spring in 2011 opened up the possibility that a liberal democratic wave might regain vigor in the Arab world, which was instead followed by a Muslim Brotherhood wave of election victories. The democratic way only found precarious purchase in Tunisia. And the Muslim Brotherhood wave was thwarted in Egypt and later overtaken by the more radical achievements of ISIS in Iraq and Syria. After the traumatic state failures, civil wars, and terrorist resurgences of recent years, there is a return of "statist" viewpoints, in countries like Egypt, Jordan, and the Gulf, which emphasizes a reassertion of state power, and the call to rally around the flag to preserve basic national order and security.

The ideological trajectory in Iran and various Arab Shi'a communities had aspects of similarity and difference with what is described below. Iran had its own liberal and constitutional period, particularly marked by the constitutional revolution of 1905. It also had its anti-colonialist leftist nationalist in the form of Prime Minister Mohammad Mossadegh, and an authoritarian national secularist dictatorship in the form of Reza Shah, and then his son Mohammad Reza. But the Islamist trend, led by Ruhollah Khomeini from exile, gained strength in the 1970s and was a driving ideological and mobilization force in the revolution that overthrew Mohammad Reza in 1979. But the revolution also comprised powerful leftist, nationalist, and liberal movements. The Islamic Republic turned against them after 1979 to create an ideologically and organizationally "cleansed" revolutionary state.

Arab Shi'a communities in Iraq, Lebanon, Kuwait, and elsewhere were very much part of the various liberal, leftist, communist, and Arab nationalist movements that animated politics between World War I and the 1970s. But as those movements lost steam, and particularly after the successful Islamist-led revolution against the shah in Iran, the region's main Shi'a country, more Arab Shi'a communities began to turn toward the Islamic Republic. This was partly the result of Arab Shi'as feeling empowered by the success of the revolution in Iran, and seeing the inspiring success of using religion for political inspiration and mobilization. It was also partly the result of deliberate and organized outreach by Iran to Shi'a communities in the Arab region following the revolution.[18]

The various dead ends that political ideological evolution has experienced in the modern Arab world, and the absence of a clear pathway to an ideologically satisfactory future, has created the charged conditions in which alternative and often radical ideological viewpoints have been given space to be heard and thrive.

THE WEAPONIZATION OF SUNNI AND SHI'A IDENTITY: THE PIVOT OF 1979

In many ways, the Middle East today is living in the shadow of 1979. Five developments that year set the stage for a ravaging conflict between radicalized and armed Sunni and Shi'a movements.

First, and as mentioned above, was the Islamic Revolution in Iran itself. This caused a dramatic reorientation of Arab Shi'a political consciousness and mobilization away from nationalist, liberal or leftist profiles, toward an Islamist, Shi'a-specific, Iran-centric profile. This was partly a natural reorientation after the satisfying success of the Islamic revolution in Iran, but it also became an integral, well-organized, and well-financed strategy of the new Iranian state. Exporting revolution and helping co-religionists — as well as the "downtrodden" in general around the world — was written into the new constitution, organized through the Islamic Revolutionary Guard Corps (I.R.G.C.) and related institutions of the state, and financed by petrodollars. Mobilizing and arming Shi'a — and some Sunni groups, like Hamas — abroad also became part of the Islamic Republic's national security strategy. Confronted by war with Iraq (and Saddam's Iraq received broad Arab backing), threats of regime change from the United States, and threats of attack from Israel, Iran resorted to asymmetric approaches and building proxy forces in Lebanon, supporting the Iraqi opposition to Saddam, and bolstering Assad's Syria. The Islamic Revolution of 1979 led to the mobilization and weaponization of Shi'a power in various parts of the Arab world.

Second, the Soviet invasion of Afghanistan led directly to U.S.-Saudi cooperation in mobilizing and arming Sunni jihadis. These included native Afghans, as well as the encouragement of thousands of Arab jihadis to join the fight. It was this cauldron that forged the modern jihadi armies, and later enabled the rise of al-Qaeda.[19]

Third, 1979 was also the year of the takeover of the Great Mosque in Mecca by armed Islamist rebels threatening to overthrow the Saudi state. Before 1979, the Saudi state had perceived the main internal, as well as external, threats as coming from nationalist and/or leftist directions. Nasser had been their most dangerous adversary in the 1960s, and other monarchies — in Egypt, Iraq, Libya, and elsewhere — had fallen to nationalist or leftist revolts or coups. In 1979, it was driven home to them that the main domestic threat to Saudi rule might come from the political right — radical Sunni Islamists — and that the main external threat would now be from an Islamist Iran.

These two conditions spurred the Saudi government, after 1979, to pivot quickly to reassert their Islamic credentials and push their version of Islam both domestically and externally.[20] Internally, this oriented the kingdom in a more conservative direction for ensuing years, while externally, the Saudis spent billions within Sunni communities around the Arab world, and further afield, training imams, funding madrasas, and buying influence and Islamic credibility. This gradually pulled Sunni institutions, media, mosques, and political movements into the Saudi orbit, and with a distinct sectarian and religious overtone.[21] It is important to note that the current Saudi Crown Prince Mohammad bin Salman has vowed to reverse this policy and turn Saudi Arabia to a more moderate and tolerant Islam.[22]

Fourth, 1979 was the year of the conclusion of the Egyptian-Israeli peace treaty. This decisively removed Egypt, which had led the Arab world for the past 50 years, from the Arab fold. It further discredited the nationalist secular model that Egypt represented, although that model had already suffered a serious blow in 1967. The departure of Egypt shifted the locus of Arab power decisively toward the Arab Gulf states. With this shift came a swing from the nationalist secularist discourse, which has a strong presence in Egypt, to the conservative Islamist, and rather Wahhabi and Sunni, discourse that prevails particularly in Saudi Arabia.

Fifth, 1979 marked the height of the oil price boom of the 1970s. For the previous century, Egypt had been the largest, wealthiest, and most advanced of the Arab countries. From 1979 onward, the center of wealth shifted decisively toward not only Saudi Arabia and the Gulf, but also to Iran. Two petro states, Saudi Arabia and Iran, would, for the ensuing decades, vie for power and influence across the Middle East.

Indeed, 1979 ushered in the current era of sectarian mobilization and conflict in the Middle East. Egypt and the United Arab Emirates (U.A.E.) have turned clearly against this approach. The crown prince of Saudi Arabia has indicated that he intends to follow suit, but it is not yet clear if that will be sustained and result in real changes in Saudi foreign policy. Turkey and Qatar still maintain fairly strong support for Sunni Islamist movements and show no signs of change in that regard. Iran's current president and foreign minister have indicated that they might be open to moving away from this policy, but that standpoint does not appear to be shared by the supreme leader and the I.R.G.C.

The Breakdown of Regional Order and the Iraqi Jihad: 2003

Until 2003, there was Hezbollah in southern Lebanon, Hamas in Gaza, and a few armed non-state actors operating in a few pockets of the Arab world. These groups did not pursue a direct global terrorist campaign, but fought localized conflicts. Al-Qaeda, which had proven its global intentions in 2001, was largely confined to Afghanistan and parts of Pakistan. The U.S.-led invasion of Iraq in 2003 changed that, which had three direct effects. First, it broke the Iraqi state and created conditions of ungoverned space, unmanaged security, and political conflict that enabled the entry and spread of both Sunni and Shi'a radical armed non-state actors in Iraq, including al-Qaeda.

Second, it broke the precarious Arab regional state order that had prevailed since World War II in which Iraq had been a buffer to Iranian power. After 2003, Iran would project immense influence in Iraq, and from there, further into Syria and Lebanon, as well as harbor ambitions in Yemen and Bahrain. The Iranian surge poured fuel on Sunni-Shi'a tensions both in Iraq and the Arab region, and caused a panicked reaction from Arab Sunni states, particularly in the Gulf, to find ways to mobilize and push back against this surging Iran. In the ensuing decade and half, Iran would maintain its strong position in Iraq and Lebanon, gain enormous new presence in Syria, and a surprising presence in Yemen through the Houthi movement there.

Third, the prolonged U.S. military occupation and presence in Iraq was the perfect ideological vehicle to mobilize jihadists. In Iraq, jihadists — both Sunni and Shi'a — could fight what they considered "Christian Crusading occupiers" of Muslim lands. For Sunni jihadists, Iraq had the added attraction of providing a venue to also fight what they considered heretical Iranian-backed Shi'as (or Safavid-backed *rawafid*, in their nomenclature).[23]

The Arab region has had four orders in the past century and half: It started under an Ottoman Turkish order; shifted to a British-French dominated order in the interwar period; then entered into an Arab order of sorts after World War II (despite an Arab cold war between Saudi and Egypt, and the Iraqi invasion of Kuwait in 1990); the region has now entered a new era in which Iran wields enormous influence in the Arab world and is particularly dominant in the Levant.

This new order has been under contestation, and will be for several years to come. It fuels much of the tension in the region that contributes to state collapse and civil war, and fuels the sectarian radicalization and mobilization that enables the rise of V.T.M.s and designated terrorist groups.

ARAB UPRISINGS, STATE FAILURE, CIVIL WAR, AND THE SYRIAN JIHAD: 2011

The revolts of 2011 were the result of a long brewing tension between growing populations and public demands on one side, and increasingly rigid, repressive, and corrupt regimes on the other. The revolts erupted in six Arab countries. In Tunisia, and only in Tunisia, did they lead to a tenuous democratic transition. In Egypt and Bahrain, revolt was eventually crushed in a state-led counterrevolution. In Libya, Yemen, and Syria revolt led to full or partial state failure and civil war.

While armed non-state actors proliferated in all three countries, it would be in Syria that the largest and most violent radical groups would take root. This is for several reasons. First, in Syria the regime survived more or less intact, blocked any path toward political negotiation, and used its full force against large swathes of its population. In Libya, Muammar Qaddafi might have wished to do the same, but was defeated through foreign intervention. In Yemen, Ali Abdullah Saleh took a softer approach, negotiating his own departure from office, then engaging in a complex civil war to fight for his, or his son's, way back into state power. The survival and ferocity of the Assad regime drove the opposition increasingly in more militant and radical directions, and was a boon for radical group recruitment.

Second, the war in Syria had a distinctly sectarian identity to it, with a minority Alawite regime, backed by Shi'a Iran and Hezbollah, fighting a Sunni majority opposition backed by Turkey and a number of Arab Gulf states.

This also indicates that, third, in addition to becoming a sectarian civil war, in which Islamist sectarian radicalization could thrive, the Syrian war was one that drew in enormous external proxy or direct intervention.[24]

There was foreign air intervention in Libya and support for rival groups between Turkey and Qatar on one side and Egypt and the U.A.E. on the other. In Yemen, there is Iranian backing for the Houthis facing off against a Saudi-led military intervention. However, those two arenas do not approach the extent to which Syria was a proxy battleground for the future of the Levant at the heart of the Middle East. Iran considered the war to defend the Assad regime and Damascus as the front line for the defense of Tehran, as well as its ability to maintain Hezbollah as a deterrent to Israel. Some Arab Gulf states felt that a Sunni recapture of Damascus would compensate for the historic loss of Baghdad to Shi'a and Iranian control as a result of the U.S. invasion of 2003.

The Iraqi jihad merged into the Syrian jihad, as al-Qaeda and the Islamic State of Iraq moved into Syria after 2011, and morphed into the Islamic State of Iraq and Sham (ISIS). This resulted in a splinter in the al-Qaeda movement, with ISIS going its own direction, while al-Qaeda itself took on a slew of different names and found a wide foothold in some pockets of the Syrian opposition.[25]

The forces and contradictions that led to the Arab uprisings are still present, and in some cases getting more acute. The needs and frustrations that these uprisings expressed, and that in many cases continue, are part of the enabling environment in which V.T.M.s thrive.

Section Conclusion

In the preceding section I have presented six enabling conditions for V.T.M.s in the Middle East and attempted to situate them in their historical context. These included low state legitimacy, the origins of legitimacy for armed non-state actors, the impasse of political ideological development, the weaponization of sectarian identity, the collapse of regional order, and the effects of the Arab uprisings of 2011. Many elements of these enabling conditions will figure again in the next section, which looks at structural drivers and factors from a more sectorial and ahistorical perspective. But it is important to look at drivers and factors from both perspectives. Elements discussed in the drivers and conditions presented in this preceding section will also figure in the third part of this essay, which proposes broad policy directions to counter V.T.M.s and reduce the drivers that provide their enabling environment.

A Consideration of Structural Drivers and Factors

Much of the valuable literature on violent extremism has repeatedly examined the structural, macro, society-wide "push" factors that enable and encourage the rise of V.T.M.s, looking for clear explanations and causal links. These factors include dire socio-economic conditions, repressive political practices, and cases of cultural alienation or marginalization. Consideration of these factors is important and fruitful, but there is no simple predictive link between these factors and the rise of V.T.M.s.[26] These factors often operate indirectly and in complex combinations. And one combination of factors that has led to V.T.M.s in one country or context might not in another. Concomitantly, every case of the rise of V.T.M.s shows a different combination of factors. It is, thus, virtually impossible to make broad macro generalizations about the drivers of

V.T.M.s across a wide spectrum of cases or countries.[27]

Examining macro conditions and "push" factors, as if they can create V.T.M.s on their own, generally grossly underestimates the "pull" factor of particular groups being effective and successful in organizing, planning, recruiting, growing, and so forth. V.T.M.s, as we mentioned at the outset of this essay, are particular organized movements with goals, organizational structures, and internal dynamics. They take advantage of vulnerabilities in a society — vulnerabilities that may be described in the literature on "drivers and factors" — to take root and grow in a particular environment. In a medical metaphor, we can think of V.T.M.s as particular pathogens that thrive in a weakened and immunocompromised host. Defeating the pathogen is a big part of curing the patient. However, examining macro push factors remains critical, because even if one pathogen is defeated, another pathogen can easily find purchase in a compromised host; or the "defeated" pathogen can mutate into a different, often more lethal, form, and take root again. This is a dynamic that we have seen in how al-Qaeda mutated into the Islamic State in Iraq, which then mutated into ISIS, and could, in future years, mutate into yet another form. Therefore, in considering the drivers and remedies for V.T.M.s, keeping the push and pull factors in mind, and understanding how they interact, is critical to gaining a more complete picture.

Socio-economic Factors

Recent research indicates that whereas most V.T.M. leaders and key cadres are not in their positions because of economic need, conditions of impoverishment in their surrounding environment greatly enhance their ability to recruit — provided, of course, they have the economic resources to do so. Conditions of dire economic need — exacerbated greatly by state failure and civil war — certainly create favorable conditions for V.T.M.s to exploit.[28] A related enabling condition might also be, not desperate material economic need per se, but a perception of socio-economic injustice vis-a-vis the state or a dominant group.[29] In that case, the socio-economic factor is one of grievance, not absolute need or deprivation, and the V.T.M. is a vehicle to redress that grievance.

In any case, in a society where socio-economic conditions have deteriorated dramatically, whether because of bad policy, corruption, state failure, or even climatic conditions, both indicators of absolute economic need and/or a sense of socio-economic grievance will rise, because in conditions of increasing scarcity and bad governance there will be a powerful few that will still be able to access or monopolize wealth and resources. And there is no doubt that challenging economic conditions in Iraq, Syria, Yemen, and parts of Libya, already strained before the uprisings and conflicts of 2011, got dramatically and desperately worse as state institutions collapsed and civil war ravaged large swathes of those countries.

It is also important to note that, unlike some powerful V.T.M.s in the last century, such as radical communist and leftist groups that identified socio-economic grievance as their main issue, most of the V.T.M.s in today's Middle East have mainly religious, sectarian, ethnic, or nationalist grievances and goals. Economics might be part of their concern and program, but it is by no means the principal one.

Nevertheless, it is quite clear that economic deprivation provides a conducive host environment for ambitious V.T.M.s, and that improving economic conditions, boosting gainful employment, and increasingly meeting the basic needs of individuals and families for shelter, food, education, and basic healthcare, is critical in strengthening the immune system of vulnerable societies.

Political Factors

We might divide political factors into three levels: (a) The regional and international environment impacting a state or society; (b) the presence or absence of national political state institutions; and (c) where they exist, the policies and performance of those institutions.

EXTERNAL ENVIRONMENT: CONTAGION WITHIN A BROKEN REGIONAL ORDER

One of the likeliest predictors of whether a country will be impacted by the entry and growth of a V.T.M. is whether it is neighboring a country or region that already harbors such a group. This partly explains why the outbreak of a V.T.M. in one country might quickly turn into an epidemic in other parts of the region. This implies that defeating the threat often requires a region-wide strategy, and might not be sustainably achieved in one country alone. The challenge is exacerbated in a region like the Middle East where there is no regional political or security order to manage or mitigate region-wide threats. To the contrary, principal states are engaged in a proxy war against each other that only fuels, directly or indirectly, radicalization and the conditions that enable V.T.M.s.[30] Of course, it doesn't help if global players, like the United States and Russia, are also not on the same page and are backing different states within a broken regional order, or different groups within one civil war.

THE STATE: STANDING OR COLLAPSED

The presence or absence of a state over a territory is the single strongest variable in determining the presence or absence of a large-scale V.T.M. Generally, the collapse of a state, or at least its partial collapse, leaves territory ungoverned or tenuously governed. It also creates security, economic, and other needs for individuals, families, and communities that resourceful V.T.M.s can exploit.[31] The full or partial collapse of a state also opens up the major questions of alternative political orders and borders, which often motivates V.T.M.s and can inspire some adherents.

While there can be lone wolf attacks and dangerous sleeper cells in any state, it is important to note that a V.T.M. has never defeated a standing state that wasn't already broken or collapsed, and that a V.T.M. cannot find purchase and conditions for significant growth except in a fundamentally broken or compromised state. It is also the case that even if a particular V.T.M. is defeated in a certain country, the victory will not be sustained unless a viable and effective state is rebuilt, with a minimal level of acceptance and sovereignty throughout that country. Failed states and V.T.M.s go hand-in-hand — where the former exist, the latter will thrive.

POLITICS

Some hardcore leaders and cadres of V.T.M.s carry alternative visions of how they define the nation and what they think the state should be. For them, even if the extant state is suddenly inclusive, fair, and well-functioning, they would still choose to be at war with it. But for most recruits, it's fair to say that they were driven to join a V.T.M. only after they met with extreme dissatisfaction, or outright threat, at the hands of the state in which they lived. In the Middle East, the rise of V.T.M.s can in no way be divorced from the policies and performance of Saddam's Iraq toward the Shi'a or Kurds, Maliki's policy toward the Arab Sunnis, Qaddafi toward Benghazi and other sectors of society, Saleh's policy toward his opposition, or Assad's government toward many of its own citizens. Those states collapsed, fully or partially, for a political reason, and people joined V.T.M.s largely to redress well-defined and egregious political offenses against them. V.T.M.s, including what we call terrorist groups, are enabled in an environment of broken politics.

A USAID study identified a number of political factors that could contribute to violent extremism and enable V.T.M. recruitment.[32] These include: (a) Basic political exclusion and denial of political rights and civil liberties; (b) more violent repression and violation of human rights (torture, assassinations, mass killings); and (c) endemic corruption in favor of a protected state-connected elite. These factors can be exacerbated if there are areas within the state that are not fully under state control and can serve as safe havens for disaffected individuals and groups to mobilize. Attempts by states to control or repress opposition might often make things worse: Either by pushing more political opponents toward radicalization and taking up arms; or through the prison system, in which torture and mistreatment also pushes toward radicalization within a ready-made prison network of discontent. Some states might think that they can repress their way toward defeating violent extremism and V.T.M.s, and that might be true in some cases in the short term. However, in the long term, unless the politics of the state are more inclusive and less repressive, the dynamics of discontent and pushing people toward the fringes are likely to reproduce conditions conducive for the growth of V.T.M.s.[33]

SECTION CONCLUSION

The literature on extremism and conditions that provide push and pull factors for V.T.M.s is rich and valuable. It repeatedly brings to the fore the range of socio-economic and political conditions that enable these types of groups and their ability to thrive. I refer the reader to those valuable studies, without making a claim to summarize them in this essay, but rather to reaffirm their main findings, and to use them as guideposts when thinking about integrated policy responses to combating V.T.M.s in the varied countries of the Middle East. I also reprise the point made in several of these studies that there is no one condition or set of conditions that consistently leads to the rise of V.T.M.s, or to their demise, but that the challenge of defeating V.T.M.s and preventing their reemergence is, like politics, a practical not a natural science.

POLICY TAKEAWAYS

IMMEDIATE POLICY URGENCIES

So far, most policy has focused on treating the symptom rather than its causes: Defeating V.T.M.s after they emerge, in a continuous game of whack-a-mole, rather than trying to address the causes that enabled their rise. While possibly irrational, this is not always completely nonsensical, for six reasons: (a) The symptom, a virulent V.T.M., can cause immediate and large-scale damage, and must be contained and defeated quickly. Much like a high fever, it can kill the patient, and must be treated immediately regardless of its underlying cause. (b) The symptom manifests as a security threat, and elicits a security counter-response. (c) Devising a policy to attack and kill terrorists is conceptually "simple" and straightforward; figuring out the long-term policies that would gradually remove the conditions that enable them is complex; few major world leaders or capitals have evinced the breadth and depth of policy appreciation to think beyond the primary level. (d) Political and security gains from whacking a V.T.M. are reaped in the short term; the gains from a more complex and sustained-gain strategy are long term, and beyond the horizon of most world leaders. (e) For major players, like the United States, the military is the swollen instrument of foreign policy; as the saying goes, when you have a hammer, most problems look like nails. (f) It has proven easier to sell publics on committing to a security response, than to committing to more complex and long-term diplomatic or political foreign policy goals.

Nevertheless, the policy of defeating present V.T.M.s, even if they are symptoms not causes, is an urgent and necessary one. This includes several "lines of effort,"[34] which have been pursued in recent years. First, working directly and with partners in the region to attack and defeat terrorist groups — this has seen progress in recent ISIS defeats in Mosul and Raqqa. Second, interdicting the flow of foreign fighters to these groups, which have been dramatically reduced, especially across the Turkish border. Third, clamping down on terrorist financing — progress has been made through actions of the U.S. Treasury, as well as policy changes in some regional capitals, and recent terrorism financing agreements. And fourth, limiting and countering V.T.M. media and online messaging through shutting down of suspected V.T.M.-linked accounts and working with partners to provide counter-messaging.

But from the analysis presented in this paper, a more comprehensive and sustained-gain strategy must address the following four longer-term components.

LONGER-TERM POLICY COMPONENTS

PRIMARY PILLARS

1. ENDING CIVIL WARS AND STANDING UP FAILED STATES

If one were to select one variable that had the biggest determinant effect on whether V.T.M.s are able to take root and thrive, or alternatively be prevented from taking root or coming back into a country, that variable would be the presence or collapse of the state. As described in this paper, the partial or full collapse of the state creates a perfect storm of security, socio-economic, and political conditions, including in many cases, civil war, that enable the entry and growth of V.T.M.s.[35] Any sustained-gain policy for defeating V.T.M.s and addressing the primary conditions that enabled their rise would have to put a very high priority on, first, bringing about an end to the civil wars that have broken out in the collapsed states, and then, post-civil-war, helping get the shattered state back on its institutional feet. The debate over how easy or hard this is, or how cheap or expensive, and what array of regional and international states and institutions should be involved, is a valid one. However, any strategy that presumes that the war against V.T.M.s can be sustainably won in the context of a sea of failed states and ongoing civil wars is deeply misguided.

2. DE-ESCALATING REGIONAL PROXY WAR AND STABILIZING REGIONAL RELATIONS

The second big ticket variable that has driven the rise of V.T.M.s in the Middle East has been the proxy war between Iran and Saudi Arabia, which erupted in 1979, and only got worse after the Iraq invasion of 2003 and the Arab uprisings of 2011. This has transformed Arab political consciousness and mobilization from the left-right divide that dominated political life in the 1950s and 1960s, to the sectarian Sunni-Shi'a divide that now dominates the political spectrum. It has torn societies apart, contributed to state failure and collapse, helped ignite sectarian civil wars, and fueled conditions that now see radical Shi'a and Sunni armed non-state actors arrayed against each other throughout the Levant and Yemen.[36]

De-escalating tension between Iran and Saudi Arabia, and working toward stabilizing regional relations, is neither easy nor straightforward, but it is also by no means impossible. Rather, it is one of the main foreign policy challenges of our time, and one whose resolution would bring about the greatest global benefits in terms of improved security and economic prosperity. Both Iran and Saudi Arabia have legitimate national security concerns, and both have an interest in a de-conflicted and prosperous region where their national security is preserved. I have written elsewhere about how this political challenge might be approached. Any strategy that presumed that the growth of Sunni and Shi'a V.T.M.s and terrorist groups could be stemmed, while Iran and Saudi Arabia continued in open and un-curtailed conflict, would also be deeply misguided.

SUSTAINING PILLARS

1. BETTER GOVERNANCE

Bad governance and repressive politics don't immediately lead to the emergence of large V.T.M.s, as long as the state is not in collapse, but they do create conditions that: (a) Drive people toward increasingly radical political and militant options; (b) enable the penetration into society of V.T.M. cells; and (c) can contribute to the fraying and eventual partial or full failure of the state. This is what happened in Syria, Iraq, Libya, and Yemen, and is the fear that some currently have regarding Egypt. While states must be resolute in fighting terrorist groups, and should be helped in doing so, they should also be encouraged, or pressed, to pull back from repressive policies that go beyond terrorist groups, reopen civic and political space, and create more inclusive and responsive politics. All the Arab uprisings were about demands for basic political rights and inclusion as well as social justice, and it was the rejection of these demands that led to partial or full state failure and civil wars in several Arab countries, providing inviting conditions for V.T.M.s. While Arab publics, in the immediate aftermath of the carnage of recent years, might tentatively tolerate a temporary reversion back to authoritarianism, the demands for basic good governance will only grow over time, particularly as key socio-economic indicators continue to add strain.

2. Economic Development

High demographic growth, a youth bulge, coupled with slow economic growth, high unemployment, and unfavorable land and water conditions were primary underlying drivers of the Arab uprisings. Those same dire socio-economic conditions were preyed upon by V.T.M.s with cash to spend. Unrest, state collapse, and civil war in several countries have only made economic conditions worse. In a long-term outlook of slow global growth, major obstacles to high MENA growth, and escalating climate change impacts, these conditions risk getting worse. While post-war Europe had the Marshall Plan, and China today is pushing investment through its One Belt, One Road policy, there is still no clear long-term economic integration and development strategy for the Middle East.[37] Unless the region's various resources and economies are better integrated together and with the global economy, and until the large population countries of the region get on a more high-growth and job-rich economic trajectory, the crises and exported risks of the region are likely to get worse.

Conclusion

The conditions that brought about the rise and spread of V.T.M.s in the Middle East are complex and have been long in the making. While particular V.T.M.s might be defeated in the field of battle, addressing the geopolitical, political, and socio-economic conditions that provide the space for their rise and the conditions for their growth is a broader generational challenge. In examining the historical, geopolitical, and other drivers that enable V.T.M.s in today's Middle East, as attempted in this essay, there is provided a helpful context for understanding their rise and thinking about strategies to reverse that trend.

Endnotes

1. I would like to thank MEI intern Mr. Yousuf Eltagouri for his valuable help in preparing the final version of this paper.

2. See, Cordesman, Anthony H. "Tracking the Trends and Numbers: Islam, Terrorism, Stability and Conflict in the Middle East." Arleigh A. Burke Chair in Strategy - Center for Strategic and International Studies, Feb. 15, 2017.

3. See, Allan, Harriet, et al. "Drivers of Violent Extremism: Hypotheses and Literature Review." *Royal United Services Institute*, Oct. 16, 2015, p. 2.

4. See, Jones, Jessica. "Drivers of Violent Extremism." *Center for International Private Enterprise*, Jan. 18, 2017.

5. See, Byman, Dan. *Deadly Connections: States that Sponsor Terrorism.* Cambridge University Press, 2007, pp. 24-26.

6. Bruce Hoffman, *Inside Terrorism* (New York: Columbia University Press, 2017), 3-17.

7. Raymond Hinnebusch, *The International Politics of the Middle East* (Manchester, UK: Manchester University Press, 2003).

8. For more, see Ruggie, J. G. "Continuity and Transformation in the World Polity: Toward a Neorealist Synthesis." *World Politics*, vol. 35, no. 02, 1983, pp. 261-285.

9. Paul C. Helmreich, *From Paris to Sèvres: The Partition of the Ottoman Empire at the Peace Conference of 1919-1920* (Columbus: Ohio State University, 1974), 65-69.

10. See, Barnett, Michael. "Institutions, Roles, and Disorder: The Case of the Arab States System." *International Studies Quarterly*, vol. 37, no. 3, 1993, pp. 280-289; Kerr, Malcolm "The Arab Cold War: Gamal Abd al-Nasir and His Rivals, 1958-1970." Oxford University Press, 1971.

11. For more, see Başkan, Birol. *Turkey and Qatar in the Tangled Geopolitics of the Middle East.* Palgrave Macmillan, 2016, pp. 96-100, 106-107.

12. Michael C. Hudson, *Arab Politics: The Search for Legitimacy* (New York: Yale University Press, 1980), 83-86.

13. See, Nahas, Maridi. "State-Systems and Revolutionary Challenge: Nasser, Khomeini, and the Middle East." *International Journal of Middle East Studies*, vol. 17, no. 04, 1985, pp. 507-527.

14. Albert Habib Hourani, *Arabic Thought In The Liberal Age: 1798-1939* (Cambridge University Press, 1962).

15. Fouad Ajami, T*he Arab Predicament: Arab Political Thought and Practice Since 1967* (Cambridge University Press, 1981).

16. Khalil Al-Anani, "Upended Path: The Rise and Fall of Egypt's Muslim Brotherhood," *The Middle East Journal* 69, no. 4 (2015): 527-543.

17. For more on this perspective, see Gerges, Fawaz. "ISIS and the Third Wave of Jihadism." *Current History*, vol. 113, no. 767, Dec. 2014, pp. 339-343.

18. Fred Dallmayr, "Radical Changes in the Muslim World: Turkey, Iran, Egypt," *Globalizations* 8, no. 5 (2011): 639-646.

19. Mohammed M. Hafez, "Jihad after Iraq: Lessons from the Arab Afghans," *Studies in Conflict & Terrorism* 32, no. 2 (2009): 73-75.

20. For more on al-Jama'a al-Salafiyya al-Muhtasiba, Juhayman ibn Muhammad ibn Sayf al-Otaybi, and rejectionist Islam in Saudi Arabia, see Hegghammer, Thomas, and Stéphane Lacroix. "Rejectionist Islamism In Saudi Arabia: The Story Of Juhayman Al-Utaybi Revisited." *International Journal of Middle East Studies*, vol. 39, no. 01, 2007, pp. 103-120.

21. Raihan Ismail, *Saudi Clerics and Shi'a Islam* (Oxford University Press, 2016), 18-30.

22. Chulov, Martin. "I will return Saudi Arabia to moderate Islam, says crown prince." *The Guardian*, 24 Oct. 2017.

23. See, Fuller, Graham E. "Islamist Politics in Iraq after Saddam Hussein." *United States Institute of Peace*, no. 106, 13 Aug. 2003, pp. 3-10.

24. See, Jonathan Spyer, "Syrian Regime Strategy and the Syrian Civil War," *Middle East Review of International Affairs* 16, no. 3 (September 2012). and Charles Lister, *The Syrian Jihad: Al-Qaeda, the Islamic State and the Evolution of an Insurgency* (Oxford University Press, 2015), 5-8.

25. Charles Lister, "The Free Syrian Army: A Decentralized Insurgent Brand," *The Brookings Project on U.S. Relations with the Islamic World*, November 2016, 4-16.

26. See, Krueger, Alan, and Jitka Maleckova. "Education, Poverty, Political Violence and Terrorism: Is There a Causal Connection?" *Journal of Economic Perspectives*, vol. 17, no. 4, 2003, pp. 141-142.

27. Graeme Blair et al., "Poverty and Support for Militant Politics: Evidence from Pakistan," *American Journal of Political Science* 57, no. 1 (2012): 40-48.

28. Susan Rice, Corinne Graff, and Carlos Pascual, "Confronting Poverty: Weak States and U.S. National Security," *Yale Journal of International Affairs*, 2009.

29. For more on this perspective, see, Moghaddam, Fathali M. "The Staircase to Terrorism." *American Psychologist*, 2005, pp. 162-166.

30. Ross Harrison, "Defying Gravity: Working Toward a Regional Strategy for a Stable Middle East," *Middle East Institute Policy Paper*, 2015.

31. See "The Jihadi Threat 5: Drivers of Extremism." *Wilson Center*, Dec. 14, 2016.

32. United States Agency for International Development. *Guide to the Drivers of Violent Extremism*. Feb. 2009, pp. 27.

33. See, Dalacoura, Katerina. "Islamist Terrorism and the Middle East Democratic Deficit: Political Exclusion, Repression and the Causes of Extremism." *Democratization*, vol. 13, no. 3, 2006, pp. 508-525.

34. See, "The Global Coalition To Defeat ISIS." U.S. Department of State, 10 Sept. 2014.

35. Stewart Patrick, "Weak States and Global Threats: Assessing Evidence of "Spillovers"," *Center for Global Development*, no. 73 (January 2006): 14-22.

36. GaUse III, Gregory F. "Beyond Sectarianism: The New Middle East Cold War." *Brookings Doha Center Analysis Paper*, no. 11 (July 2014): 5-15.

37. For more on this perspective, see Fardoust, Shahrokh. "Economic Integration in the Middle East: Prospects for Development and Stability." *Middle East Institute Policy Paper*, no. 5, 2016, pp. 17-22.

CHAPTER TWO

AL-QAEDA VERSUS ISIS:

COMPETING JIHADIST BRANDS IN THE MIDDLE EAST

CHARLES LISTER

INTRODUCTION

When people took to the streets in their masses across the Middle East in late 2010 and early 2011 to demand liberal reforms and democracy, the assumed conclusion was that jihadist militancy was witnessing its existential defeat. Having long presented themselves as the best, and often as the only alternative model for how to replace repressive and corrupt dictatorships, al-Qaeda and other likeminded groups were suddenly faced with a non-violent rival model, which was displaying a far greater effect. The conclusion drawn in Western governments was that the dramatic success of democratic protest finally proved that jihadists had lost their long-sought-after base. As many saw it, the fish suddenly found themselves swimming in a hostile sea, to draw upon Mao's famous phrase.

What many failed to foresee, during what was auspiciously labelled at the time as the Arab Spring, was that the advent of popular protest and political change had opened the gates to unprecedented instability, and jihadists were preparing to exploit the resulting chaos. Al-Qaeda's central leadership had since 2008 already been internally discussing the need to soften its image in order to gain the trust of the masses, and the empowerment of revolutionary sentiments gave al-Qaeda's local affiliates invaluable opportunities to test out this more locally-focused, politically savvy, and pragmatic approach. This approach was attempted first in Yemen and Mali at the outset of the first Arab Spring protests,[1] but the transition from protest to civil conflict in Syria gave al-Qaeda an opportunity to perfect its new long-game jihadist model.

While political protest and regional instability provided al-Qaeda with an opportunity to test out and refine its pragmatic localism model, it also provided conditions in which the Islamic State in Iraq (I.S.I.) could both recover from its de facto military defeat by U.S. military forces in 2009-10, and reassert its ultra-violent model of jihadist extremism and Islamic state-building project. Beginning in Iraq in 2011 and overtly expanding into Syria in mid-2013, ISIS developed and implemented a dramatically different model of jihad, focused on sowing chaos and tearing sovereign countries and communities apart through the use of unilateral sectarian hyper-violence, with the eventual objective of replacing chaos with a centrally-controlled Islamic State.

Consequently, the Middle East was faced with the emergence of two divergent models of jihadist militancy — one focused on embedding within existing, local revolutionary dynamics in order to pursue a long-term Islamization of opposition movements; and another focused on using existing instability to sow even greater disorder in order to pave the way toward a rapid and savage establishment of a jihadist proto-state. Both of these contrasting models of jihad have proven to be effective mechanisms for exploiting pre-existing socio-economic weaknesses in the Middle East, and in leveraging power vacuums resulting from Arab Spring instability.

However, while ISIS and al-Qaeda have both benefitted from pursuing these divergent strategies in the near term, both have also presented their own unique disadvantages and vulnerabilities. This paper will seek to explain in more depth how these divergent models of jihad came to exist; what underlying drivers and trends they sought to exploit; how the emergence of two competing brands has driven the expansion of jihadist terrorism; and how evolving dynamics may see one model triumph over the other, or a reunification of both into a single, doubly-evolved strategic vision. This explanation and analysis will be undertaken through two separate case studies that will detail the differing models practiced by al-Qaeda and ISIS, and highlight the respective drivers that the groups sought to utilize and exploit to further their success. After assessing the two divergent models and the drivers fueling their success, a succeeding section will then lay out the most influential drivers and policy recommendations tailored toward countering them.

AL-QAEDA'S STRATEGIC REORIENTATION

Al-Qaeda has changed significantly since the dramatic attacks on September 11, 2001. Whereas at that time it was a centrally led and commanded organization operating covertly under the de facto protection of a semi-recognized state in Afghanistan, the al-Qaeda of today is more accurately described as a movement of loosely connected locally unique factions operating in the open within broader revolutionary insurgencies.[2] Al-Qaeda's central leadership had become increasingly distant from its globally distributed affiliates under Osama bin Laden, but Ayman al-Zawahri's time at the helm appears to have catalyzed an acceleration of this decentralization of the al-Qaeda movement, with localized affiliates taking more responsibility for their own tactical and strategic operations, and the central leadership assuming a more distant, inspirational role.

This evolution of al-Qaeda's structure and modus operandi was something largely forced upon it by the consistent U.S. counter-terrorism pressure placed on its leadership heartlands in Afghanistan and northwestern Pakistan since late 2001. With less room to maneuver, and at constant threat of detection and targeting by drones, the time taken for al-Qaeda's leadership to respond to even the most significant strategic issues relating to its formal affiliates around the world steadily increased. Micromanaging affiliate operations was out of the question. Thus, as their global leadership became increasingly distant, the local affiliates themselves embraced an increasingly central role over their own decision-making, which consequently created yet more distance from the central command in Afghanistan and Pakistan.

The one mechanism used to avoid this decentralization from going too far was the appointment of a global deputy leader operating out of al-Qaeda's most strategically valuable zone of jihad. For a time, this status was given to Yemen, where the leader of al-Qaeda in the Arabian Peninsula (AQAP), Nasr al-Wuhayshi, was al-Qaeda's deputy from 2013 until his death in June 2015. However, the opportunities provided by a seemingly intractable civil conflict in Syria and the growth there of a highly effective and popular al-Qaeda linked group, Jabhat al-Nusra, meant that Wuhayshi's successor was to be Syria-based. After his release from Iran in spring 2015 and his smuggling to Syria, that man was Abdullah Mohammed Abd al-Rahman (Abu al-Khayr al-Masri), a veteran Egyptian jihadist close to Zawahri.[3] This time, however, al-Qaeda's deputy leader was not a member of a local affiliate as Wuhayshi had been, but was deployed to Syria to operate separately and re-energize al-Qaeda's central leadership, not in South Asia but this time on Europe's doorstep.

STRATEGIC VISION

Al-Qaeda's ultimate strategic objective is to establish a global caliphate, composed of many localized Islamic emirates formed through a military and propagation struggle. For al-Qaeda, however, this is a very long-term goal, potentially necessitating centuries of effort. In the more immediate term, al-Qaeda exists in order to pursue three lines of interrelated effort: To join or to start localized insurgencies against local rulers deemed to be corrupt and insufficiently Islamic; to peacefully spread the fundamental notions of Islam through *dawa*, or religious outreach; and to conduct a covert terror campaign against "the far enemy" (the United States, Europe, and Israel).

At different times throughout its existence, al-Qaeda has attached different levels of priority to these three facets of operations, but since the Arab Spring's eruption in late 2010, the local has steadily gained more traction over the international. In other words, al-Qaeda's global and local leaderships have focused more heavily on attaching themselves to, and embedding themselves within, local dynamics of instability, seeking to drive local change and exploit existing instability in order to better the al-Qaeda brand.

Brand awareness was not a reality that emerged solely after the Arab Spring, as al-Qaeda's affiliation with its branch in Iraq had begun causing detrimental effects on the global image of the movement as early as the mid-2000s.[4] Al-Qaeda in Iraq and later I.S.I. embraced a particularly sectarian strategic vision based on utilizing mass violence that, in al-Qaeda's mind, risked damaging its ability to gain traction elsewhere in the world. Since the Arab Spring, and especially after its public split with the expanded I.S.I. known as ISIS since 2013, al-Qaeda has sought to clearly differentiate themselves from this brutalism by amalgamating the first two of al-Qaeda three lines of effort: Local insurgency and *dawa*.

The dramatic split with ISIS did not represent the point of substantive change in al-Qaeda's strategic thinking, however. That came as early as 2011, when senior al-Qaeda strategists and leaders had begun discussing the need to substantially soften its image, particularly in areas where it has newly arrived. In early 2012, al-Qaeda in the Islamic Maghreb (AQIM) leader Abu Musab Abdul Wadud (Abd al-Malik Droukdel) wrote to his forces in Mali, ordering them to treat its people like babies:

The current baby is in its first days, crawling on its knees, and it has not yet stood on its two legs. If we really want it to stand on its own two feet in this world full of enemies waiting to pounce, we must ease its burden, take it by the hand, help it, support it until it stands. ... One of the wrong policies that we think you carried out is the extreme speed with which you applied shari'a. ... Our previous experience proved that applying shari'a this way ... will lead to people rejecting the religion and engender hatred toward the mujahideen.[5]

While such pragmatic advice was too late to arrive in Mali, similar language was subsequently used in Yemen, where AQAP rebranded itself as Ansar al-Shariah in an attempt to rid itself of the notorious al-Qaeda label.[6] Although more effort was expended there to provide services and introduce a semblance of stability to otherwise chaotic areas of southern Yemen, a tendency toward harsh restrictions and penal measures eventually provided the space for a state-backed tribal uprising. It was only in Syria from late 2012 that this evolved al-Qaeda model began to demonstrate discernible success. A year later, Zawahri himself codified some of this thinking in his *General Guidelines for Jihad* document, in which repeated reference was made to the need to avoid killing civilians and other Muslims, as well as to avoid targeting public areas or members of "deviant sects," unless in defense.[7]

OPPORTUNITIES

Given the ongoing evolution in strategic thinking and the increasing focus on embedding within local struggles, al-Qaeda perceived the onset of political protest and instability in early 2011 as an opportunity, not a challenge. Early that year, al-Qaeda's then deputy leader, Atiyah Abd al-Rahman, wrote an urgent letter to bin Laden suggesting that leading operative Younis al-Mauritani "send his brothers to Tunisia and Syria and other places" in order to exploit the newly favorable circumstances. Bin Laden himself favored "patience," as he believed that soon enough, political Islamists would end up filling the political vacuums, which itself would provide opportunities for *dawa*-based exploitation by al-Qaeda.[8]

As 2011 developed, al-Qaeda was presented with multiple opportunities ripe for the picking, with instability and/or civil conflict in Libya, Egypt, Syria, Iraq, and Yemen. Each provided their own unique dynamics, with all producing new or emboldening pre-existing insurgencies, and all taking place in areas where al-Qaeda maintained pre-existing networks and active operations. In Syria, al-Qaeda was presented with an area in which it had rarely been kinetically active, but where it had established extensive foundational infrastructure during the 2003-10 war in Iraq.[9] Not only was Syria already well placed to be a theater in which al-Qaeda could rapidly establish a new area of operations, but its proximity to Jordan, Lebanon, Turkey, and Iraq ensured that whatever jihadist group developed there would have easy access to recruits and black market supplies.

Yemen also provided al-Qaeda with considerable opportunities, given that it already hosted the global movement's most capable and potent affiliate, AQAP, and was home to swathes of disenfranchised Sunni tribes well-known to AQAP and Ansar al-Shariah operatives. Likewise, the rapid escalation of Libya's situation from protest to civil conflict presented al-Qaeda with opportunities to expand AQIM's regional operations, and to replicate the localism model that was being experimented with at the time in Mali and Yemen. Libya's vast array of weapons depots, and the rapid militarization of the population also played into the hands of extremist groups like those who affiliated themselves with the al-Qaeda movement.

Beyond any single theater, the collective sense of infectious regional change meant that significant numbers of people across the Middle East were naturally susceptible to those advocating alternative social, religious and political models. Poverty, unemployment, corruption, economic and political mismanagement, security repression, and even climate change provided specific conditions for locally-focused jihadists like al-Qaeda to harness. In areas where protest had turned to violence, it was often those with a simple and less corruptible religious foundation that ended up successfully gaining the most credibility. Al-Qaeda was operating in fertile ground.

CHALLENGES

Al-Qaeda faced two significant immediate challenges amid the early phases of the Arab Spring: One political and one military. As mass protest gave way to dramatic political changes in countries like Tunisia and Egypt, it was political Islamist movements like the Muslim Brotherhood that stood in the wings as the best prepared and socially established organizations to fill the vacuums. The populist movements that uprooted Hosni Mubarak and Zine el-Abidine Ben Ali from power were not pursued in order to replace repressive dictatorships with any form of Islamic governance. However, it was organizations like the Muslim Brotherhood that had worked most effectively to mobilize as social movements within and often underneath the controls of those outgoing dictatorships. They therefore stood to benefit the most, as they were comparatively better positioned.[10] As Islamists of a more moderate nature, they presented a serious challenge to al-Qaeda's vision of exploiting not only the instability in places like Egypt and Tunisia, but also the opening for new socio-political and religio-political models for governance.

Al-Qaeda was also challenged, or perhaps more accurately threatened, by domestic and foreign attempts — both real and anticipated — to suppress and contain its pre-existing and newly developing presences across the region. In Yemen in particular, intensified U.S. attention upon AQAP's activities and its continued focus on plotting external attacks on the homeland played at least some role in encouraging the government-led tribal counter-offensive against its holdings in the south. On a local level, many of the early anti-Qaddafi militias in Libya, particularly those which enjoyed support and protection from the U.S. and U.K.-led coalition intervention, actively sought to isolate fledgling jihadist factions and separate them from the broader strategic gains made on the ground.

Finally, and arguably most importantly, was the challenge al-Qaeda faced from ISIS and its dramatic gains in Iraq and proclamation of a caliphate in mid-2014. Initially in Syria in late 2013, ISIS was a direct military threat to Jabhat al-Nusra, which in effect was al-Qaeda's Syrian affiliate at the time. That threat translated into a military adversary in early 2014, and then an international strategic competitor after the announcement of the caliphate. That latter development, and the fact that ISIS demonstrably controlled territory spanning across what had been a sovereign boundary between Syria and Iraq, posed an existential threat to al-Qaeda's jihadist preeminence. That pre-existing jihadist groups across the region and further afield then pledged their allegiance to this ISIS caliphate further undermined al-Qaeda's claim to be the representative of global jihad.

OUTCOMES

In 2017, al-Qaeda arguably found itself in a more favorable position than its jihadist rival, ISIS.[11] Whereas the latter's brutal violence and bold declarations had attracted dozens of governments to coalesce into a coalition seeking its destruction, al-Qaeda's comparatively quieter and more locally-focused approach meant it had been given several years to consolidate progress made prior to ISIS's caliphate proclamation in mid-2014. Consequently, al-Qaeda had achieved a discernible re-energization of a portion of its central leadership now based in northwestern Syria, where it was surrounded by a highly effective, if not dominant jihadist group, Hay'at Tahrir al-Sham (H.T.S.). H.T.S.'s overwhelming emphasis on the local, however, appeared by mid-2017 to have induced a distance between it and al-Qaeda, at least in terms of command loyalty. In Yemen, meanwhile, al-Qaeda had successfully embedded itself within the Sunni tribal revolution against the Houthis, and effectively exploited the Saudi-led military intervention. Elsewhere, al-Qaeda appeared to be attempting a recovery in Afghanistan, while sustaining operations in Pakistan, Bangladesh, North Africa, Somalia, and affiliated operations in many other areas of the Islamic world.

Events since 2011 had also ensured that al-Qaeda's process of decentralization had continued unabated, and affiliate tactics and strategy had become more of a local issue. This process may have provided local al-Qaeda factions with the ability to better embed themselves within local dynamics, and insulate themselves from external threat, but over time, this approach was also revealing serious disadvantages. In Syria for example, where affiliate Jabhat al-Nusra had thrived in an unprecedented way, the pressure to continue seeking local credibility in order to embed further into the local revolution meant more concessions were necessary. The rebranding to Jabhat Fateh al-Sham through a claim to have broken external ties to al-Qaeda was one such concessionary move, which divided the movement's leadership and, later through a complex series of events, led to a further rebrand (to H.T.S.) and aggressive attacks on former opposition allies. Within six months, al-Qaeda's reputation for trustworthiness within the broader Syrian armed opposition movement had discernibly declined, and Zawahri had begun speaking a different language than that used by his forces in Syria, calling for its forces in Syria to revert to a traditional model of guerilla warfare based on a transnational vision.[12] Al-Qaeda's future in Syria appeared to present two possible scenarios: Either further concessions and splits in al-Qaeda's senior circles, or a more aggressive assertion of dominance and a further loss of trust within portions of the opposition.

Despite these challenges, the evolution of al-Qaeda's brand to something perceived locally as being more appreciative of local dynamics meant that continued instability in the Middle East promised to present more opportunities for exploitation. It also raised the possibility that this evolved jihadist thinking could begin to "mainstream" its way into acceptability among some conventional circles in the region, including even within governments. Perceptions of U.S. isolationism combined with regional state frustration at continued Iranian expansionism produces the kind of dynamics that could feasibly catalyze some to consider localized al-Qaeda affiliates as de facto acceptable actors. The evolution of Jabhat al-Nusra into H.T.S., and the resulting distance between it and al-Qaeda's central leadership, looked in June 2017 to have potentially set the group up for possible formal relations with at least one regional government, Qatar. Doha had worked directly with the group for several months to negotiate a population swap in Syria that eventually took place in April.[13] Such developments represent the dangerous start of a slippery slope for counter-terrorism strategy, but a major victory for groups whose roots lay, at least originally, within al-Qaeda.

THE ISLAMIC STATE'S RESURGENCE

STRATEGIC VISION

Just like al-Qaeda, ISIS's ultimate strategic objective has been to establish a global caliphate. However, unlike al-Qaeda, ISIS rapidly sought to attain this step, beginning in 2011 with a covert entry into Syria and recovery in Iraq, and ending in its public proclamation of a caliphate across those two countries in mid-2014. Although a definitive break between al-Qaeda and ISIS did not take place until February 2014, ISIS and its predecessor, the I.S.I., had been operating to a markedly different strategic hymn sheet to al-Qaeda since the mid-2000s, when its brutal sectarian practices in Iraq incurred repeated criticism from al-Qaeda's global leadership.

ISIS's preference for violence, mass murder, intimidation, and other brutal behaviors is founded in its belief that ultra- or hyper-violence is the only tool available to create chaos, to split Westphalian states, and to purify communities from the inside out. Of particular ideological importance in this respect are the writings of Abu Bakr Naji, who spoke of a phased "management of savagery" to first create chaos and then a just and righteous Islamic rule. Naji also stressed that it was only through the "crucial" use of violence and the avoidance of any "softness" that a sufficient sense of strength would be presented as to allow the complete introduction and imposition of shari'a upon the people.[14]

In order to achieve its self-proclaimed caliphate status, ISIS framed itself as its name implied: As an Islamic movement that was explicitly seeking to build a pure Islamic state that Muslims from around the world could emigrate to. Whereas al-Qaeda sought to build alliances and avoid enemies, ISIS acted unilaterally and in the interests only of itself and its objective to establish a state-like entity. Territory was almost entirely unshared with others, and rivals were either aggressively managed or violently suppressed. While ISIS was undoubtedly focused on the local, and spent considerable resources trying to demonstrate its ability to provide civilians with services and other governance-related needs, its eyes were ultimately fixed on the global. The establishment of an Islamic State crossing Syria and Iraq then presented ISIS with the fuel to catalyze an expansion by proxy across the Islamic world and further afield, as supporters sought to ride ISIS's wave of apparent success.

With the state project and caliphate a reality, ISIS's strategic vision shifted to its expansion and defense from external attack. As the international gained more importance, ISIS activated plans to deploy fighters into Western countries to strike what al-Qaeda had called the "far enemy." When the international community united to roll back the territorial caliphate in Syria and Iraq, ISIS responded further by encouraging its supporters across the world to launch their own attacks using whatever means available.[15] Even despite suffering substantial losses on the ground, the concept of an ISIS caliphate became stronger on a virtual level, meaning ISIS could continue to draw upon supporters of its strategic vision, who had themselves witnessed its potential and, it hoped, would fight for its eventual return.[16]

ISIS had therefore established for itself an alternative model of jihad that stood in competition to al-Qaeda. The significant differences of these competing models of jihad, and ISIS's rapid demonstration of success between 2011 and 2014, potentially presented the ISIS model as the benchmark for a new, younger, and hyper-extremist generation of jihadists. Whereas al-Qaeda had gained a reputation for traditionalism and a tendency to resort to extensive theological debates over even minor issues, ISIS presented itself as a jihadist movement that gave no concessions and would achieve its objective as quickly as possible, whatever the consequences.

OPPORTUNITIES

ISIS's predecessor in Iraq, the I.S.I., suffered a strategic defeat following the U.S. military "surge" from 2007-10, with 34 of the group's 42-man senior leadership either killed or captured, and all territory controlled by the group recaptured by Iraqi authorities.[17] However, an insurgent group is only as weak as its opponent is strong. The most important U.S.-led efforts to roll back the Islamic State during the surge were led by Sunni Arab tribal fighters in Iraq's western Anbar province. They had been collectively known as the Sons of Iraq coalition and depended at the time upon military support and financial payments from the United States.

When President Barack Obama announced his decision to "end" the combat mission in Iraq in August 2010, it was assumed that these tribal fighters would continue to enjoy the necessary support from the Iraqi central government in Baghdad. However, with the U.S. military effectively no longer a player in the country, Iraq's then Prime Minister Nouri al-Maliki gave little support to the Sons of Iraq, who were left to dwindle into irrelevance.[18] Just as al-Qaeda in Iraq and the I.S.I. had enjoyed the recruitment boost provided by America's decision to pursue de-Baathification in Iraq, so ISIS enjoyed the benefits provided by Maliki's refusal to continue to pay the Sons of Iraq. ISIS recruitment steadily increased, as did its credibility as an alternative to a central government widely perceived within Sunni Arab communities as overly influenced by Iran and hostile to Sunni communities. ISIS subsequently experienced a significant recovery and regrowth in Iraq through 2011-14, peaking with its dramatic capture of Mosul in June 2014.

The I.S.I. was also presented with clear opportunities when Syria devolved into chaos in the first half of 2011, and as an indigenous armed resistance movement began to form there that summer. In fact, just as the very first armed resistance groups began to form in Syria, the I.S.I. leadership in Iraq decided to secretly dispatch a cell of commanders to neighboring Syria to create a Syrian wing of the I.S.I.[19] That wing, Jabhat al-Nusra, was covertly formed in October 2011 and announced publicly in January 2012. Until its public break-up in April 2013, Jabhat al-Nusra had been operating — at least on paper — under the authority of the I.S.I. and its leader, Abu Bakr al-Baghdadi. The I.S.I. in Iraq had even been covering half of Jabhat al-Nusra's monthly financial costs.[20] As a result of its split with Jabhat al-Nusra in the spring of 2013, ISIS emerged as a transnational entity operating in both Iraq and Syria, and proceeded to pursue an aggressive strategy of expansion across northern and eastern Syria.

Just as was the case with al-Qaeda, ISIS also benefited more broadly from the collective sense of change that swept across the Middle East amid the Arab Spring protests. However, ISIS did not seek to ride the wave of change and use it as a conveyor belt like al-Qaeda; rather, ISIS sought to use the wave of change as a catalyst to sow division and chaos, and destroy nation-states from within. In other words, the change that the Arab Spring brought about was not just pointed in the wrong un-Islamic directions, but it was also far too insufficient in scale. ISIS sought to entirely transform the world in as short a time and in as destructive a manner as possible.

The final opportunity provided to ISIS post-Arab Spring was the perception amongst some circles of the global jihadist movement that al-Qaeda had failed to achieve any clear territorial or state-building objective, and had in fact become weaker and less united over time. ISIS's model of jihad was internally oriented toward presenting an image of intense unity of purpose, guided through an organizational structure that was intensely controlled and ruled by total allegiance to one's leadership. The fact that al-Qaeda's core leader Zawahri was rarely seen in public and that on the occasions when he did show himself, it was normally to give long-winded theological monologues on video, provided ISIS with an opportunity to demonstrate that it represented a more pro-active movement, capable of collective action and constant results.

CHALLENGES

The biggest challenge ISIS has faced in recent years has been from determined attempts by the international community to challenge its territorial holdings and defeat its ability to identify as a "state." ISIS's use of hyper-violence to achieve its goals, and its singling out of minority communities like Iraq's Yazidis, generated the kind of global outcry that necessitated international action. And by identifying so explicitly as a state-like movement whose very existence is predicated on controlling territory and governing populations, those actions have resulted in a self-incurred threat.

Following the U.S. military intervention in Iraq in August 2014, and then in Syria in September 2014, the international coalition against ISIS has grown to 68 member states. The collective military action subsequently undertaken by the coalition had by late September 2017 successfully recaptured a combined total of 83 percent of ISIS territory in Iraq and Syria, including the cities of Mosul and Raqqa.[21] Although ISIS has created an image in its supporters' minds of what a jihadist caliphate looks like, and proven the fact that one can exist, the extent and pace of these territorial losses represents a serious challenge to ISIS's ability to present itself as a military force protected by God. They also demonstrate opportunity costs to potential supporters of the group in local zones of instability like Syria and Iraq, who will view joining ISIS at any point in the present or future as carrying with it considerable risks.

In addition to the clear disadvantages resulting from its violent action and rapid pursuit of grand objectives, ISIS is also likely to face the challenge of maintaining its reputation among communities now liberated from its iron grip and past victimization. As with most insurgent movements, territorial defeat rarely results in the neutralizing of the ideology underpinning the movement itself. The drivers motivating the insurgency will, more often than not, continue to exist, even if among a smaller proportion of the base community. However, the particularly intense violence employed by ISIS, and the deeply repressive nature of its governance, will not stand ISIS in good stead to mount a comeback amongst the same communities at one point in the future. Moreover, the crumbling caliphate of 2017 is the result of ISIS's second comeback, after its first experiment with "state"-building in the mid-2000s was defeated. Trying a third time and hoping for the same level of successful outcomes will arguably face significant challenges.

Finally, ISIS's various *wilayat* that consist of pre-existing jihadist groups who have pledged allegiance to ISIS and its caliphate since late 2014 may begin to stray when the caliphate heartland in Syria and Iraq becomes more negligible. While the "virtual caliphate" may well persist in supporters' minds on the internet, the ability of surviving ISIS leadership figures to sustain a tight-knit organization with many thousands of fighters distributed across the world will be severely challenged. Al-Qaeda may have managed to survive this same challenge in years past, but it enjoyed the advantage of not having proclaimed the existence of a discernible territorial entity from which part of its authority derived.

Outcomes

By October 2017, ISIS found itself as its weakest point since the start of the Arab Spring and its power looked set to diminish further as coalition forces consolidated victories in Mosul and Raqqa and as a pro-Assad coalition pressed on toward al-Mayadin and al-Bukamal in Deir Ezzor. Thus far, ISIS's particularly violent brand of jihad appears to have reduced their appeal as a potential alternative for disenfranchised Sunni populations in the region. Even in Iraq, where in some cases Iran-backed Shi'a militias were a lead force in liberating territory from ISIS, the local communities remained either indifferent to ISIS, or openly hostile to it. It is in this sense in particular that al-Qaeda appears to have trumped ISIS, in that its focus on adapting to local sensitivities has provided it with a more durable insurance policy if and when faced with a major external threat.

Consequently, ISIS's future prospects as a self-declared territorial entity look bleak. Seemingly irreversible losses in Syria and Iraq are compounded by the detrimental effect they will have upon the confidence and obedience of allied or affiliate movements elsewhere in the world. The only remaining source of hope in the medium term is that ISIS's caliphate has been established for all to see as a once discernible reality and as an idea, or aspirational vision. Not only did it exist, but its reality sparked the formation of one of the most significant global military coalitions in recent history.

That that caliphate "idea" remains in existence will be ISIS's main source of strength as its territorial project continues to crumble. Should ISIS successfully continue to encourage or "inspire" terrorist attacks in the heart of Western cities, then its brand will live to fight another day. Should one or more affiliates elsewhere in the world — such as Wilayat Gharb Ifriqiyyah in Nigeria or Wilayat Sinai in Egypt — manage to sustain a high tempo of operations and continue their strong affiliation with the original ISIS brand, that may also help tide over the losses sustained in its heartlands. Nevertheless, ISIS's future still appears to be existentially tied to its existence in Iraq and Syria, and it is there that its fate is most at risk.

Key Drivers and Counter-Measures

Political Failure, Weak States, and Instability

Clearly, the most significant driver responsible for fueling the recent rise, expansion, and consolidation of jihadist militancy, and for the emergence of two divergent, competing models of jihad, has been the rife political and social instability across much of the Middle East. Crippling issues of governance failure, corruption, economic mismanagement, high levels of youth unemployment, and more were all brought to the surface during the Arab Spring protests of 2010-11. Mass protest, state repression, and foreign intervention and interference all then contributed toward an environment in which change was deemed the key dynamic of the region. For some, that trend toward change meant an opportunity not for democracy, but for a radical transformation of local or regional governance. Jihadists pounced.

For ISIS, the prevalence of opportunities provided by political failure, and the resulting proliferation of weak states and instability, was something to exacerbate. In keeping with Abu Bakr Naji's strategic thinking, mere instability was not enough of a reality to bring about total change — debilitating chaos was necessary. In Iraq and Syria, ISIS took advantage of instability, conflict, societal divisions, political oppression, and corruption to tear communities, governments, and borders apart. That expansionist project then — for a period of time — expanded at a rapid rate, thanks in part to ISIS's success in Syria and Iraq, but also due to the prior existence of the same driver conditions of political failure, corruption, economic mismanagement, and so forth.

While ISIS sought to further intensify pre-existing drivers of instability, al-Qaeda aimed to exploit them as part of tailor made locally-embedded and locally-sensitive strategies. Al-Qaeda presented aggravating conditions as a reason for why a positive change was necessary and it posited only al-Qaeda had the ingredients for that positive change. Whereas al-Qaeda and its regional affiliates remained determined to establish Islamic states, or emirates, it calculated that doing so too quickly would spark a secondary popular demand for change, when communities rejected something they were fundamentally unprepared for. Instead, al-Qaeda thought, it would take time to inculcate the suitable conditions for such a proclamation. In the meantime, energy was best invested in siding with the masses and inserting itself within broader revolutionary movements with more short-to-medium term resiliency.

Combating this set of drivers is a long-term challenge that will require deep and determined investment from governments in the Middle East and from the international community. Strong diplomatic relationships and resulting financial investments must be made more strictly in accordance with demonstrated attempts to improve socio-political freedoms, to eliminate state-linked corruption, and ensure full ethnic and sectarian political representation. Favoring "strong" leaders more prone to oppressive behaviors may promise a semblance of short-term stability, but it in fact serves only to further emphasize the underlying drivers that fuel extremism and instability.

SECTARIANISM DRIVING REGIONAL COMPETITION

Another key driver that jihadists of all stripes — including Shiites — have exploited to maximum effect in recent years is the intensifying sectarian dynamic that appears to be mobilizing people behind a great power struggle between Saudi Arabia and Iran. Although sectarianism has not necessarily been the defining factor behind the Saudi-Iran competition, it has been used by both states to mobilize popular support and militia or proxy recruitment to fight it out in civil conflicts across the region. From Iraq to Syria to Yemen, different regional governments have used the Shi'a versus Sunni dichotomy to shape and drive conflict, hoping to eventually win out and acquire greater influence over the other.

That regional governments have played this dangerous and destabilizing game has directly fueled the very reasons for the existence of groups like al-Qaeda and ISIS. Both jihadist movements have focused their operations in much of the Middle East, and especially in conflict hotspots like Syria, Iraq, and Yemen, as being part of a grand sectarian struggle for primacy in the Islamic world. Although no substantive evidence exists to suggest regional governments have directly provided support to al-Qaeda or ISIS, the significant provision of assistance to other, less extreme armed movements has undoubtedly added to the ability of jihadists — especially those linked to al-Qaeda — to play a prominent role as battlefield "partners." When conflicts in these countries appear to be defined primarily in sectarian terms, then the greatest benefactors will be extremists on all sides. Jihadists then have an interest in sustaining those conflicts, to further their narrative and real-world gains.

Tackling the prevalence of sectarian narratives as driving and mobilizing forces behind regional rivalries is also a long-term challenge, especially given the historical nature of this dynamic. It is also hard to imagine a Middle East in which Saudi Arabia and Iran no longer perceive themselves as determined rivals or competitors for influence. Therefore, the international community's best efforts would be spent de-escalating existing conflicts; limiting and eventually preventing external interference in them; and putting far greater effort into political dialogue and multilateral diplomatic initiatives aimed at resolving or preventing conflict. Economical and overly risk-averse policies of conflict containment or isolationist decisions to avoid any involvement altogether have proven especially insufficient in recent years, as revealed in the scale of the conflict in Syria, Iraq, Yemen, Libya, and elsewhere.

GLOBALIZATION AND ITS EFFECTS

Another key driver behind the recent growth of jihadist militancy is globalization and its various effects, including the loosening of international borders; easier and more affordable access to international travel; the speed of information sharing through the internet; the proliferation of social media and encryption technology; and the resulting hyperactive, feverish nature of international news and current affairs.

As events unfolded in the region, whether in Tunisia or Egypt as long-standing regimes fell to protests; in Libya where an international intervention secured the defeat and death of Moammar Qaddafi; or in Syria, Iraq or Yemen where civil war disintegrated portions of the state, news of all kinds spread fast and jihadists found a market for their own propaganda. For the first time, a teenager sat in his bedroom in Paris or London could follow battlefield events virtually minute-by-minute, and when ISIS chose to decapitate Western hostages or to conduct mass executions on video, it found a willing and vulnerable audience online.

Extremist materials thus moved from complex, member-only web forums to easily accessed social media platforms, where written material, photos, and high-definition video could all be uploaded, for free. As more potentially recruitable individuals were reached online, they also found themselves able to communicate with on-the-ground jihadists, using freely available cell phone applications, on which they could coordinate their planned arrival to Syria, Iraq or elsewhere. That globalization and the loosening of international borders had made airline travel less prohibitively expensive, made the actual act of joining a terrorist group a lesser leap that it would have been only a decade earlier. Consequently, the conflicts in Iraq and Syria sparked the greatest movement of jihadist militants ever recorded, far eclipsing the state-backed recruitment of the Afghan mujahideen in the 1980s.

Globalization and all of its effects are an inevitable, irreversible reality of the modern world, but they raise a number of substantial challenges from a law enforcement and intelligence perspective. The nature of the airline travel industry in particular demands a greater level of intelligence sharing between governments, and individual government border controls — by air and land — should be more stringently monitored and controlled. Beyond any other sphere, the internet has become an arena of invaluable activity for jihadist groups, and the public and private sectors must sustain, if not intensify, their efforts to prohibit extremists from having any easy or sustained use of the online space. Increased effort could also be invested in creating large numbers of "mole" accounts, impersonating extremists and spreading disinformation. In an age of 24-hour news in which patently fake content finds its own readership, the responsible news industry also has an increased duty to serve people best, with credible, verified, and serious content. Glorification of warfare and mythologizing of extremists like ISIS do the counter-extremism industry and counter-terrorism community no favors.

INTRA-JIHADIST COMPETITION

Another important driver that contributed toward the recent dramatic expansion of jihadist militancy in the Middle East, but that is also a consequence of it, is the intensive dynamic of enmity and competition between the world's two Sunni jihadist "brands," al-Qaeda and ISIS. The emergence of these divergent models of jihad was a long time coming, with al-Qaeda's central leadership having been unhappy at ISIS's predecessor movement's brutal violence in Iraq as early as the mid-2000s. That ISIS and al-Qaeda would have come to a divorce may potentially have been foreseeable, but the unique dynamics in existence post-Arab Spring certainly provided the space for differing strategic approaches and military rivalries on particularly important battlefields, such as Syria. The opportunities presented by the post-2010 instability and sense of collective change across the region also spurred on jihadist movements to dig their heels in and pursue bold strategies.

Once the dynamic of intra-jihadist competition had been established from mid-2013, and once the two jihadist movements had begun fighting each other in Syria from early 2014, the lines of differentiation were drawn and both movements sought to out-compete the other on the local and international stages. ISIS's success attracted unprecedented international counter-terror intervention and in response it pursued an intensive direct and indirect foreign attack strategy, coordinating and inspiring dozens of attacks in Europe, America, and elsewhere in the region. Al-Qaeda, on the other hand, focused overwhelmingly on the local in an apparent attempt to present itself as the favored and more durable jihadist brand, operating not solely in its own self-interest, but in pursuit of popular demands. With both divergent brands in full operation, the international community faced a complex set of threats, forcing it to preeminently devote its resources to combating the immediate one posed by ISIS, leaving al-Qaeda to embed itself further, in Libya, Yemen, Mali, Syria, and elsewhere.

To most effectively tackle this multifaceted jihadist threat, the international community must acknowledge that countering terrorism and extremism is a long-term struggle that encompasses more than mere military means. Granted, in a dynamic of intra-jihadist competition, an initial emphasis should be placed on combating both movements' territorial holdings; targeting their leaderships; restricting their access to finance; and blocking the movement of prospective foreign jihadist recruits. In pursuing such short-term and aggressive objectives, one would be aiming to weaken the groups' structures and to undermine their credibility, thereby simultaneously de-escalating the cyclical competition between them and weakening both of their capacity for even limited successes.

In conjunction with pursuing the above aggressive policies, there is also an argument for a geographically limited containment strategy, allowing jihadists a small territorial entity in which extremist practice and oppressive rule will "let them rot" from the inside. This strategy would have the added benefit of better ensuring that such groups would not be welcomed back, should they attempt a comeback years later. In such a scenario, the international community would be presented with invaluable opportunities to sponsor locally-led and managed counter-messaging campaigns, in order to undermine the ideology and the name of the jihadist group in question.

Beyond these short-to-medium term measures, the international community would be best advised to pursue the other policy recommendations set forth in the first three driver sections. These actions focus more on the structural and environmental drivers that could otherwise fuel violent extremism for many more years to come, and which must be tackled determinedly and consistently if we are to have any hope of pulling the rug out from under jihadists' feet.

OUTLOOK

The instability that swept across the Middle East since the Arab Spring has provided jihadist movements with durable futures, albeit ones based on differing foundations and seeking the same objective through differing means. The short-termist strategy operationalized by ISIS may have sparked an unprecedented international coalition response, but the rapidity with which ISIS's caliphate was established and the idea placed in its supporters' minds means it has created a cause that is likely to live on long after the territorial caliphate is rolled back. Al-Qaeda, meanwhile, appears to have pursued a long-term project in a more durable fashion, building trust and relationships beyond the traditional jihadist sphere in an attempt to secure a protective blanket around any future external threats.

However, al-Qaeda's successful implementation of this "controlled pragmatism" in Syria and Yemen may be beginning to reveal shortcomings, particularly in the apparent inability to push beyond al-Qaeda's negative brand image to secure anything close to a "uniting of the ranks" and a transition to a genuine mass movement. In struggling to attain this goal, al-Qaeda's Syrian affiliate has been forced to announce concessionary rebranding initiatives that both failed to convince Syrians of its intentions and enraged portions of al-Qaeda's most traditional and veteran figures in the region. Consequently, the latest iteration of al-Qaeda in Syria, H.T.S., appears to have distanced itself from al-Qaeda and likewise, al-Qaeda's senior leadership has been publicly at odds with H.T.S.'s tactics and strategy.[22] With that same al-Qaeda leadership purportedly preparing Osama bin Laden's son Hamza for a future leadership role, the prospects for a return to the jihadist group's ultra-extremist and transnational ways were on the rise. That Hamza bin Laden's public statements clearly avoided any criticism of ISIS — as was not the tradition for other senior al-Qaeda figures — also suggested the possibility of a future al-Qaeda rapprochement with, or re-co-optation of ISIS.[23]

The region's instability has also fueled unprecedented competition between great regional powers, principally Saudi Arabia and Iran, both of which have utilized their Sunni and Shi'a identities as sources for sectarian mobilization to pursue rival interests in weak and fragile states. That geopolitical dynamic of mutually escalatory action has directly empowered actors that operate based on religious foundations, including and in particular those on the more extreme end of the spectrum, like ISIS and al-Qaeda. Intense and intractable conflict; regional competition based in part on sectarian foundations; the rise of multiple competing jihadist movements; and the lack of international will to determinedly put an end to the cycle of violence have all played into the hands of extremists coming to the fore in driving violence. Within that existing context, al-Qaeda and ISIS have been competing against each other to emerge as the dominant representative of jihadism worldwide.

Some experts have suggested that continued instability in the Middle East combined with intensive international pressure against ISIS may encourage an eventual rapprochement between al-Qaeda and ISIS, and the creation of an even more capable and dangerous jihadist movement. This scenario remains highly unlikely, given the extent to which both movements have fought each other and declared the other to be religiously illegitimate and worthy of destruction. Unless a substantial proportion of both movements' existing leaderships are killed, a continued state of competition between the two is most likely. However, it is possible that a territorially weaker ISIS may maneuver itself into a position of not *having* to fight al-Qaeda.

ISIS, as a transnational movement, will seek to exploit the virtual level of its caliphate identity to continue to encourage terrorist actions beyond Syria and Iraq. Meanwhile, the long-game approach embraced by al-Qaeda affiliates in Syria and Yemen may catalyze a further distancing between operational al-Qaeda factions and the movement's central leadership in Afghanistan-Pakistan. In this case, al-Qaeda would in effect be continuing along the already laid path of decentralization, which on the one hand means al-Qaeda would represent even less of an organization, but on the other, would mean that Middle Eastern states and the broader international community would face an even more diverse and adaptable set of jihadist adversaries.

ENDNOTES

1. Charles Lister, "Intra-Jihadist Competition: Combating an Unprecedented Threat," *The Annals of the American Academy*, Vol 668, Issue 1 (October 2016): 53-70, and: Charles Lister, "Jihadi Rivalry: The Islamic State Challenges Al-Qaida," *Brookings Institution* (January 2016).

2. Charles Lister, "The Dawn of Mass Jihad: Success in Syria Fuels al-Qa'ida's Evolution," *CTC Sentinel* (September 2016).

3. Charles Lister, "Al Qaeda Is About to Establish an Emirate in Northern Syria," *Foreign Policy*, May 4, 2016.

4. Emily Hunt, "Zarqawi's 'Total War' on Iraqi Shiites Exposes a Divide Among Sunni Jihadists," *Washington Institute for Near East Policy*, November 15, 2005; and Jack Moore, "Osama Bin Laden Letters Warned Against the Pillars of ISIS's Strategy," *Newsweek*, March 2, 2016.

5. Rukmini Callimachi, "In Timbuktu, al-Qaida left behind a manifesto," *Associated Press*, February 14, 2013.

6. Aaron Zelin & Patrick Hoover, "What AQAP's Operations Reveal About Its Strategy in Yemen," *War on the Rocks*, April 23, 2015.

7. Ayman al-Zawahri, "General Guidelines for Jihad," *As-Sahab Media* (September 2013).

8. Lister, "Intra-Jihadist Competition: Combating an Unprecedented Threat."

9. Charles Lister, *The Syrian Jihad: Al-Qaeda, the Islamic State and the Evolution of an Insurgency*, (London: Hurst Publishers, 2016), 31-50.

10. Shadi Hamid, "Islamism, the Arab Spring, and the Failure of America's Do-Nothing Policy in the Middle East," *The Atlantic*, October 9, 2015; and "Shadi Hamid & William McCants, "Islamism after the Arab Spring: Between the Islamic State and the Nation-State," *Brookings Institution*, January 2017.

11. "The Jihadi Threat: ISIS, Al-Qaeda and Beyond," Washington D.C.: *United States Institute of Peace*, 2017.

12. "Al-Qaeda's Zawahiri calls for 'guerrilla war' in Syria," *Al Jazeera*, April 24, 2017.

13. Martin Chulov, "Qatari royal family members used as leverage in Syrian population swap," *The Guardian*, April 14, 2017.

14. David Martin Jones & M.L.R. Smith, "The Strategy of Savagery: Explaining the Islamic State," *War on the Rocks*, February 24, 2015; Hassan Hassan, "ISIS has reached new depths of depravity. But there is a brutal logic to it," *The Guardian*, February 7, 2015; Martin Reardon, "ISIL and the management of savagery," *Al Jazeera*, July 6, 2015; Lawrence Wright, "ISIS's Savage Strategy in Iraq," *The New Yorker*, June 16, 2014; David Ignatius, "The manual that chillingly foreshadows the Islamic State," *The Washington Post*, September 2014.

15. Abu Mohammed al-Adnani al-Shami, "Indeed, Your Lord is Ever Watchful," Al-Furqan Media, September 9, 2014; "Islamic State calls for attacks on the West during Ramadan in audio message," *Reuters*, May 22, 2016.

16. General Joseph L. Votel, LTC Christina Bembenek, Charles Hans, Jeffrey Mouton and Amanda Spencer, "#Virtual Caliphate: Defeating ISIL on the Physical Battlefield Is Not Enough," Washington D.C.: Center for a New American Security, 2017; Harleen Gambhir, "The Virtual Caliphate: ISIS's Information Warfare," *The Institute for the Study of War*, December 20, 2016; Charlie Winter, "Documenting the Virtual Caliphate," *Quilliam Foundation*, October 2015.

17. Lister, *The Syrian Jihad*, 46.

18. Miriam Benraad, "Iraq's Tribal 'Sahwa': Its Rise and Fall," *Middle East Policy*, Vol. 18, Issue 1, Spring 2011: 121-131; Priyanka Boghani, "David Petraeus: ISIS's Rise in Iraq Isn't a Surprise," *PBS Frontline*, July 29, 2014; Ehab Zahriyeh, "How ISIL became a major force with only a few thousand fighters," *Al Jazeera America*, June 19, 2014.

19. Lister, *The Syrian Jihad*, 55-59.

20. Lister, *The Syrian Jihad*, 58.

21. CJTF, "OIR Monthly Civilian Casualty Report," Kuwait: CJTF, 2017.

22. Charles Lister, "Al-Qaeda's Turning Against its Syrian Affiliate," *Middle East Institute*, May 18, 2017.

23. Ali Soufan, "Hamza Bin Laden, Osama's Son, Is Helping Al-Qaeda Stage a Deadly Comeback," *Newsweek*, June 19, 2017.

CHAPTER THREE

JIHADIST PROPAGANDA, OFFLINE:

STRATEGIC COMMUNICATIONS IN MODERN WARFARE

CHARLIE WINTER, HAID HAID

INTRODUCTION

Propaganda has long been central to revolutionary warfare. However, never has it been used more aggressively and effectively than it is today. In Syria in particular, in-theater propaganda has come to be of foundational importance to non-state actors operating across the political spectrum. Few groups have been as adept at offline outreach as ISIS and Hay'at Tahrir al-Sham (HTS), each of which used propaganda and offline public diplomacy to systematically entrench itself within the local body politic, whenever and wherever conditions allowed.

Understanding how and why these organizations use strategic communication is a necessary step toward stabilizing Syria, yet the issue remains under-researched, with most analysis of jihadist communication operations focusing on propaganda disseminated over the Internet, and how its online consumption contributes to the radicalization of would-be foreign fighters and terrorists. With this paper, we hope to help correct this imbalance in the research. Comparing and evaluating the in-theater communication operations of ISIS and HTS, we shed light on an aspect of the Syrian war about which little information is publicly available. Using a qualitative mixed-methods approach incorporating semi-structured interviews with activists and journalists operating inside northern Syria, longitudinal propaganda research, and in-depth content analysis, we examine how each organization used strategic communication operations to further their respective insurgent aims.

The paper proceeds as follows: First, we focus on communication infrastructure and delivery, contrasting ISIS's once-sophisticated and extensive network of propaganda kiosks and recruitment centers with HTS's own institutionalization efforts, which have tended to be subtler, more rudimentary, and, arguably, more effective. The second section explores how both groups worked to restrict the flow of information in their heartland territories between 2013 and 2018. We conclude the paper with a discussion of the strategic principles that underpin each organization's understanding of and approach toward offensive and defensive strategic communication, noting that it is imprudent to assume similarities based on ideological inclination alone.

Manufacturing Public Discourse

Islamic State In Iraq and al-Sham

Between 2013 and 2018, ISIS deployed both consumed and performative propaganda in Syria. The former consisted of audio-visual media products, everything that was broadcast and distributed in-theater through its bespoke communication infrastructure — documentaries, current affairs features, radio programs, photograph reports, newspapers, magazines, operation claims, theological literature, infographics, posters, billboards, and so on. The latter — performative propaganda — relied on direct interpersonal engagement and was primarily delivered by outreach officials working on the ground in Syria. This latter form of propaganda involved constant face-to-face interaction between representatives of ISIS and its civilian constituents, and, while it was most obviously encapsulated in public spectacles like executions and amputations, it appeared in more benign contexts, too, from town fairs and mosque gatherings to school lessons and competitions.

ISIS evidently recognized the power of physical presence, and that the act of media dissemination could itself become a form of propaganda. With that in mind, its consumed propaganda was always a supporting act to its performative counterpart, a way for it to fight, in its own words, "on an internal front to bring the truth" to the population over which it ruled.

The most crucial physical components of its propaganda activism were the *nuqtah i'lamiyyah* (literally, media point) — a caliphate-wide institution that facilitated in-theater propaganda dissemination — the Center for Proselytization and Mosques, and the Ministry for Education. Regarding the nuqat i'lamiyyah, a March 2016 article in ISIS's official newspaper, *al-Naba'*, provides some revealing information. Established in places that were "lacking in communications mechanisms," media points were intended to "present the media in all of its forms to the ordinary people" and serve as a "coupling link" between the ISIS organization and its civilian constituents. At one and the same time, media points delivered news updates on ISIS's war effort and projected its utopian narrative. Wherever they were, they screened propaganda films, and served as satellite publishing houses, radio listening points, and digital distribution centers. Attendance was assured by blatant intimidation, as well as the host population's desire to appear loyal. What's more, they were not limited to towns and cities — mobile kiosks were also rigged up so that the caliphate's audio-visual output could reach even the remotest areas of Iraq and Syria.

In Raqqa, which was the symbolic seat of the caliphate until 2017, activists asserted that there were "many [media points] in the city and its environs." According to the aforementioned *al-Naba'* article, each kiosk "provide[d] a full media archive in a number of languages, from English, French and Kurdish to Turkish, Farsi and Bangla, and so on." The same article went on to claim that ISIS's media officials in the city intended to set up a new "kiosk in every neighborhood and on every important street."

The media point initiative was complemented by ISIS's Center for Proselytization and Mosques, a caliphate-wide outreach unit that was dedicated to in-theater recruitment operations. Concerned with enlisting both civilians and soldiers to the group's ideology, the center worked doggedly across Iraq and Syria between 2013 and 2018 to entice locals to its cause. The scope and sophistication of its activities were encapsulated in a May 2016 video from northern Syria, which followed a team of its recruiters as they engaged in a two-week enlistment drive. First, they are shown distributing leaflets in mudbrick villages. Next, there is an account of their *da'wah* and shari'a courses, which are shown to have put particular focus on the education and recruitment of children: Young boys are depicted being coached in *tahfidh* — learning the Quran by rote — as well as being taught how to write. The narrator explains that there are similar courses on offer for women and girls, something that had, he claims, resulted in mothers signing their own children up to volunteer for military and even suicide operations. The campaign concludes with a sight familiar to ISIS, a da'wah caravan party, at which villagers are shown rapturously pledging allegiance to Abu Bakr al-Baghdadi before tucking into boiled sweets and bursting into song. This is just one example of the Center's in-theater recruitment drives — as many other propaganda videos and photograph reports attest, they happened continuously across ISIS's territories between 2013 and 2018.

Operating alongside these efforts was the Ministry for Education, which for a time presided over public schooling in parts of Syria that were controlled by ISIS. After its sweeping victories of 2014, ISIS commandeered the pedagogical infrastructure that was already in place in its new territories — teachers were re-educated or, failing that, cast off, and entire curriculums were revised. When the schools eventually reopened their doors to the trickle of students that voluntarily returned, they worked to normalize the ISIS cause — arithmetic was taught with reference to AK-47s and hand grenades alongside a revisionist history of Islam and "Islamic" geography. Besides these more indirect forms of outreach, candidates for *shibl* (cub) camps were cultivated in ISIS-run schools. Upon selection, *ashbal* (plural of cub) were dispatched to boarding facilities in rural areas, provided with weapons training and intensive ideological coaching. There, they would be indoctrinated through a mixture of education, hardship, and social support, a cocktail of measures capable of turning many of them into some of the caliphate's most committed fighters.

Adopting a highly sophisticated approach toward in-theater outreach between 2013 and 2018, ISIS used pre-existing social structures in Syria as well as its own infrastructural institutions to interact with the civilian population over which it ruled. Its efforts were expensive and expansive — they crossed genders and did not discriminate according to age.

Hay'at Tahrir al-Sham

Contrasting with the above, HTS's offline outreach operations have tended to rely much less on infrastructure. Whereas the self-proclaimed caliphate invested thousands of dollars in establishing hundreds of media points across Syria and Iraq — many of which were outfitted with widescreen televisions and laser printers — HTS's media output, which comprises the videos, photograph reports, and literature produced by in-house media centers like the Ebaa Agency and Amjad Foundation, is markedly less flashy, and so too is its distribution methodology. While, like ISIS, its outreach operations are split between consumed and performative propaganda, the relative weight of each category differs significantly; HTS tends to spend much less time and effort on consumed propaganda operations.

Instead, it usually opts for a more personal mode of dissemination, chiefly in the form of the media cadres it sends to mosques to hand out literature after Friday prayers. These officials are also in regular attendance at public da'wah gatherings and events. The literary materials they distribute are more variable than those of ISIS, tending to adapt to the group's immediate priorities in the area in question. Sometimes, they consist of leaflets working to mobilize specific groups against specific events — like, for example, the political negotiations in Astana — whereas at others they consist of shari'a guidance promoting HTS's rigid interpretation of Islam, and not much else. These cadres also distribute compact disks and flash drives loaded with lectures and leadership statements. However, compared to ISIS, there are far fewer of them.

Alongside its semi-formalized media distribution infrastructure, HTS has co-opted a number of already-extant structures and institutions in its territories in northern Syria, something that enables proxy media officials to propagandize on its behalf while masquerading as independent actors. By outsourcing its public diplomacy through *mudafat, du'at al-jihad*, and public gatherings, the details of each of which are outlined below, the group has been able to save on resource expenditure and become a more decentralized — and therefore elusive — target for counter-strategic communication operations.

One of the most important arenas for HTS's everyday outreach is its network of mudafat — large guest rooms set up and administered in rural areas that are used to host social gatherings. According to interview respondents currently residing in HTS-held territory, there are a number of different mudafat, each of which is used for a distinct purpose. The two most prominent manifestations are those that are devoted to the *muhajirin* (foreign fighters) and those that serve the interests of the *umara'* (leaders). The former is used exclusively by foreign fighters, the groupings of which are based on place of origin or tribal affiliation (there are, for example, both Tunisian mudafat and Yemeni mudafat). These facilities offer a center of gravity for social and ideological incubation among HTS fighters and are also important nodes for fundraising and recruiting. The latter, the doors of which are open to everyone, are reserved for hosting engagements between HTS elites and representatives from the local population. Usually, they are presided over by HTS's local military *amir* (leader) or some other influential figure from the organization. These institutions in particular are central to the group's public outreach: Through them, it is able to maintain channels of communication with local dignitaries and allow people to air their concerns, make recommendations, and voice demands. Attendance is incentivized more than it is coerced — in much the same way as ISIS's Center for Proselytization and Mosques draws crowds, HTS periodically lays on public feasts at its mudafat, often following up with da'wah sessions or speeches from designated officials.

In tandem with the above, HTS also presides over a network of religious education centers, which are administered by its volunteer corps, the du'at al-jihad (callers to jihad). These institutions differ from the schools and camps of ISIS because they are less holistic in their approach and rarely fall under the official HTS rubric. Instead, they usually operate semi-autonomously, augmenting the group's official outreach operations under the watchful eye of the Saudi jihadist cleric, 'Abdullah al-Muhaysini. With tacit encouragement and endorsement from HTS, du'at al-jihad education centers and even a radio station have proliferated across northern Syria over the past few years. Although their staff-members are always cautious to distance themselves from group affiliations, locals interviewed by the authors widely consider them to be part and parcel of the organization.

Some centers, such as Dar al-Arqam in the Idlib countryside, focus their efforts on young children, coaching them in tahfidh and shari'a jurisprudence. Just like ISIS, they too offer physical activities such as martial arts classes. Others, such as the al-'Izz bin 'Abdulsalam Center, target teenagers and younger men, seemingly hoping to develop them into HTS-sympathetic preachers for eventual deployment at local mosques and da'wah centers. These centers are somewhat akin to ISIS's boarding schools — they provide their students with food and accommodation, and offer two tiers of ideological education. The first lasts four months and focuses on introductory shari'a sciences (*al-'ulum al-shari'ah*); upon completion, the second tier opens up, allowing students to engage in more advanced shari'a courses for a further six months. Besides this, there are also women-only du'at al-jihad centers, such as the 'Umar bin al-Khattab and Umm 'Ammarah Institutions, wherein female attendants are provided with similar theological training. Just as is the case in the context of ISIS, the aim appears to be to use female supporters as a vector for ideology, a way to diffuse it and its accompanying worldview into both public and private spheres. After all, if the mother is a committed adherent of the jihadist ideology, then she is more likely to radicalize and recruit her own children to its cause. Teaching staff often float between more than one center — for example, the Dar al-Arqam and al-'Izz Bin 'Abdulsalam Centers share at least two teachers, each of whom have featured prominently in their respective graduation videos.

Besides the mudafat and du'at al-jihad initiatives, HTS also hosts regular public gatherings. Unlike ISIS, these rarely showcase the implementation of corporal or capital punishments. Instead, HTS seems to prefer consensual communication between it, or its affiliates, and the local population. For that reason, it uses the carrot more than it does the stick, something that is particularly apparent at its da'wah parties, where it organizes tahfidh contests, comedy evenings, and general knowledge quizzes. At the quizzes, the use of the carrot is most liberal: HTS quizmasters are renowned for asking deliberately easy questions so that they have a pretext to distribute more rewards, and therefore appear to be more generous. Those in attendance receive constant positive reinforcement and are encouraged to sign up to go to more regular classes, a possible first step toward their eventual recruitment.

All this is complemented by HTS's control of local mosques, something that gives it a direct line of contact with the masses over which it rules. In order to exert the requisite level of control, HTS has worked systematically to exclude all preachers that do not adhere to its particular reading of Islamism, replacing them with handpicked imams that are directly affiliated with it. Sometimes, this is done immediately, using coercive means; at others, though, the takeover has been known to be more gradual. In any case, once it has seized control of a mosque, HTS uses its sermons (Friday prayers in particular) to send a unified — and, rather like ISIS, strictly regulated — message, broadcasting its ideological and political position. Interview respondents noted that mosque outreach has been a particularly important factor in HTS's efforts to mobilize the masses against peace talks and cease-fires, as well as its local rivals.

Instead of creating its own infrastructure, then, HTS favored already-extant structures and institutions in northern Syria; by outsourcing its propaganda activism like this, it has been able to save on resource expenditure and become highly decentralized, two qualities that stand in stark contrast to ISIS.

As the above pages have shown, both ISIS and HTS have adopted concerted strategies for in-theater outreach in Syria. Using a combination of bespoke infrastructure and co-opted local institutions, each group invested a huge amount of time and energy in communicating with the local population. The groups differed most in their reliance on the production and distribution of official media products. Whereas ISIS worked to fetishize its brand through a constant flood of propaganda, HTS was both more conservative and more subtle — it preferred to diffuse its ideological principles and sociopolitical values through long-term education and mosque outreach, and its output was seemingly borne more out of an ad hoc need to steer public opinion than anything else.

RESTRICTING PUBLIC DISCOURSE

ISLAMIC STATE IN IRAQ AND AL-SHAM

During its proto-state tenure in Syria, ISIS incrementally worked toward establishing an information monopoly. Like other totalitarian movements, it considered external channels of information that ran against its party line to be a long-term destabilizing threat. Hence, from 2014 onward, it set about removing or discrediting them. Cognizant of the fact that immediately withdrawing civilian access to the outside world would risk irreparably harming its local appeal, it opted for a gradualist approach — it was only in mid-2016 that it began to fully implement its censorship program, inhibiting

Internet access, jamming radio signals, and banning satellite dishes (which it at one point condemned as *'adu min al-dakhil* — "an enemy within").

We should not overstate the extent of its censorship success; enforcing these policies was easier said than done and, for that reason, it had to be far more flexible than its edicts suggested. That being said, the group did eventually manage to severely constrict the information space in large parts of Syria and Iraq. For example, activists living in ISIS-held Raqqa last year reported that, while it was relatively easy to access the Internet in early 2014, "it became harder to do so in 2015, and even harder in 2016." By early 2017, Raqqa's once myriad Internet cafes had been whittled down to just a handful, each of which was administered by ISIS-vetted individuals who recorded their customers' names and facilitated regular police inspections.

The group's stance on satellite dishes followed a similar trajectory. After years of ambiguity — and apparent ambivalence — toward the consumption of satellite television, it began to take a more proactive stance toward the end of 2015, eventually threatening citizens in Raqqa with "severe punishment" if they were caught watching it. So, once again, while its stated position had long been clear, it was quite some time before it actually came to implement it.

Whereas in its heartlands ISIS proceeded cautiously, seemingly intent on preserving the fragile acquiescence of the local and muhajir population, the same cannot be said of towns and cities that were of lesser strategic value to it — especially those that were seized after protracted military campaigns. For example, in Tadmur (also known as Palmyra), it circumvented any pretense of censorship gradualism and enforced a de facto ban on Internet communication by refusing to repair the cyber infrastructure that had been so crippled during its first capture of the city in May 2015. Incidentally, in the Iraqi city of Ramadi, it banned the Internet by the same means, though it did eventually permit some limited access alongside mobile telephony, provided it took place in custom-built, ISIS-monitored "halls."

As a cumulative result of its policy of information restriction, credible news that ran contrary to ISIS's official media was, by late 2016, structurally inhibited in Syria: Verifiable reports about the coalition's efforts were scarce, and the rumors that did get past its firewall were often obscured by disinformation. While it was not enough to stop the group from being ousted from most of its urban holdouts there, this meant that conspiracy theories ran amok, and confusion as to its enemies' real aims blossomed.

Hay'at Tahrir al-Sham

For its part, HTS has tended to be more cautious than ISIS when it comes to censorship. Indeed, it has been demonstrably aware of its inability to ban outside channels of communication, whether at once or gradually, and its efforts have been more selective — only certain individuals, groups, and forms of communication are targeted by its censors. The precise details of how it engages in its restriction measures are difficult to discern, but locals have noted that the group has its own specialized apparatus — informally referred to as the *fira' al-ma'lumat* (literally, information branch) — which is said to monitor the media distributed in its immediate sphere of influence. It is, according to interview respondents in northern Syria, this unit that has the final say on what does and does not get circulated in HTS territory.

Notwithstanding its existence, HTS is significantly more permissive than ISIS. For example, it has long allowed dozens of pro-uprising newspapers and magazines to be circulated in its territories, publications over which it has no direct oversight whatsoever. While it frequently levels accusations of secularism at them, it only bans those which criticize it specifically or threaten its ideological hegemony. One of those banned was the *Enab Baladi* newspaper, which was cut off in January 2017 after it published an article criticizing the group for dominating Idlib and providing a pretext for the Syrian regime to attack the city. Furthermore, back in early 2015 — when HTS still referred to itself as Jabhat al-Nusrah — it famously banned a series of other pro-revolution newspapers, among them *Sada al-Sham*, *Tamaddon*, and *Souriatna*, after they published a message of solidarity with the murdered journalists of *Charlie Hebdo*. After accusing them of attacking Islam, it confiscated and incinerated all the editions it could lay its hands on, framing its actions as an attempt to defend the interests of the religion. The editors of the "offending" newspapers considered this to be a cynical effort to opportunistically leverage local people against channels of information that were unsympathetic to its jihadist cause.

In the context of radio stations, HTS has been less ambivalent. It has, for example, raided a number of rival broadcasters in northern Syria after accusing them of committing acts forbidden under Islam. In January 2016, it stormed the facilities of Radio Fresh, a station run by local activists in the town of Kafranbal. In its immediate aftermath, the station was taken off-air, its manager arrested, its electronics confiscated, and its archives wiped clean, all under the pretext that it had been broadcasting "immoral" programs with women announcers and music.

Besides this, HTS has also aggressively competed for visual dominance in northern Syria. Like ISIS once was, it is a profligate producer of billboards, signposts, and posters, and has attempted to render its iconography ubiquitous across its territories. As one respondent reported to the authors, "When you only see one logo all over the place, you unconsciously start assuming the dominance of that group." To this end, it has systematically worked to erase any symbols or signs of which it disapproves, whether that is because they are "un-Islamic," or because they are deemed to be an ideological threat to the group and its leaders. Subversive anti-HTS slogans — which often appear covertly overnight — are immediately expunged and replaced with pro-HTS slogans, as are posters and billboards produced by rival organizations fighting for the same outcome goals. By way of example, HTS frequently defaces the billboards of Hizb ut-Tahrir and has even banned printing presses from working with it, even though it too intends to instate shari'a law and establish an Islamic caliphate.

In sum, through gradual and selective censorship, HTS and its antecedents have worked methodically to become one of few hegemons in northern Syria's information landscape. While, like ISIS, it remains far out of reach of a true information monopoly, the targeted damage it has done to public discourse in its territories is likely to have lasting consequences.

While both ISIS and HTS have had an uneasy relationship with outside channels of information, each responded to this challenge differently. Whereas ISIS was more radical in its approach, which eventually came to consist of censorship of anything that was not published by the group, HTS has tended to be more cautious, preferring to preserve relationships through more targeted negative measures.

Conclusion

As the above pages have shown, ISIS and HTS deployed a carefully thought-out cocktail of consumed and performative propaganda in Syria between 2013 and 2018, one that was calibrated to the needs of both the general population and active group members. Weaving together media distribution and media restriction in a range of ways, each group invested a significant amount of time in the deployment of domestic influence operations, working to enhance, stabilize, and entrench their respective insurgent governments.

However, despite their shared ideology and similarly strategic understanding as to the importance of in-theater communication, ISIS and HTS are highly distinct at the tactical level. Unlike ISIS, which expended huge amounts of resources in media production, HTS has been more unobtrusive. A 2012 interview with one of the HTS movement's former commanders, a man named Abu 'Adnan who was a shari'a official at the time, gives a glimpse into how the group has historically viewed audio-visual propaganda. In it, he states, "We don't care about the press. It's not a priority to us." As such, instead of flooding the world with a constant torrent of on- and offline propaganda like ISIS has done, HTS portrays itself to be more interested in actions than in words. So, whereas ISIS invested heavily in propaganda and infrastructure, using consumed and performative operations in almost equal measure, HTS has tended to rely more on the performative side of the equation, focusing more on co-opting institutions and engaging in regular face-to-face outreach. This difference in the proportionate reliance on consumed and performative propaganda lies at the heart of what makes the two groups so distinct from one another.

In any case, it is imperative that policymakers and military practitioners develop a better understanding of how both organizations have used — and differed in their use of — offline strategic communication operations in Syria. In the context of modern-day revolutionary warfare, the information space is increasingly seen as a "decisive battlespace," and, for that reason, far more research needs to be done on how it is leveraged in-theater. While studying the impact and influence of online propaganda is important in its own right, it has distracted the world from what could be an even greater challenge. The above pages, which are just an initial step toward filling this gap in knowledge, hint at the scale of the mass-indoctrination operations that have occurred in Syria in recent years, the cumulative impact of which will not simply evaporate, even after both ISIS and HTS have been militarily defeated.

ENDNOTES

1. The group's name has changed several times since its rise in 2013. In July 2016 it changed its name from Jabhat al-Nusrah to Jabhat Fatah al-Sham after breaking ties with al-Qaeda. The group renamed itself Hayat Tahrir al-Sham in January 2017, making a large-scale merger with other Syrian rebel groups. For consistency, this paper always refers to the group as Hayat Tahrir al-Sham (HTS).

2. This article draws on primary data collected from five semi-structured interviews with journalists and experts familiar with HTS. These were conducted online in February 2018 by the author over Skype and/or WhatsApp.

3. This analysis on ISIS's media kiosk infrastructure draws on research undertaken by the first author for a United States Naval War College case study project. For more detail, see Charlie Winter, "Totalitarian insurgency: Evaluating the Islamic State's in-theater propaganda operations," *Naval War College Center for Irregular Warfare and Armed Groups*, January 2018.

4. ISIS, "The media point: A window inside the media of the Islamic State," Al-Naba' XXI, March 8, 2016.

5. ISIS, "Aspect of the work of the media point in the city of Raqqa," Raqqa Province Media Office, April 19, 2017; ISIS, "Aspect of the work of the media office in the province — the media point," Khayr Province Media Office, March 8, 2017; ISIS, "Establishing a media point in the city of Tadmur," Homs Province Media Office, June 5, 2015; ISIS, "Opening a media point in the city of Sirte," Tripoli Province Media Office, September 2, 2015; ISIS, "A screening of Allah and His Messenger spoke the truth at the media point in the city of Raqqa," Raqqa Province Media Office, April 22, 2017.

6. ISIS, "The media point," 12.

7. As of December 19, 2015, al-Naba' has been disseminated in electronic form, too, through ISIS's official propaganda disseminator, Nashir.

8. ISIS, "Distributing the weekly al-Naba' newspaper to ordinary Muslims," Nineveh Province Media Office, November 19, 2016; ISIS, "Distributing al-Naba' and video materials in south Shirqat," Dijla Province Media Office, July 23, 2016; ISIS, "Distributing al-Naba' in the city of Tal'afar," Jazira Province Media Office, April 14, 2017.

9. Interview between author and Raqqa Is Being Slaughtered Silently, June 15, 2017.

10. ISIS, "The media point," 13.

11. ISIS, "The media point," 13.

12. ISIS, "Raiding the villages to spread guidance," Aleppo Province Media Office, May 2016.

13. See, for example: Quentin Somerville and Riam Dalati, "An education in terror," *BBC News*, August 2017.

14. See, for example: Pamela Engel, "Inside the textbooks that ISIS uses to indoctrinate children," *Business Insider*, August 21, 2016.

15. Asaad Almohammad, "ISIS Child Soldiers in Syria: The Structural and Predatory Recruitment, Enlistment, Pre-Training Indoctrination, Training, and Deployment," *International Center for Counter-Terrorism*, The Hague, February 19, 2018.

16. Author interview via skype with Ali El Yassir; Middle East analyst focusing on violent extremist groups, February 2018.

17. Author interview via Skype with Mustafa, a freelance trainer focusing on peace-building, February 2018.

18. Author interview via skype with Ali El Yassir; Middle East analyst focusing on violent extremist groups, February 2018.

19. Author interview via skype with Orwa Khalifa, a Syrian journalist, February 2018.

20. Author interview via Skype with Mustafa, a freelance trainer focusing on peace-building, February 2018.

21. Author interview via skype with Orwa Khalifa, a Syrian journalist, February 2018.

22. Author interview via Skype with Mustafa, a freelance trainer focusing on peace-building, February 2018.

23. Author interview via skype with Orwa Khalifa, a Syrian journalist, February 2018.

24. Author interview via Skype with Mohammed, the coordinator of 24CR, a civil resistance group against extremism, February 2018.

25. Author interview via Skype with Ahmed, a Syrian journalist, February 2018.

26. The official soundcloud account for du'at al-jihad radio station, du'at al-jihad.

27. Author interview via skype with Orwa Khalifa, a Syrian journalist, February 2018.

28. Dar al-Arqam Center, "Graduation ceremony

of the first course at Dar Al-Arqam center," Dar al-Arqam Center, August 23, 2017.

29. Author interview via skype with Ali El Yassir; Middle East analyst focusing on violent extremist groups, February 2018.

30. Al-'Izz bin 'Abdulsalam Center, "Graduation ceremony of the eighth course at al-'Izz bin 'Abdulsalam Center," al-'Izz bin 'Abdulsalam Center, February 14, 2018.

31. Umar bin al-Khattab Center, "Graduation ceremony of the first course at Umar bin al-Khattab Center," Umar bin al-Khattab Center, September 14, 2017.

32. Umm 'Ammarah Center, "Graduation ceremony of the fourth course at Umm 'Ammarah Center," Umm 'Ammarah Center, September 11, 2017.

33. Author interview via Skype with Ahmed, a Syrian journalist, February 2018.

34. Author interview via Skype with Mohammed, the coordinator of 24CR, a civil resistance group against extremism, February 2018.

35. Dar al-Arqam Center, "Graduation ceremony of the first course at Dar Al-Arqam center," Dar al-Arqam Center, August 23, 2017.

36. al-'Izz bin 'Abdulsalam Center, "Graduation ceremony of the eighth course at al-'Izz bin 'Abdulsalam Center," al-'Izz bin 'Abdulsalam Center, February 14, 2018.

37. Author interview via skype with Orwa Khalifa, a Syrian journalist, February 2018.

38. Author interview via skype with Orwa Khalifa, a Syrian journalist, February 2018.

39. Author interview via Skype with Ahmed, a Syrian journalist, February 2018.

40. Author interview via skype with Orwa Khalifa, a Syrian journalist, February 2018.

41. Author interview via skype with Ali El Yassir; Middle East analyst focusing on violent extremist groups, February 2018.

42. Author interview via Skype with Mohammed, the coordinator of 24CR, a civil resistance group against extremism, February 2018.

43. Elements of this section are drawn from research undertaken by the first author as part of a United States Naval War College case study project. For more detail, see Winter, "Totalitarian insurgency."

44. On December 2, 2015, ISIS's Department of Hisba released a statement banning satellite TV transmitters on account of their insidious spreading of "deceit, lies and defamation." By the end of the month, this statement had been officially translated into English and Farsi. In the weeks that followed, al-Naba' featured an infographic detailing the seven central evils of satellite transmission, which was subsequently translated into English. ISIS, "The banning of satellite receivers," Department of Hisba, December 6, 2015; ISIS, "The banning of satellite TV receivers," Diwan al-Hisbah, December 30, 2015; ISIS, "al-Naba' XI: Wait, we are also waiting," December 29, 2015; ISIS, "Purifying the homes of the Muslims from satellite dish receivers," Hisba Committee, May 17, 2016.

45. Interview between author and Raqqa Is Being Slaughtered Silently, June 15, 2017.

46. Interview between author and Raqqa Is Being Slaughtered Silently, June 15, 2017.

47. Interview between author and Raqqa Is Being Slaughtered Silently, June 15, 2017.

48. Interview between author and Raqqa Is Being Slaughtered Silently, June 15, 2017.

49. As signified by the release of ISIS, "Destroying the satellite devices," Raqqa Province Media Office, May 31, 2016.

50. Interview between author and Khaled al-Homsi, May 31, 2017.

51. Interview between the author and Waleed al-Fahdawi, June 4, 2017.

52. "Satellite Dishes Reconnect Post-IS Mosul to World," AFP, April 20, 2017.

53. Author interview via Skype with Ahmed, a Syrian journalist, February 2018.

54. Author interview via Skype with Ahmed, a Syrian journalist, February 2018.

55. Enab Baladi, "The administration of Bab al-Hawa crossing confiscates Enab Baladi newspaper because of an article criticising al-Nusra," Enab Baladi, January 31, 2017.

56. Al-Souria Net, "al-Nusra executes a second woman on charges of prostitution and Ahrar al-Sham confiscates pro-opposition newspapers," al-Souria Net, January 20, 2015.

57. Enab Baladi, "The administration of Bab al-Hawa crossing confiscates Enab Baladi newspaper because of an article criticising al-Nusra," Enab Baladi, January 31, 2017.

58. Syria Untold, "Syrian newspapers attacked for standing with Charlie Hebdo victims," Syria

Untold, January 27, 2015.

59. Mustafa Hussien, "Radio Fresh suspends its broadcasting due to threats from al-Nusra," *Smart-News Agency*, June 16, 2016.

60. Ibid.

61. Author interview via Skype with Mustafa, a freelance trainer focusing on peace-building, July 2017.

62. Haid Haid, "Resisting Hayat Tahrir al-Sham: Syrian Civil Society on the Frontlines," *Adopt a Revolution*, November 10, 2017.

63. Ibid.

64. Author interview via Skype with Mustafa, a freelance trainer focusing on peace-building, February 2018.

65. Rania Abouzeid, "Interview with Official of Jabhat al-Nusra, Syria's Islamist Militia Group," *Time Magazine*, December 25, 2012.

CHAPTER FOUR

THE PRIMACY OF PRAXIS:

CLERICAL AUTHORITY IN THE SYRIAN CONFLICT

SHIRAZ MAHER

INTRODUCTION

Since its inception in 2011, the Syrian conflict has presented a carousel of actors, movements, and propositions to the outside world. While well-known jihadi organizations arrayed against the Syrian government captured the most international attention, such groups were among a much broader cast competing for authority within the opposition. In order to understand how and why political groups rose to prominence at different times, this paper explores the manner in which clerical authority is derived from praxis. Put another way, this paper demonstrates how a range of actors on the ground tried to establish authority through action, rather than theoretical abstraction.

Examining competing claims by different scholars and groups in the Syrian conflict shows three distinctive periods of authority during which the influence of particular groups rose and fell. A group of indigenous Syrian scholars first injected religious language into the revolution, followed by Salafi scholars predominantly from the Gulf along with countries like Egypt and Jordan, and lastly came then-millenarian jihadi organizations such as ISIS and Jabhat al-Nusra. This paper will account for why these actors lost support in the conflict when they did, and why differing constructions of theology came to triumph at specific moments.

The Dutch scholar Roel Meijer has previously explored the role of praxis — understood here as the process by which theoretical ideas are actualized in the pursuit of social change — with regard to the Saudi jihadi Yusuf al-'Uyayri, a topic which remains vastly understudied.[1] Within the Syrian context, contestations of religious authority borne of praxis have produced a heavily splintered and fragmented Sunni opposition. This is true for Sunni Islam in general but is particularly evident among the constellation of Salafi actors who have, at different times, aligned themselves with the Syrian cause.

In the broadest sense, three phases of established clerical authority can be identified. The first instance took place as parts of the uprising transitioned from peaceful protest to armed resistance in the form of groups like the Free Syrian Army (FSA). At this time, indigenous Syrian clerics who supported the uprising tried to establish a strict framework of military law to govern the armed opposition, for example by codifying rules of engagement. As the crisis persisted and conflict worsened, most of these clerics found themselves forced into exile, issuing edicts from abroad and losing the support of those actually fighting on the ground. This gave rise to the second wave of mainly Gulf Salafi clerics — supported by others in countries such as Egypt and Jordan — who internationalized the conflict and precipitated the unprecedented wave of foreign fighters who flooded into the country. Much like their predecessors, however, these clerics suffered from the same problem of remoteness, having limited themselves to inciting others to jihad from the relative comfort of Riyadh, Cairo, or Doha.

A vacuum of authority had then begun to emerge for the new international jihadis gathering in Syria and Iraq, who soon comprised the third wave. This space was quickly dominated by the most brutal jihadi actors operating in that conflict: ISIS and, to a lesser extent, al-Qaeda. Members of the former even underscored how their authority was derived from actions by chanting the group's popular refrain: *Baqiyya wa tatamaddad,* meaning "remaining and expanding."

CONTROLLING THE FIRE

Although the Syrian conflict is far from resolved, it is already the subject of fierce revisionist history. Supporters of the Assad regime, among others, have attempted to portray the entire uprising as extremist in nature, an attempt by

Sunni radicals to revive the Muslim Brotherhood's agitations of the 1970s.[34] These accusations either misunderstand or deliberately misrepresent the nature and dynamics of the original uprising. As was commonplace across the Middle East, mosques became the starting point for many of the so-called *ayam al-ghadab,* or "days of rage," providing a concentration point from which popular unrest became manifest. This is hardly unsurprising and should not necessarily be taken as an indicator of religious sentiment, let alone extremism. The centrality of mosques as a focal point of gatherings is best understood as a reflection of political realities in the Middle East, a region where public congregations of any kind are heavily restricted. The only way for large numbers to gather naturally is during prayer, making mosques natural starting points for the protest movements that swept the region. Syria was no exception.

The idioms of defiance are important here. Syria's uprising was initially defined by the same language that framed anti-regime opposition in Tunisia, Egypt, and Libya, with generic calls for the overthrow of the regime like *al-sha'b yurid isqa al-nizam,* meaning "the people want to overthrow the regime." The language of Syria's revolution was indisputably secular during its incipient phases, as each Friday was given a particular theme, such as dignity, glory, martyrs, steadfastness, persistence, greatness, or rage.[5] When the Syrian Muslim Brotherhood's exiled leadership called for protests in April 2011, their calls went largely unanswered, even in the group's traditional strongholds of Aleppo and Hama.[67]

As the crisis persisted, however, Syrian Sunni clerics found themselves playing increasingly important roles in the uprising. Their mosques quickly became the front line of anti-regime agitation, with government forces frequently attacking the worshippers inside. On one occasion at the ancient Omari mosque in Daraa, one of the main centers of the uprising, soldiers fast-roped onto the mosque roof during prayer before opening fire. Many of the worshippers were trapped for more than 90 minutes, coming under assault from tank shells and machine gun fire. Four people were killed, among them the imam's son.[8] The symbolism of the event was every bit as offensive as the assault itself.

The mosque was among Syria's oldest, built in the seventh century after forces commanded by the Prophet Mohammed's companion, Omar bin al-Khattab, conquered Daraa.

Episodes such as this began to unravel the delicate accommodation Bashar al-Assad had reached with some Sunni groups since coming to power in 2000.[9] He had hoped to reverse some of the animosities created by his father, leading to a number of delicate engagements with groups and Islamic traditions that the Syrian state had traditionally been uncomfortable with, although the precise contours of this arrangement are beyond the scope of this paper.[10] For present purposes, what matters is that when the pressures of the uprising took hold, an indigenous and restless body of clerics was already within the country, injecting a language of religion that eventually replaced that of revolution.

As the military campaign against Assad's regime took hold, clerics who had backed the rebel movement sought to control the newly emerging armed groups. Arab experiences throughout the late 20th and early 21st centuries — from the Lebanese and Algerian civil wars to the war in Iraq and Libya's revolution — suggested that anything other than a tightly controlled armed opposition would quickly descend into chaos. To an extent, this was inevitable. The decentralization of the Syrian uprising, with its lack of national coordination, ensured that highly localized characteristics dominated the behavior of different groups in different areas.

The first serious attempt at creating a national umbrella movement to coordinate the opposition, the first wave of praxis in the Syrian conflict, came from the former imam of the Umayyad Mosque in Damascus, Moaz al-Khatib. He had vocally backed the opposition and was subsequently detained by the regime several times before fleeing the country in July 2012. Along with others, including secular activists, he helped create the National Coalition for Syrian Revolutionary and Opposition Forces, often referred to as ETILAF, and served as its first president.[11]

Another prominent member of Syria's clergy is Sheikh Muhammad al-Yaqoubi, who comes from a celebrated family of Islamic scholars. He took a strident line against the regime from the earliest days of the uprising and condemned the government's heavy-handed treatment of protesters, the killing of innocent people, and its assault on mosques, particularly after Friday prayers. Yaqoubi also issued a series of *fatwas* for rebel fighters that counselled against extremist interpretations of jihad, including a prohibition on the use of suicide bombers and land mines.[12] These injunctions might seem ridiculous when examining the trajectory of the Syrian conflict today, but they had an important role to play in 2012 before groups like ISIS emerged. For a while, it certainly seemed as though the message of Yaqoubi and others managed to hold the line against millenarian militancy. For example, in the first two years of Syria's conflict only 22 suicide bombings were conducted,[13] compared with 247 during the first two years of the conflict in Iraq.[14]

However misplaced it may now seem, there was an optimism in the early stages of the war that fighters in the battlefield could be relied upon not only to restrain themselves but also to refer to clerical authorities for guidance. "I urge everyone in the war to remember their [pure] intentions," argued another prominent Syrian scholar, Sheikh Abdul-Hadi al-Kharsa. "You should refer to the scholars to see if what you are doing is valid in Islam."[15]

Although many of these clerics were forced into exile, they still hoped to exert some influence over the armed opposition as the crisis spiraled out of control. Even influential Salafi-jihadi theorists of Syrian origin repeatedly condemned the emergence of avowedly jihadi organizations such as Jabhat al-Nusra and urged Syrians to support the FSA.[16] Among them was Abu Basir al-Tartusi, whose real name is Abd al-Mun'am Mustafa Halima. Tartusi is even known to have entered Syria on short trips alongside the FSA to advise its fighters in Homs, rather than align himself with extremist jihadi groups. He did, however, later develop relations with more austere groups such as Ahrar al-Sham and Suqour al-Sham.[17] In 2011, Tartusi told Point of Order, a show on Gulf satellite TV channel Al-Arabiya, that the FSA was an "arm of the revolution" of which he was "proud."[18]

With the exception of Tartusi, the presence that these clerics had inside Syria invested their opposition to the regime with authority. Their hopes of inserting religious scholars in each of the revolutionary military councils were dashed as the potency of their influence faded along with their detachment from the conflict. For example, for those on the ground, Moaz al-Khatib eventually came to exemplify the kind of pragmatism that only those divorced from the everyday privations of the conflict could allow themselves. While the exiled leadership was already causing resentment because of their relative security and proclivity for conferences in comfortable hotels, Khatib issued a statement on Facebook in 2013 saying that he was ready for dialogue with the regime to bring the crisis to an end.[19] The statement was met with immediate and widespread uproar. Even the National Coalition, whose presidency Khatib had resigned by that stage, issued a statement distancing itself from his remarks for fear of losing their support base inside the country.

INTERNATIONAL JIHAD

With much of the original Syrian leadership exiled from the country, the conflict took on an international dimension among predominantly, though not exclusively, Salafi clerics from the Gulf. This happened for two reasons. The first relates to the audacity of the Assad regime, which had unleashed a barbarous assault against protesters. Cases such as Hamza al-Khatib, a 13-year-old boy from Daraa who disappeared into the bowels of the regime's dungeons in April 2011, exemplified this. After a month of being held incommunicado, his badly mutilated corpse was eventually returned to his family. Covered in bruises, his family discovered bullet wounds in his kneecaps, which his tormentors had filled with cigarette butts and ash. Khatib's penis had also been cut and mutilated.[20] This was hardly an isolated case. The regime's loyalist apparatchiks flooded social media with horrific videos of state-sanctioned abuse from across Syria, spawning sympathy for the nascent armed opposition that had emerged. The systematic nature of Assad's killing machine was later confirmed by a Syrian army defector, known as Caesar, who documented more than 50,000 deaths of those held in Syrian detention centers.[21]

While news of such atrocities inflamed domestic opposition and caught the attention of international observers, it did not adequately account for the internationalization of the conflict that took place, first to others in the region and later further afield. After all, it was hardly news to anyone that the Syrian regime tortures its political opponents. That much was well known for years and was, of course, already a significant motivating factor for the original uprising. Moreover, for Arabs in neighboring countries, repressive tactics used by the Syrian regime against its opponents did not differ in any meaningful way from the types of repression they would have faced in their own countries. Why, then, did Syria so dramatically capture the imagination of jihadi actors abroad?

For Salafi clerics across the broader Levant, North Africa, and Gulf, the Syrian tinderbox represented their worst fears. They watched the same videos of protesters being tortured that provoked widespread condemnation from Western powers but were witnessing with their ears — not their eyes. What mattered was not the torture itself, but what was being said to victims. Here, regime soldiers directed uniquely loaded sectarian insults against normative Sunni beliefs and figures, such as the Prophet Muhammad's wife, Ayisha, or against his companions, known as the *sahaba*. In other cases, protesters were forced to commit blasphemy by answering "Bashar" when asked questions such as "who is your God," "who created you," or "who is better, Allah or Bashar?" Protesters were also made to prostrate and kiss Assad's picture while being asked: "Who is your Lord?"[22,23] The injection of sectarian framing into the conflict by the Syrian regime has been extensively documented in a study by Daniel Corstange and Erin York, revealing how the overriding notions of civic identity and unity that dominated the earliest stages of the revolution were overwritten by the indelible brushstrokes of sectarian distrust.[24] The result was that minorities were scared into retreat, while the passions of Sunni radicals were both ignited and unleashed.

Moreover, these sectarian insults inflamed the fears of those who had come to regard the deteriorating situation in Syria not as a struggle for human rights, but as one for the future direction of Islam itself. Those fears were only accentuated by the Iranian regime's unconditional support for Assad. In a not atypical statement from a Gulf Salafi cleric, the Kuwaiti preacher Sheikh Nabil al-Awadi slammed the Syrian Ba'athists and their supporters.[25] He repeatedly pronounced *takfir*, the claim that another is impure or a non-Muslim, against the regime and its allies because Assad belongs to Islam's heterodox Alawite sect and is backed by Shi'i Iran. He therefore concluded they had,

... distorted Islam, in fact, they left Islam and did not even believe in it for a day. ... The Syrian crisis is not an issue of the poor or oppressed. Instead, it is a battle for survival, O nation of [Sunni] Islam! You people of the true and pure religion, you must unite to support your brothers in Syria.[26]

Awadi could not have painted a more desperate situation. Within months he was inciting jihad in Syria, offering advice to those participating in the fighting there, and praying for Allah to "accept the jihad of our people in Syria."[27, 28]

Open calls for jihad began shortly after. The highly influential Saudi cleric Mohammed al-Arifi, who has built a large following on social media, also echoed Awadi's message. During a sermon in June 2013 at the historic 'Amr bin al-As mosque in Cairo, Arifi declared that Muslim scholars had agreed on the necessity of jihad in Syria.[29] Within days of Arifi's speech, Egyptian President Mohammed Morsi attended a large public rally alongside popular Salafi scholars such as Muhammad Hassan, from the northern Dakahlia governorate, who also declared jihad in Syria to be an obligation.[30] When Morsi took to the podium after Hassan, he began by declaring to an already enraptured crowd, "Here I am [at your service], Syria."[31]

A flood of Salafi scholars began declaring jihad in Syria. Salman al-Awda, a prominent Saudi Salafi who was active in the kingdom's *sahwa*, or "awakening," movement of the late 1980s and early 1990s, has enjoyed a large following both at home and abroad for decades. Awda wrote a book called "Revolution Questions" in the aftermath of the 2011 uprisings and encouraged Arab citizens to seek their rights through social engagement rather than revolutionary change.[32] Yet, even in the Syrian context, Awda reasoned that jihad was necessary. When asked on Twitter about whether the fighting in Syria is jihad, he replied, "Fighting in Syria for the Syrian people is jihad and is resistance to a tyrannical regime and whomever stands with it."[33]

Perhaps the most wild-eyed denunciation of the Syrian regime came from an exiled cleric, Adnan al-Aroor, who had left the country after the failed Islamist uprisings of the early 1980s, which were primarily led by the Muslim Brotherhood. Aroor was another Salafi cleric who had been based in Saudi Arabia since leaving Syria and declared the need for armed opposition to the regime from the earliest stages of the attempted 2011 revolution. During a particularly boisterous appearance on the Islamic TV channel Wesal — whose regional office in Saudi Arabia was closed by the authorities in 2014 for its promotion of sectarian content — Aroor famously declared that those from the Alawite sect would be subjected to a "harsh and painful" punishment.[34] "By Allah," he said, "we shall mince them in meat grinders and we shall feed their flesh to the dogs." Like Tartusi, Aroor also tried to bolster the FSA with support, but he spoke in much more intemperate and unguarded language than his counterpart.

These clerics, and many others like them, enjoyed authority for two reasons. The first was due to their reputations, stature, and standing among an internet audience of millions. Arifi, for example, has more than 21 million followers on Twitter, more than 24 million followers on Facebook, and more than a million subscribers to his YouTube channel.[35] Although he is at the more popular end of the spectrum, he is not atypical, with many foreign scholars who called for jihad in Syria enjoying a support base in the millions. Both Awadi and Awda have more than 11 million followers on Twitter. Meanwhile, Yusuf al-Qaradawi, widely regarded as the most important spiritual influence on the Muslim Brotherhood, has a relatively modest following of just over 2 million, though his findings are amplified much more widely through organs of the Muslim Brotherhood around the world.[36] Secondly, the impassioned tones with which these preachers conveyed a sense of urgency about the conflict in Syria won them wide accolades during a phase of the conflict when praxis was primarily demonstrated through talking about the conflict and inciting passions against the Assad regime. After all, the flow of foreign fighters was only just beginning at this stage, and preachers who vocally denounced Assad could claim to be doing their bit as a result.

Yet the very thing that gave these scholars an opportunity to promote the Syrian cause — their presence outside the country and fame achieved through social media and satellite television — also provided the means for their unravelling. As ever-growing numbers of foreign fighters flocked to Syria and Iraq throughout 2013-15 to participate in jihad alongside militant groups, the inevitable question arose: If fighting the regime was an individual religious obligation required of every Muslim, then why weren't the scholars advocating such jihad also present on the battlefield? Although Tartusi and Aroor had made short, sporadic visits into Syria, this did little to protect their reputations. Aroor's own son Jaber pointed out the hypocrisy of his father's position on live TV, arguing that while he implored others to jihad he was himself sitting in comfortable television studios.[37] It was an awkward, deeply uncomfortable moment for Aroor, who was present on the same show when the remarks were made.[38] The clip undermined Aroor with all constituencies. For those who worried about his angry sectarian rhetoric, whether they supported Assad's regime or not, the clip laid bare the hypocrisy of his position. It also served the same purpose among those who not only agreed with him about the necessity of jihad in Syria but who were also engaging in it themselves.

Arifi attracted similar criticism when he flew to London just days after giving his fiery speech in Cairo. Having arrived in the UK, he was photographed strolling casually along a high street in the capital wearing trousers and a shirt, rather than the flowing robe and headdress commonly worn in the Gulf. It provided a sharp visual metaphor for the divergence between the angry rhetoric that conveyed a sense of impending doom within the walls of the 'Amr bin al-As mosque in Cairo and the more sedate environment of a British high street. Widespread ridicule followed on social media with the hashtag "Arifi's summer residence in London."[39] Twitter users mockingly circulated images of him talking with a woman in the street, describing it as a "picture of the *mujahid* field commander of the Brigades of the Islamic nation's [*umma*] scholars."[40] The apparent hypocrisy was also widely reported in both the Arabic and English press at the time, again undermining Arifi's claims to authenticity.[41]

JIHADI PRAXIS AS AUTHENTICITY

An unprecedented mobilization of foreign fighters occurred through 2013-16 as tens of thousands of individuals from across the world migrated to Syria in support of jihadi organizations. The most prominent among these organizations were ISIS and Jabhat al-Nusra, with both groups establishing claims to authenticity and legitimacy primarily through praxis, rather than scholarship.[42,43] While the scholars already discussed may have encouraged jihad or spread intemperate views which could be considered indistinguishable from those espoused by ISIS or Jabhat al-Nusra, they nonetheless relied upon their scholarly credentials to establish their authority. This was not the case with the militant groups.

ISIS, for example, sought to ensure that its claims to authenticity were derived from military dominance on the ground. Consider the visual dynamics of this first. Whenever ISIS projected images of its key leadership figures, they almost always appeared in military fatigues, wearing tactical vests and surrounded by arms. The most vivid example of this came from Abu Muhammad al-Adnani, the former spokesman of ISIS who was portrayed in precisely that guise on the front cover of the group's English-language magazine, *Rumiyah*, after he was killed in a drone strike.[44]

From a leadership perspective, the only significant exception to this was Abu Bakr al-Baghdadi, whose carefully choreographed appearance in the Nuri mosque of Mosul was designed for different ends. Baghdadi appeared not as a soldier, or even as a member of ISIS, but as the caliph of all Muslims. His claim to have revived this ancient Islamic institution therefore required a different form: A powerful man dressed in simple robes. Yet, even this orchestrated theater demonstrated the primacy of the practical. First was the sheer audacity of what was transpiring. Here was the hunted leader of a barbarous terrorist movement appearing so brazenly in public to deliver a sermon and lead congregational prayers. Of course, when Baghdadi finally dismounted the pulpit to join the congregants, he was surrounded again by the imagery of ISIS with a row of AK-47s propped up against the walls around him as he led the prayer. That much had been spelled out in his sermon moments before. "This is the establishment of the religion," he said, "a book that guides and a sword that supports."[45] The corollary was clear: Here is a group whose members don't just talk, they also get things done.

At least Baghdadi could claim some pedigree standing within the broader jihadi movement. He had participated in the insurgency against Western troops after the invasion of Iraq in 2003 and held a Ph.D. in Islamic studies from Baghdad's Islamic University, since renamed Iraqi University, with a specialty in sharia law.[46] That potency of praxis, however, resounded through the entire group. Even clueless foreign fighters, who unlike Baghdadi had no credentials to speak of, suddenly found themselves supremely empowered. Within months of arriving in Syria, an 18-year-old former butcher from Sydney named Abdullah Elmir appeared in a propaganda video aimed at his peers in the West. Released in October 2014, the video showed Elmir dressed in combat gear and surrounded by at least a hundred other fighters who were similarly attired and armed. Elmir proceeded to deliver an address to Western nations participating in the anti-ISIS coalition:[47]

> *Bring your planes, bring everything you want to us, because it will not harm us. Why? Because we have Allah, and this is something you do not have. Is it not apparent to you, how are these victories possible? These victories come only from Allah and that is how these small numbers of soldiers that we have, we take these massive victories.*[48]

Countless videos like this appeared, most of which featured men dressed in combat gear performing military roles.[49] This is not limited to ISIS. The group's greatest rivals in the Syrian jihadi arena have been Jabhat al-Nusra or its various incarnations and, more specifically, its leader Abu Mohammed al-Jolani. While ISIS dominated international headlines and pulled focus with its actions in the eastern parts of the country, Jolani's supporters ensured their figurehead was not forgotten.

Aleppo had been the jewel in the rebel movement's crown ever since parts of the east fell beyond Assad's control in mid-2012. This was not for any strategic or military purpose but because of its symbolic value, the emblem of a movement with momentum on its side. For Assad, reclaiming Aleppo was an urgent priority and occupied his planning throughout most of 2016, not long after Russia formally entered the conflict. By the summer, Aleppo was essentially besieged, with the exception of a few short-lived revanchist rebel campaigns, and the likelihood of Aleppo falling back into regime hands grew increasingly inevitable.

By this point, Jabhat al-Nursa had rebranded to Jabhat Fateh al-Sham and released a series of pictures showing Jolani along with the group's alleged military leaders sprawled over maps, presumably planning a way to break the siege.[50] Pictures like these had been clearly staged and designed to boost morale, but there was broader messaging at play too. These pictures were designed to show jihadi leaders as intrepid warrior-scholars, their names always prefaced by the honorific title of "sheikh," who were risking and sacrificing their lives on the front lines.

That became even more obvious when further pictures of Jolani were released in early 2018 almost immediately after Hay'at Tahrir al-Sham (HTS) — which Jolani led after Jabhat Fateh al-Sham ceased to exist — lost the Abu al-Duhur Military Airbase. Located in Idlib governorate, the capture of the base had been one of the group's (then Jabhat al-Nusra) most significant victories in the province. HTS had been widely criticized for not putting up enough resistance and withdrawing from the base, essentially gifting it back to Assad. Within days, pictures were released of Jolani on the front lines, talking to his men and rallying the troops for their next fight.

CONCLUSION

The study of praxis within jihadi circles points to the much broader crisis of legitimate authority within Islam. Which scholars and, by extension, interpretations of Islam, receive traction? Why? These are questions that have dominated policy debates in Western capitals ever since the terrorist attacks of 9/11. The topic is an iridescent one. Yet, what this brief essay demonstrates is that, even within militant or conservative contexts, there are intra-group competitions for authenticity and following. For those prioritizing action either through necessity due to the privations of war or for ideological reasons, it is those actors on the ground whose words are likely to resound most effectively. Herein lies the potency of praxis. More than scholarly merit or standing, it is the ability of an actor or group to deliver through action that becomes the ultimate marker of authenticity, and, by extension, piety. Similar lessons are drawn from studies evaluating the success of countering violent extremism (CVE) movements, where those operating through credible interlocutors at the grassroots are often shown to be much more effective than those adopting more abstract approaches.

For those who have watched the constant ebb and flow of the Syrian opposition's fortunes, the corollary is clear: Only those on the ground can control what takes place there. Western officials who have sought to work with the opposition have consistently failed to appreciate this. As a result, they continued to support and bolster organizations long after they grew disconnected and detached from the unconscionable realities of Syria's brutal war. Such miscalculations were evident even during the early stages of the conflict when groups like the FSA remained a credible force on the ground, but were supported with only "non-lethal aid." Their jihadi competitors, by contrast, were better equipped and armed, and thereby able to project power and prowess to prospective recruits. In this event, these organizations grew like a hydra while a lack of support for moderate actors condemned them to obscurity.

Sunni Islam is particularly vulnerable to this crisis of authority because it has no established clergy or formally recognized system. As such, there are no structural firewalls inherent to the religion that could automatically undercut the claims to authority made by one actor or institution versus another. The Syrian crisis offers a perfect microcosm of this, demonstrating why arguments about the lack of religious learning or scholarly ability within an extremist movement does little to undermine its support base. Thus, when Abu Bakr al-Baghdadi stood up to declare himself a reluctant caliph in the Nuri mosque, tens of thousands from across the world accepted him as such. For almost two years afterward, both Baghdadi and the so-called caliphate he ruled over proved to have an almost hypnotic effect on people across the world, hopelessly drawing them in like Homer to the sirens. Entire families packed their bags and abandoned their lives in response to Baghdadi's message, acting on a belief that Muslims must obey the caliph and live in the caliphate wherever and in whatever circumstances it exists. The question remains — who could have ever convinced them otherwise?

ENDNOTES

1. Roel Meijer, "Yūsuf Al-'Uyairī and the Making of a Revolutionary Salafi Praxis," *Die Welt Des Islams 47* (2007): 422-59.

2. A simple transliteration method has been adopted here, broadly in line with the conventions outlined by the *International Journal of Middle Eastern Studies*, but without diacritic markings. Names of people, groups, and commonly established words in the English language, such as jihad, are afforded their given renderings.

3. Raphael Lefevre, *Ashes of Hama: The Muslim Brotherhood in Syria*. London: Hurst & Co, 2013.

4. Shiraz Maher and John Bew, "Syria's World War," *New Statesman*, Apr. 11, 2018.

5. A full list is painstakingly maintained at:https://notgeorgesabra.wordpress.com/2013/10/18/every-friday-new-slogans-of-the-peoples-revolution/.

6. "Scores killed on Syria's 'day of rage,'" *Al Jazeera*, Apr. 29, 2011.

7. Joshua Landis, "As quiet returns, Syrians ponder future," Foreign Policy, Apr. 5, 2011.

8. Alyssa Newcomb, "Syrian Troops Take Omari Mosque in Daraa, 4 Dead," *ABC News*, Apr. 30, 2011.

9. Line Khatib, *Islamic Revivalism in Syria: The Rise and Fall of Ba'athist Secularism*. London: Routledge, 2011, 111-144.

10. Ibid, chapters 6-9.

11. "Kalimat al-shaykh Moaz al-Khatib, r'aiys al'itilaf al-suwri fi al-doha" [Speech of Shaykh Moaz al-Khatib, President of the Syrian Coalition in Doha], YouTube, Nov. 11, 2012.

12. "Fatwa on using land mines in urban warfare by His Eminence Shaykh Muhammad Al-Yaqoubi," Facebook, Aug. 25, 2012. The fatwa prohibiting suicide bombing has since been taken down; see original link here.

13. The figures for Syria were compiled by the author using media reports.

14. For Iraq an authoritative source is: www.iraqbodycount.org

15. "Shaykh Kharsa on the Free Syrian Army," Free Halab WordPress Blog, Jan. 8, 2013.

16. Aron Lund, "Holier Than Thou: Rival Clerics in the Syrian Jihad," *The Jamestown Foundation, Terrorism Monitor*, Volume 10, Issue 14, July 16, 2012.

17. "Al-shaykh, Abu Basir al-Tartusi fi burj al-diymows ma al-jaysh al-hur," [The shaykh Abu Basir al-Tartusi at the Diymows tower with the Free Army], YouTube, Mar. 12, 2014.

18. Abu Basir al-Tartusi, Daftar al-thawra wa-l-thawar: kalimat kutibat lilthuwrat al-'arabiya wa bihasa minha al-thuwrat al-suwriya [Notebook on the revolution and revolutionaries: words written on the Arab revolutions and specifically on the Syrian revolution]. Volume 1, 250.

19. "Al-Khatib 'must'ad' lilhiwar ma al-nizam al-suwri [Khatib 'ready' for dialogue with the Syrian regime]," *Sky News Arabia*, Jan. 2013.

20. Shiraz Maher and Nick Kaderbhai. "Bashar al-Assad is still the problem," *Telegraph*, Sep. 26, 2015.

21. "Syrian Army Defector, 'Caesar,' Briefs Committee, Shows Photographs Documenting Atrocities by Assad Regime — Chairman Royce Opening Statement," House Foreign Affairs Committee, July 31, 2015.

22. "Khatiyr jidan min rubuk Bashar al-Assad min shida al-t'adhyb bihalab thaman alhuriyat ghaly, [Very dangerous, 'who is your Lord, Bashar al-Assad' under intense torture in Aleppo, the price of freedom is expensive]," YouTube, Dec. 14, 2016,

23. "Rughm al-t'adhyb tifl yubsiq 'alaa suwrat Bashar al-Assad [Despite the torture of a child, (he) spits on a picture of Bashar al-Assad]," YouTube, Oct. 31, 2011.

24. Daniel Corstange and Erin York, "Sectarian Framing in the Syrian Civil War," *American Journal of Political Science*, Volume 62 (2018): 441-455.

25. For al-Awadi's personal website see: http://www.emanway.com/. He also dedicates a section to informing readers of developments in Syria called silsilat suwriya…miylad 'umma [Syria series…birth of a nation]: http://www.emanway.com/serie/41/

26. "Syria - Sh. Nabil Al-'Awdhi," YouTube, Dec. 13, 2011.

27. Nabil al-Awadi, "Allahuma tuqubal jihad a'hlana fi suwriya" [Oh Allah, accept the jihad of our people in Syria]," Twitter, Mar. 15, 2012.

28. Al-Arifi yud'au liljihad fi suwriya min masjid 'amru [Al-Arifi calls for jihad in Syria from 'Amr mosque]," YouTube, June 14, 2013.

29. "Muhammad Hassan, al-jihad fi suwriya wajib [Muhammad Hassan, the jihad in Syria (is a) duty]," YouTube, June 15, 2013.

30. "Al-r'aiys Mursi lubayk ya suwriya [President Mursi, here I am (at your service), oh Syria]," YouTube, June 15, 2013.

31. Salman al-Awda,'As'ilat al-thawra [Revolution Questions], *Beirut: Namaa Center for Research and Studies*, 2012.

32. Salman al-Awda, "Al-qital fi suwriya li'ahl suwriya jihad wa muqawamat linizam ghashim wa limun yaqif fi sufh [Fighting in Syria for the Syrian people is jihad and is resistance to a tyrannical regime and whomever stands with it]," Twitter, Aug. 1, 2012.

33. "Syrian Sunni Cleric Threatens We Shall Mince The Alawites in Meat Grinders," YouTube, Sep. 12, 2015.

34. These figures are accurate as of Apr. 2018. See: https://twitter.com/mohamadalarefe; https://www.facebook.com/3refe; https://www.youtube.com/user/AlarefeTV

35. Again, these figures are accurate as of April 2018. See: https://twitter.com/NabilAlawadhy; https://twitter.com/salman_alodah; https://twitter.com/alqaradawy

36. "Ibn Shaykh Aroor, yud'a walidih fi mawqif muhrj lilghaya [Son of Shaykh Aroor puts his father in a very embarrassing position]," YouTube, Aug. 6, 2012.

37. Jaber later stated on the same show that he had only been joking and that he supported his father.

38. The original Arabic hashtag was: العريفي_ مصيف_في_لندن#

39. "Suwrat al-mujahid al-qa'id al-miydaniy likuta'aib 'ulema' al-'umma [Picture of the holy warrior, the field commander of the Brigades of the Islamic nation's scholars]," Twitter, June 18, 2013.

40. "Intiqadat l-al-Arifi 'alaa Twitter: d'aa liljihad fi suwriya wa rah yasiyf fi London [Criticism of Arifi on Twitter: (he) called for jihad in Syria and went to summer in London]," *al-Masry al-Youm*, June 17, 2013.

41. Although some foreign fighters joined Jabhat al-Nusra directly, others worked with groups that supported it, bringing them under the broader umbrella of the group's influence and command. The Islamic State has been referred to by a number of acronyms including ISIS, ISIL, and Daesh.

42. "Fight or flight? Saudi cleric heads to London after call for jihad in Syria," *Al-Arabiya English*, June 22, 2013.

43. Rumiyah, Issue 1, September 2016.

44. The full video of Baghdadi's speech has now been removed from the internet. A copy is held in the ICSR archive of the Syrian civil war and was used for this citation. Transcripts of the speech exist online.

45. "A biography of Abu Bakr al-Baghdadi," *SITE Insite Blog on Terrorism and Extremism*, Aug. 12, 2014

46. The official name of the coalition is The Global Coalition Against Daesh.

47. This video has been removed from the internet but is held in the ICSR archive of the Syrian civil war and was used for this citation. Partial copies of it exist on news websites, such as here: "Australian teen Abdullah Elmir warns Tony Abbott in Isis message — video," *The Guardian*, Oct. 21, 2014.

48. "There Is No Life Without Jihad," al-Hayat Media Centre, June 2014.

49. "Sheikh Abu Mohammed al-Jolani checks military developments and discusses them with military leaders within the camp during the siege of Aleppo," Twitter, Oct. 29, 2016.

CHAPTER FIVE

OUT OF THE DESERT:
ISIS's STRATEGY FOR A LONG WAR

HASSAN HASSAN

INTRODUCTION

In both Syria and Iraq, the insurgency landscape has undergone a notable transformation. Various militant groups have largely been forced to turn from holding and defending population centers to retreating into rural areas or ungoverned spaces, or even temporarily melting away. ISIS has lost almost all of the territory it seized in 2014. Similarly, Syrian factions opposed to the regime of Bashar al-Assad have struggled to hold on to the many populated strongholds that they held in 2012 and 2013, including sizeable garrisons in Deir Ezzor, Raqqa, al-Hasakah, and Homs in 2014; eastern Aleppo in 2016; and various areas in Homs, Hama, Idlib, and southern Syria since.

The collapse of ISIS's caliphate could open the door for other groups to operate in the terrain it once controlled uncontested. Rival groups and individuals are already preparing to return to eastern Syria and Iraq as ISIS loses ground. The space where various forces could compete in the future stretches contiguously from the Euphrates and Tigris rivers in central and northwestern Iraq to northwestern and southwestern Syria. In this complex terrain, it is unlikely that existing power vacuums will be filled quickly. As a result, insurgent groups will continue to operate there while forces loyal to central governments will likely maintain a tenuous grip, at least for the foreseeable future.

In this scenario, an expansive theater of operations will emerge, in which militants could feasibly carve out safe havens, regroup, and stage attacks locally, regionally, or internationally. Contrary to common perceptions, jihadis placed high importance on rural areas early on in 2011, while simultaneously focusing on major population centers. One al-Qaeda ideologue envisioned the possible state of jihadis in Syria as "mercurial in nature," where rural insurgency would challenge the local governments and their foreign allies that largely remain unprepared to face insurgency effectively. Forces fighting the Syrian and Iraqi governments have already articulated strategies for operating in such an environment.

The contiguous terrain linking Iraq and Syria is comparable both in value and threat to the militant hub existing along the Afghanistan-Pakistan border region. The area acquired the moniker "AfPak" and began being perceived and treated as a single theater that required an integrated or holistic approach. Concurrently, the "Syraq" space extends deep into Syria and Iraq with favorable sociopolitical conditions for jihadis to endure, entrench, and emerge again.

This region is the soft underbelly of both Iraq and Syria, a fact unlikely to change in the foreseeable future. In this region, no socially viable or sustainable local forces have been utilized by the U.S.-led coalition against ISIS to capture and hold towns previously controlled by ISIS. Instead, these Sunni-majority areas are now dominated by Shi'i and Kurdish forces. Adding to the future challenge, much of the region ISIS once controlled now lies in ruins.

This paper seeks to situate the next phase of ISIS in this context. For ISIS, rural insurgency is no less important than urban warfare as a means to degrade enemies, recruit members, and lay the groundwork for their long-term survival or next return if defeated. A key objective of this paper is to demonstrate that rural insurgency is not an afterthought for ISIS and other jihadis who are currently on the defensive. Rather, rural insurgency is a strategy that they have long thought about and planned for, even before the U.S. launched Operation Inherent Resolve in the summer of 2014. ISIS has prioritized the borderlands where both the Iraqi and Syrian governments have more limited reach, and it is here where the jihadi project will either die or flourish.

ISIS's Formula for Survival

ISIS has a strategy to resume its insurgency after the collapse of its government, namely from rural areas. The plan is often expressed in three terms used in its Arabic-language publications — *sahraa* or "desert;" *sahwat* or "Sunni opponents;" and *sawlat* or "hit-and-run operations." These terms deal with the where, who, how, and why of the next phase of insurgency.

SAHRAA, OR "DESERT"

Since the summer of 2016, even before the battles in Mosul and Raqqa began, ISIS began to talk about the desert as a viable place to launch its post-caliphate insurgency. Since then, ISIS propaganda has frequently featured desert combat to show that it could still inflict damage on government forces in remote areas and on vital highways linking Syria and Jordan to Iraq. Invoking the desert also draws parallels to the last time the organization was deemed defeated in Iraq after 2008.

SAHWAT, OR "SUNNI OPPONENTS"

Sahwat was originally restricted to the tribal Awakening Councils established in western Iraq to fight ISIS's predecessor, the Islamic State of Iraq (ISI), during the 2007 U.S. troop surge. The term has since been broadened to include any and all opponents and collaborators coming from Sunni communities.

SAWLAT, OR "HIT-AND-RUN OPERATIONS"

Headquartered in the desert or hidden in populated areas, ISIS aims to run a far-reaching and ceaseless insurgency in rural areas and urban centers to deter and stretch thin its opponents and to abrade any fledgling state-run governance or security structures in areas it previously controlled.

ISIS began to publicly articulate its post-caliphate strategy in earnest in May 2016, when its former spokesman Abu Muhammad al-Adnani gave his last speech before being killed in Syria in late August 2016. In his speech, Adnani prepared ISIS's followers for the fall of "all cities" under the group's control. Throughout the speech, he depicted the rise and fall of the group as the latest stage in a historical flow, continuing as a preconceived and preordained process from the early days of the Iraq War in 2003-04 until the current day. Territorial demise, to him, was merely a change of mode in which the process of depleting the enemy would continue apace, if in different forms. If and when an opportunity for another rise presented itself, the process of enemy degradation would have laid the groundwork for an even deeper influence than the previous round. In his May 2016 speech, Adnani proclaimed: "Do you think, O America, that victory is achieved by the killing of one commander or more? It is then a false victory." He added:

Victory is when the enemy is defeated. Do you think, O America, that defeat is the loss of a city or a land? Were we defeated when we lost cities in Iraq and were left in the desert without a city or a territory? Will we be defeated and you will be victorious if you took Mosul or Sirte or Raqqa or all the cities, and we returned where we were in the first stage? No, defeat is the loss of willpower and desire to fight.

Since Adnani's speech, ISIS has repeatedly released videos and articles featuring similar themes. An editorial published by its weekly *Al-Naba* newspaper in August 2016 — a publication that tends to be relatively in sync with daily life under the caliphate — echoed its former spokesman's statements about how the group understood its 13-year history. In the editorial, the authors summed up the group's strategy after its expulsion from former strongholds in Iraq in the wake of the troop surge with the support of Sunni tribesman:

In the years that followed the rise of sahwat *in Iraq, the* mujahideen *retreated into the desert after leaving behind tens of concealed* mujahideen *from among the security squads [i.e. sleeper cells], which killed, inflicted pain, drained, and tormented them, and confused their ranks, and exhausted their army, police, and their security apparatus, until God willed that the Knights of the Desert return to storm the apostates inside their fortresses after they had worn them out through* kawatim *[gun silencers],* lawasiq *[sticky bombs], and martyrdom operations.*

ISIS has also focused on the role of Sunni collaborators in its demise in 2008-09 and vowed to keep up the pressure against any newly emerging ones. "America was defeated and its army fell in ruins, and began to collapse had it not been salvaged by the *sahwat* of treason and shame," roared Adnani in his May 2016 speech. The August 2016 editorial also warned the Syrian *sahwat* of the same fate as the Iraqi insurgents, claiming that the group's *mafariz amniyah,* or "secret security units," have since become even more skillful in "the methods of deceiving the enemy and thwarting its security plans."

Together, these three elements shape ISIS's formula of survival after the caliphate. Even though the group suggested it would withdraw to the desert, future attacks will still focus on urban centers, with rural areas acting as pathways between the two terrains. As the group retreats from its last strongholds, ISIS operations will target new governing structures and Sunni collaborators in order to prevent the establishment of alternatives to ISIS rule that might appeal to local communities in predominantly tribal and rural areas. Hit-and-run attacks would demonstrate that nothing is out of ISIS's reach, even if its ability to control territory has plummeted.

ISIS's Insurgency Strategy

ISIS's recent discussions of a post-caliphate insurgency are consistent with a strategy that the group's previous incarnation, ISI, expressed in a 2009 document entitled the "Strategic Plan to Improve the Political Standing of the Islamic State of Iraq," a defining study of the factors that led to ISI's near-defeat and how it planned to recover. The analysis and prescriptions in the document shaped the group's strategy, and its success has subsequently come to define how ISIS perceives its chances of recovery today. The group believes that what worked before will work again. For this reason, a closer examination of the document, along with the group's narrative around the caliphate's recent crumbling, could provide the best available insights into what ISIS intends to do next.

The document makes it clear that the popular uprising launched against ISI in Sunni areas with American help was overwhelming and devastating for the group. It discusses how tribesmen driven by tribal solidarity turned against ISI, and does not shy away from acknowledging that the uprising was inclusive of all tribes.

Around the time the document was being drafted, ISI had begun to see the momentum against it decline, due again to tribal dynamics. Quickly, ISI saw signs of new opportunities begin to emerge. Young people who had joined the U.S.-backed Awakening Councils were becoming disillusioned with their leaders. Tribal elders were restless about the rise of rival overlords coming up from within their own tribes. The Councils gradually began to crumble, and ISI slowly regained renewed, if quiet, relevance. "That does not mean the calamity and adversity will stop, it will undoubtedly continue," the document underlined. "But, as historical precedents show, it will not be as encompassing and large. They [the Awakening Councils] are decreasing substantially."

The view within ISI suggested that the group had weathered the storm of the Awakening Councils. This is how the document described the supposed process of bringing the councils down:

> *With the spread of the Awakening Councils, it became clear that ISI focused on this pathological phenomenon and on trying to target the heads of their founders. This would resemble a large tree whose roots are cut off so that its branches die out on their own. This intensive military policy culminated in the near-collapse of the Awakening Councils, a great and significant accomplishment, which proves that ISIS has become a political and military power capable of dealing with internal problems effectively.*

The purpose of ISI's 55-page treatise was to offer a diagnosis of the tribal uprising that upended its primacy and to suggest how best to prepare for the U.S.'s departure from Iraq. The group's war minister at the time, Abu Hamza al-Muhajir, said of the preparations of ISI's competitors in Iraq that "The timing of the withdrawal of the occupier is the worst timing, as the experience in Afghanistan has shown, and we have become certain of that. There are parties storing weapons and preparing [secret security units] for the day when the occupier leaves. They shoot one rocket and store ten others."

Having contained the U.S.-led tribal uprising, the next phase was to prepare for U.S. withdrawal:

> *After our emancipation from the circumstances around the* sahwat *and with the end of that phase, in which the* sahwat *presented a real danger to the* dawlah *[ISI] … this period emerges as a period of planning and preparation for what comes after the American withdrawal … the real victor of this battle will be the one who knows how to plan and prepare for the post-withdrawal period.*

This preparation phase, as outlined in the document, involved the use of various tactics that would enable the group to consolidate itself within Iraq and abrade the capabilities of its rivals. The focus would be to prevent the emergence of local structures capable of filling the vacuums left behind after U.S. withdrawal. Such tactics included targeting police and army units to maximize the cost of joining their ranks. To achieve its goals, ISI suggested three courses of action for the group's clandestine campaign.

The first focused on targeting Iraqis — particularly Sunnis — seeking to enroll in the military and police forces. ISI proposed "nine bullets for the apostates and one bullet for the crusaders" and a range of soft propaganda portraying enrollment in state agencies as both socially shameful and religiously sinful. The reason for the 9:1 bullet ratio was twofold. The Americans had already made a choice to leave Iraq, so it was pointless to focus on them. Instead, the document's authors believed that the U.S. planned to use local Iraqis as proxies for a continued occupation. Therefore, placing a focus on eroding functioning state institutions would push the U.S. further from its commitment to building a new Iraq that served its interests. By disrupting the creation of effective security institutions, ISI's logic went, the U.S. would give up and leave Iraq to its own devices, and thus open up new opportunities to the *mujahideen*, or fighters:

"When will a building be completed when what one builds is being destroyed by another," the document said, citing Arabic poetry. "This great wisdom is one of the most important policies that should be applied in the jihadi work, especially in this critical period."

Furthermore, the document explained that the U.S. had pinned its hopes on the ability of Iraq's army and police forces to fully control the security situation without the need for direct American support. This, the authors added, would enable the U.S. to withdraw from Iraq. Incessant attacks against the police and army would render the U.S. "torn between getting themselves out of the conundrum as soon as possible and staying in it while unable to complete the building that they began working on."

ISI's second proposed tactic was to purge areas in which the group operated from any sustainable rival military presence. This process would involve targeting security bases and gatherings in order to deplete the government forces and divert their attention. Such attacks would increase the group's influence and mobility in as many areas as possible, and thus enhance its ability to conduct operations in a wider area.

The goal here, according to the document, was manifold. It would supplement ISI's effort to prevent the construction of functioning army and police institutions; it would also further deplete government forces, forcing them to constantly worry about rebuilding bases or finding new areas to construct facilities, which would drain the security forces' ability to fully control population areas. In this context, the authors cited Sun Tzu's maxim: "Reduce the hostile chiefs by inflicting damage on them; and make trouble for them, and keep them constantly engaged."

ISI's third proposed course of action was to focus assassination attacks on key nodes within the security forces. Such figures included operationally effective officers, engineers, and trainers, since these skilled cadres were critical to the expanding objectives of Iraq's security forces and would be difficult to replace. The document also cited unspecified reports that most of Iraq's forces were unable to conduct operations without close American support, and therefore proposed that targeting those elite forces capable of operating independently be a top priority. "Although such targeting requires a great deal of time and effort, it is worth the focus," the document stated. "Even a small number of this type of concentrated targeting is better than a large number of other targets."

In this context, other specified targets included political leaders. By attacking effective and influential political figures, the document said, ISI would create power vacuums and sow confusion among other leaders. Since such targets were difficult to reach, the document suggested that ISI work patiently to infiltrate political circles and recruit moles and bodyguards to conduct attacks on its behalf. Successful targeting would erode the public's trust in the government's ability to defend ordinary citizens.

Retreating to Rural Areas

Throughout the U.S.-led campaign against ISIS that began in the summer of 2014, the U.S. pursued a disjointed strategy in Iraq and Syria. The campaign initially had an Iraq-first approach in which professional, tribal, and Kurdish forces were trained and equipped to fight ISIS. In Syria, the effort to train an anti-ISIS force from within mainstream opposition factions was halfhearted and swiftly crumbled. Therefore, the U.S. continued to rely heavily on an effective yet insufficient Kurdish militia, the People's Protection Units (YPG). In October 2015, the Syrian Kurds announced the establishment of the Syrian Democratic Forces (SDF), which included a growing number of Arab fighters.

After ISIS was driven out of most of central and northern Iraq and northern Syria in mid-2017, the war's center of gravity shifted toward the two countries' hinterlands. Local forces there were relatively less-equipped to fight ISIS, and more battle-hardened Kurdish-dominated forces had to travel to towns where they tended to be viewed with even more distrust than elsewhere. Deir Ezzor, for example, has almost no Kurdish population, which would otherwise have provided the legitimacy or justification for the YPG's local involvement.

Meanwhile, the weakening northern and southern Syrian opposition were coming under enormous strain, as former al-Qaeda affiliate Hayat Tahrir al-Sham (HTS) exploited their weakening to further entrench itself. In late January 2017, HTS launched a consolidation campaign in the northwestern province of Idlib. HTS claimed that opposition forces — with foreign backing — planned to turn against the group after peace talks were organized by Russia in Astana, Kazakhstan, enhancing its control of territory. By the time the campaign ended in February, several groups had either joined HTS or had been forced to join Ahrar al-Sham to shield themselves from it. HTS tightened its grip in Idlib and the mobilization against it by some sections of the opposition failed. The group then went on to assert itself as the leader of the rebellion, first through a number of suicide attacks against regime targets in the heart of Homs and Damascus, and later through offensives it led in Hama and southern Syria.

To make matters worse for the non-jihadis, the opposition's backers were shifting their priorities in the conflict. In late August 2016, for example, Turkey began to work closely with Russia after the former launched its operation to expel ISIS from west of the Euphrates River and to block any further expansion of the YPG in northern Syria. The operation, dubbed Euphrates Shield, was a game-changer in the Syrian conflict, marking a critical shift in Turkish priorities away from the removal of Assad. Countries such as Qatar have since had little room to bankroll groups they previously backed, especially after both Turkey and Jordan moved closer to Moscow, and since the regime recaptured eastern Aleppo in December 2016.

With backers either changing priorities, exiting the conflict, or being locked out of it, the resulting loss of territorial strongholds placed non-jihadi insurgents under increased pressure, either from HTS or ISIS. In Syria, the loss of urban bases was more damaging to mainstream opposition fighters. These fighters are less prepared than jihadis to conduct long-term rural warfare operationally and ideologically, given jihadis' experience in other battlefields in the decades before the ongoing Syrian conflict, especially in Syria and Afghanistan in the 1970s-80s, in Algeria in the 1990s, and in Iraq since 2003. Politically, withdrawal from populated urban centers also dealt a further blow to the opposition's attempts to win international recognition and support as a viable alternative to the Assad regime.

This situation as it stands has favored jihadis and positions them well to inherit what remains of anti-government sentiment. For ISIS and HTS alike, the erosion in support for the anti-Assad rebellion empowers their respective strategies, principally the objective of presenting themselves as the only available alternative to the populations they seek to control. Interestingly, ISIS's desire to present itself as the true defender of Syria's anti-regime insurgency became even more pronounced in the spring of 2018, as mainstream opposition forces agreed to a series of surrender agreements near Damascus.

Starting in October 2017, there were signs that ISIS had begun to shift its strategy in traditional key strongholds, namely the Euphrates River Valley, extending from Deir Ezzor in eastern Syria to Anbar in western Iraq.

With the fall of Mosul in mid-2017, the writing appeared to be on the wall for ISIS's caliphate. Notwithstanding ISIS's emerging weakness, the speed of its subsequent retreats from places like Tal Afar, Hawija, and even Raqqa, were a surprise to many. Even more unexpected was ISIS's retreat from areas long perceived to represent its strategic base — the Iraq-Syria borderlands and the Euphrates River Valley, where it had a decade or more of experience fighting or operating and from where it re-emerged in 2014.

ISIS's continued presence in that region, combined with assertions by local sources and U.S. officials about the volatility of the border areas, underscored the significance of these borderlands as hideouts and a potential launching pad for future operations. These areas became the center of ISIS's remaining concentration of forces, comprising die-hard foreign and local fighters and key commanders preserved from previous battles. By late summer of 2017, they were also host to at least 550 ISIS fighters who had been given safe passage to travel from Lebanon and Raqqa in deals with Hezbollah and the SDF, respectively.

But despite their apparent strategic significance, some of these areas fell abruptly from ISIS hands with little fighting in October 2017. For example, after ISIS's defeat in al-Mayadin, local sources speaking to Deir Ezzor 24, a grassroots organization specializing in documenting violations by both the regime and jihadis, denied the city had been retaken by forces loyal to Assad. The local skepticism underlined the extent to which ISIS's sudden withdrawal had surprised locals, who along with U.S. officials had seen the city as a critical ISIS base amid the ongoing assault on Raqqa to the north.

ISIS fighters also appear to have melted away in al-Bukamal and al-Qa'im, border towns that face each other in Syria and Iraq, respectively. After earlier shaping operations, the Iraqi push into al-Qa'im was relatively swift and lasted less than two weeks. Similarly, the Syrian regime and Iran-backed militias announced they had recaptured al-Bukamal in November 2017, shortly after a campaign to fight the group was launched there in September. It was after the defeat in al-Bukamal — which ISIS denied at the time — that the regime and its allies declared the jihadi group to have been destroyed, on Nov. 9, 2017.

One possible explanation could be found in ISIS's own publications. *Al-Naba* hinted at a major change of strategy in a series of articles published between September and October 2017 on dealing with the U.S. air campaign. In two reports published in September 2017, *Al-Naba* explained that having suffered heavy losses — particularly in Kobane — ISIS militants were internally debating how to evade the "precision" of U.S. airstrikes while pursuing ground assaults on multiple fronts. Ideas included disguising weaponry and engaging in military deception, such as waging fake attacks to distract enemies. The article concluded that it would be a mistake for ISIS to continue engaging forces that enjoyed air support from the U.S. or Russia because the function of these forces was not to serve as conventional fighting forces, but mainly to provoke the militants and expose their whereabouts and capabilities in order for sophisticated drones and aircraft to strike them.

In order to avoid the depletion of its forces by overwhelming air power, the article pushed for ISIS to adopt a counter-strategy in which it would begin to refrain from engaging in sustained clashes in urban centers, a notable departure from established strategy. Given that ISIS quickly retreated from urban areas in places like Tal Afar and Hawija in the weeks following the liberation of Mosul, it appears likely the article reflected an actual change in strategy by ISIS's leadership after the loss of Iraq's second largest city in July 2017.

This change of tactics was also reflected in the early stages of the battle of Raqqa, where, as *Al-Naba* revealed, ISIS divided the city into small, self-sustained, and autonomous localities in order to enable militants to defend their areas with minimal movement and without the need for resupply from other districts. ISIS allowed these small groups of fighters to make autonomous decisions, dictated by their own circumstances and needs. According to the *Al-Naba* article, another precaution taken in Raqqa and then more generally was to avoid gathering in large numbers at entry points to a battlefield, as such positions had typically been struck from the air, weakening any attempt by ground forces to advance into an urban environment. "In modern wars, with precision weapons, everyone tries to avoid direct engagement with his enemy to minimize losses," the article declared.

In another *Al-Naba* report issued on Oct. 12, 2017, ISIS suggested that it had again been forced to switch to insurgency tactics as it had back in the spring of 2008, then under the leadership of Abu Omar al-Baghdadi and his war minister, Abu Hamza al-Muhajir. The article related how the group's predecessor, ISI, had been forced to dismantle its fighting units in March 2008 and pursue a different strategy aimed at preserving what was left of its manpower. Providing details never before disclosed, it described how the ISI had become exhausted and depleted after two years of fierce fighting against U.S. and Iraqi troops, so much so that it was no longer able to stand and fight for long. "In early 2008, it became clear it was impossible to continue to engage in conventional fighting. That was when Abu Omar al-Baghdadi said: 'We now have no place where we could stand for a quarter of an hour.'" The article argued the situation in late 2017 was comparable to 2008 and that this justified a switch of approach.

ISIS's apparent decision to conserve forces for a durable insurgency in the region stretching from Deir Ezzor in eastern Syria to Anbar province in western Iraq makes strategic sense, given that it has frequently highlighted the area as being key to its survival and best suited for a guerrilla war. For ISIS, rural and desert-based insurgency are as important as urban warfare in any sustained effort to deplete an enemy, to recruit new members, and to lay the groundwork for a future comeback. The geographic and human terrain of the Deir Ezzor-Anbar region would provide ISIS with an area in which it could regroup, coordinate sleeper cells, regain financial autonomy through extortion, and plot attacks.

Tactical changes within key sanctuaries also comport with patterns that predated the group's military weakness. Nibras Kazimi, an Iraqi security expert, has noted that ISIS used particular tactics in these areas. He has explained that, in areas like al-Rutbah, Palmyra, eastern Qalamoun, and west Samarra, ISIS's fighting was restricted to deflection, probing, and attrition even before their territorial collapse. ISIS's "well-developed and functioning" bases of operations in the desert, according to Kazimi, remained intact because the group refrained from engaging in costly battles, as had happened elsewhere in Iraq and Syria, near desert areas throughout the campaign against it since 2014.

However, this tactical evolution could be unrelated to an ISIS loss of territory. Kazimi explained that the group's operation in the desert could also be the result of an earlier strategy developed to facilitate attacks further afield, in neighboring countries like Jordan and Saudi Arabia. Even at the height of its power in 2014 and 2015, the desert remained a core component of the group's fighting strategy, and thus was not only left in place but also reinforced with new fuel and water depots, transportation routes, and alliances with desert nomads and smugglers. "The desert fighting force was developed with generous financial allocations, increased training, innovative camouflage techniques, surveillance equipment, and its own iconography and symbolism within the ISIS narrative of jihadi glory," Kazimi added.

RECOVERY SIGNS

In fact, during the early months of 2016, well before it lost Mosul, ISIS had increasingly transitioned to insurgency tactics. General Joseph Votel, commander of U.S. Central Command, told reporters in May 2016 that ISIS "may be reverting in some regards back to their terrorist roots." Indeed, in early 2016 the group had stepped up hit-and-run attacks in towns it had lost, without any indication that the limited number of militants involved in these operations sought to regain control of the towns. The tactic was a notable divergence from the group's traditional tendency — particularly at the height of its expansion in 2014 — to engage in conventional attacks, including armed convoys and artillery barrages. These new tactics tended to involve small units attacking from behind enemy lines or through hasty raids. In early 2016, as it began to combine insurgency tactics with conventional army tactics while holding territory, ISIS could be described as pursuing a hybrid strategy of territorial control and insurgency tactics.

The group also began to mount attacks in areas it had previously failed to enter as a more conventional armed force, such as in Abu Ghraib, west of Baghdad, and in the coastal region of western Syria. By reverting back to the old insurgency and terror tactics, ISIS found itself more capable of penetrating otherwise well-secured areas. Previous attempts to attack such areas through conventional fighting units had failed even while the group was at the height of its power.

By the spring of 2016, the emergence of these new tactics, combined with ISIS's continued control of territory, raised questions among U.S. officials about the versatility and adaptability of allied Iraqi and Syrian forces and the kind of training they received relative to that of ISIS. As one senior U.S. official conceded to this author in May 2017, it was not yet possible for the U.S.-led coalition to focus on countering asymmetric or insurgent tactics while ISIS still controlled significant territorial sanctuaries.

ISIS's reversion and reliance on insurgency tactics increased further as it lost more territory. Hit-and-run attacks and high-profile assassinations returned to newly liberated areas, such as in Salah ad-Din, Diyala, Anbar, and Raqqa, although such attacks were rarely accounted for in official and public statements by the U.S.-led coalition related to progress against the group.

In Iraq, the return of ISIS operations to areas newly liberated from its control was a reality long before the group lost its hold of Mosul. In October 2016, as Iraqi troops prepared for the battle in Mosul, Iraqi officials told Al Sumaria TV that ISIS had already begun to recruit new members among displaced civilians in areas secured since late 2014 in the city of Samarra, in Salah ad-Din province. Officials' fears were triggered by new findings by local intelligence and a series of suicide attacks in areas between the Balad district and Samarra, which officials attributed to the inability of security forces to hold and secure the liberated areas, especially near the Tigris River.

One Iraqi military intelligence official, Hayder Abdulsattar, told Al Sumaria at the time that ISIS's numbers and activities were growing again and, along with sleeper cells, the group had begun facilitating the movement of its operatives across the Euphrates River. "We use ambushes [to catch ISIS operatives crossing the river], but it is not enough because that requires the support of a whole brigade," Muhammad Abbas, the commander of the Sixth Brigade of Hashd al-Shaabi, or the Popular Mobilization Units (PMUs), told the channel.

Signs of ISIS recovery already appear to be emerging in areas from which the group was expelled early on in late 2014 and early 2015. This could be attributed to the time the group has spent regrouping since, or the fact that as these areas calm, they become less of a focus of U.S. or coalition airstrikes. As noted last year by Michael Knights, ISIS was already involved in intense insurgent operations in several parts of the country a year after it declared a caliphate, and especially in Diyala province, with the level of violence in June 2017 remaining at around the same level as in 2013. In fact, in Diyala, which was never overrun by ISIS, an insurgency against Shi'i militia forces had been gathering pace since 2015, and steady attacks ranging from ambushes to assassinations have been regularly reported in and near the province.

Knights' research pointed to a full-fledged insurgency in Diyala province being led from an adjacent ungoverned space north of the Diyala River. "The insurgency has attained a steady, consistent operational tempo of roadside IED attacks, mortar strikes, and raids on PMF outposts, and attacks on electrical and pipeline infrastructure," Knights wrote. He added, "In Diyala, the Islamic State is already engaged in the kind of intimate violence that was seen across northern Iraq in 2013: Granular, high-quality targeting of Sunni leaders and tribes working alongside the PMF."

There have been similar patterns of insurgent operations over the past two years in the borderlands straddling Iraq and Syria, in which ISIS benefits from geographic and social terrain that's more challenging for counterinsurgents. Since 2017, ISIS fighters have carried out several hit-and-run attacks on military bases in the area, some of which have killed high-ranking Iranian and

Russian officers.

For ISIS, the return to these activities was also designed to demonstrate that its existing, new generation of leaders was capable of following in the footsteps of their previous generation. Wilayat Salah ad-Din, for instance, released a video in May 2016 entitled "Craft of War," seeking to replicate its previous comeback. The video addressed how much the group's new leadership had absorbed skills obtained from founding leaders like Abu Abdulrahman al-Bilawi, who planned the takeover of Mosul before he was killed in June 2014. The 30-minute video showed operations targeting "the enemy's rear lines" in the province, on the Baiji-Haditha road, between the Tigris and Euphrates rivers, as well as inside the city of Tikrit.

As in other combat videos posted by ISIS, the video details various armed attacks, the forceful dispersal of the enemy, and the seizure of arms and vehicles from the bases of enemy forces. The video featured the killing of Tikrit's counterterrorism chief along with 31 people, including 14 policeman, after seven ISIS fighters entered the city's central Zuhur district in a police car wearing suicide vests and police uniforms before storming the counterterrorism chief's residence. The video's commentator then claimed the attacks demonstrated the current leadership's ability to plan and execute effective attacks, just as the old guard had done previously when they brought the group back to life after it was thought dead:

> *These operations brought to mind the planning of the ISIS's early leaders. The qualitative operations in Tikrit, Baiji, al-Siniyyah, Samarra, and others … are an extension of the methodology of the commanders and leaders who had previously led the war of attrition and kept the enemy occupied, and who laid the groundwork for a long war. Men of honesty carried the banner after them to destroy their enemy, and the first sign of glad tidings appeared at their hands (showing) that Salah ad-Din was and remains a deterring place for the apostates.*

ISIS has an extensive plan to exploit this region. It is also conscious of the advantages presented to it today in being able to focus its energies on guerrilla or insurgent-type operations, rather than on seeking to maintain control over approximately one-third of Iraq and half of Syria. ISIS has spoken occasionally, for example, of the enhanced abilities of its clandestine network to resume a post-caliphate insurgency to exhaust and erode its enemy. This network is led by the worst of the worst within ISIS, namely the *amniyat*, or "security units."

Even at the height of its strength in 2014, ISIS's *amniyat* continued to operate underground. Such units were typically tasked with clandestine work within local communities, behind enemy lines, and even within the organization itself. Thus, they are the most likely to melt back into the population by virtue of their anonymity, expertise, and mobility. While locals who lived under ISIS had varying access to those within the organization's military, police, clerical, and services sectors, *amni* or "security operatives," were largely unknown to the local population.

WRONG LESSONS LEARNED?

The overall goal of the strategy proposed in 2009, and echoed in recent years, was to deplete the enemy and preempt any effort by central or local authorities to create security or social structures capable of entrenching rival government political orders and challenging the presence of jihadis. The campaign of incessant attacks to debilitate the enemy, which ISI fighters launched inside Iraq following the U.S. withdrawal in 2010, is a process jihadis refer to as *nikayah* or "a war of attrition."

These tactics distinguish ISIS even from its ideological sibling, al-Qaeda. While the concept of *nikayah* was first popularized within al-Qaeda circles, mainly by the Jordanian jihadi theorists Abu Qatadah al-Filistini and Abu Muhammad al-Maqdisi, such tactics have emerged as the organizing principle of ISIS's insurgent campaign. Al-Qaeda operatives conduct similar attacks against specific targets for similar reasons, but these attacks are significantly less comprehensive and wide-ranging than those of ISIS. The latter does not shy away from publicly targeting individuals who collaborate with governments. It also has no qualms in apostatizing and killing clerics or community leaders who work against them. Conversely, in its attempt to win hearts and minds, al-Qaeda tries to avoid alienating local communities. Instead, it focuses on de-emphasizing its ideology and embedding into the social or insurgent fabric of a given country, depending on the circumstances, as it has attempted to do in Yemen, Syria, and Libya.

The tactics that ISIS followed after it was dislodged from Sunni towns in Iraq before 2008 are arguably unique across the Islamic jihadi landscape. Its extreme, unequivocal, and comprehensive targeting of all potential opponents or rivals enabled it to achieve results that al-Qaeda in Syria, for example, struggled to achieve. In another example, the absence of viable Sunni insurgent groups that could rival it in Iraq is in large part due to its pre-emptive campaign against them over the years, along with other factors, notably the withdrawal of American support from the Awakening Councils and the targeting of those councils by the former prime minister, Nouri al-Maliki. Al-Qaeda in Syria, on the other hand, has been repeatedly checked or challenged by local resistance precisely because it has sought to accommodate dissent and avoid being compared to ISIS, tactics that limited its ability to react forcefully and adequately to competing factions and voices in the same way that ISIS did.

One major gap in the connection between ISI's post-2008 campaign and ISIS's dramatic rise in 2014 is that the group was affiliated with al-Qaeda from August

2011 to April 2013, a crucial period fueling its rise the following year. During that period, Jabhat al-Nusra's operations in Syria began, driven by members of ISI. Jabhat al-Nusra was bankrolled by the group until April 2013, when the latter unilaterally announced the merger of the two branches and the resulting creation of ISIS, which Jabhat al-Nusra swiftly rejected. Instead, Jabhat al-Nusra pledged its allegiance directly to al-Qaeda's leader, Ayman al-Zawahiri. Those were formative months for ISIS's expansion into Syria.

In the first two years of its operations in Syria, Jabhat al-Nusra built some of its most successful strongholds in rural Deir Ezzor. The effort to entrench its presence in rural areas in particular was neither arbitrary nor was it limited to eastern Syria. Despite the fact that it operated effectively in urban centers, al-Qaeda's affiliated presence in Syria was largely based in rural areas for the better part of its existence in the country.

In February 2014, Jordanian Sami al-Aridi, who had earlier replaced Iraqi Abu Mariyah al-Qahtani as Jabhat al-Nusra's top clerical authority, wrote a series of tweets about his group's strategy in Syria. Aridi, who Nusra leader Abu Mohammed al-Jolani had described to Al Jazeera in 2013 as being the authoritative voice on the group's ideology, listed 19 strategic recommendations originally developed by prominent Syrian jihadi theorist, Mustafa Abdul Qadir Setmariam (Abu Musab al-Suri). Among those recommendations was to pay special attention to rural areas and build networks in remote areas.

What if, then, ISIS drew the wrong conclusions about its rise in 2014, a development that owed a great deal to the networks and geographic reach that its former Syrian branch had established? While most of Jabhat al-Nusra's network chose not to defect during the infighting with ISIS in 2013, ISIS benefited from an influx of a sizeable number of the group's commanders, members, and resources. In other words, much of the infrastructure and some of the manpower that laid the groundwork for ISIS's expansion had been built by another group operating under different guiding principles.

Another potentially misconstrued lesson that ISIS may have internalized is a related one. In the strategy document detailed earlier, the group spoke unfavorably toward the idea of winning hearts and minds, which jihadis call *hadhina sha'biyah* meaning "communal or popular incubation." This could be attributed to the sweeping popular uprising against it circa 2008, as the authors describe how initial attempts to win hearts and minds delayed any pre-emptive moves against their fellow insurgents' counter-uprising. The lesson, the document stated, should be to nip such internal challenges in the bud without paying any undue attention to alienating people as a result.

The group followed this lesson after it broke away from Jabhat al-Nusra, immediately declaring war against the *sahwat* in Syria, by which it meant opposition fighters opposed to the regime in Damascus. Its war against the opposition caused many inside and outside Syria to see it as collaborating with the regime. That is when the group became known as "Daesh," a pejorative term based on the Arabic acronym for ISIS. It was also during that time when the group was labeled widely in the region as *khawarij* or "outliers," a reference to a similarly extreme group that emerged in early Islamic history.

Whether ISIS has learned the right lessons from its history will determine the prospects of it rising again. But that does not in any way make its next choice of tactics any less deadly. The group will continue to model its post-caliphate strategy on what it is convinced worked the last time. Significantly, the area poised to be the testing ground for the group's strategy in the coming years includes previous strongholds where al-Qaeda paved the way for ISIS's rise: Areas near the Syrian and Anbar deserts and the Euphrates and Tigris rivers in eastern Syria and northern and western Iraq.

Conclusion

As the group has made clear since the Adnani speech in May 2016, ISIS intends to replicate the experiences envisaged in its 2009 document. Adnani's comparison of ISIS's recent military defeats to the last time the group (in the form of ISI) was pronounced defeated in 2009 reflects how the group perceives these current defeats. The 2009 strategy was summed up in Adnani's definition of defeat as "the loss of willpower and desire to fight." The group's incessant, ceaseless, and targeted attacks serve a carefully calculated function. The pursuit of this strategy, the group believes, led specifically to the sweeping gains made in 2014. Mosul collapsed swiftly not because the militants were powerful; it fell because its defenders were weak, a weakness the group seems to attribute to its insurgency campaign between 2008 and 2014.

ISIS's focus is unlikely to diverge from what was described in the 2009 document. It will focus on targeting burgeoning government structures, military bases, individuals who cooperate with the government, as well as government or foreign business interests. Another obvious target will be Shi'i and Kurdish militias, now spread out throughout Iraq's central and northern Sunni communities, the diffuseness of which make them soft targets.

In Iraq, none of the Sunni insurgents that once competed with ISIS's predecessors for territory and influence exist today in a meaningful way. In Syria, meanwhile, ISIS will likely conduct a campaign focused mostly on Kurdish and regime forces that have inherited control of its former caliphate in eastern Syria. Elsewhere, especially in southern, central, and northwestern Syria, much of ISIS's efforts will likely focus on infiltrating and fighting rebel forces. The flow of arms and existing sanctuaries could position northern and northwestern Syria as lucrative financial areas for jihadi groups like ISIS.

For this reason, a priority there could be to lay low. A senior jihadi based inside Syria also told this author that some jihadi operatives had moved to zones currently overseen by Turkey in the hope of benefiting from expected reconstruction plans there. Several rebel sources have also spoken of suspected ISIS sleeper cells in Idlib.

However, the main battle will likely be concentrated in Iraq and Syria, extending from central Iraq to northern Syria. In such geographic spaces, jihadis could focus their attacks on their enemies while their opponents find it harder to sustain a counterinsurgency. The terrain also offers jihadis rear bases in which they could regroup, run sleeper cells, extort, and plot attacks on highways and in urban centers.

Remote, rural areas are also populated and jihadis could still use them to sustain themselves and to conduct urban guerrilla warfare, acting as "land pirates" sailing through an archipelago of desert areas, river valleys, rural towns, and small urban centers. Even at the height of the U.S. troop surge in Iraq, when Syria was a stable and occasionally cooperative country, the U.S. struggled to effectively target jihadi networks along the border, according to a former senior official involved in the surge.

The situation on the both sides of the border is worse today than a decade ago, with both the Syrian regime and U.S.-backed forces unable to fully secure the borders or blunt jihadi mobility. Moreover, state control of those areas has receded as jihadis have worked studiously to fill the vacuum and eradicate rivalries and any state infiltration and influence there. This means the Syrian and Iraqi governments' abilities to police these areas and to gather intelligence on local networks is seriously strained. This erosion of state reach necessitates the rebuilding of local leadership and governance to stabilize their areas and effectively challenge jihadi networks.

In addition, competing agendas complicate the ability of governments and other affiliated forces to work together on border security. These include the seemingly irreconcilable Kurdish-Turkish tensions and other ethnic and sectarian rivalries in Iraq and Syria. As such, this paper recommends an integrated American role in both countries to manage tensions and competing agendas and to ensure a coherent strategy to defeat jihadis and prevent their resurrection, while respecting the existing national borders. The U.S. is better placed than other countries to play this oversight role in the "Syraq" region, considering its presence on both sides of the border and because of its relations with countries like Iraq and Turkey.

Whether jihadis succeed in rebuilding their influence will hinge greatly on whether the U.S. is ready to anticipate jihadi strategies and to pursue actions founded upon a long-term and clear guiding policy rather than being guided by a largely reactionary approach.

ENDNOTES

1. Two senior leaders of Jabhat Fateh al-Sham, previously Jabhat al-Nusra, in December 2016 and January 2017 suggested al-Qaeda was looking for ways to expand in eastern Syria and inside Iraq as ISIS retreated. In August 2016, Ayman al-Zawahiri also called on Sunni Iraqis to prepare for a long guerrilla war after their rivals in the Islamic State lost ground. Maher Chmaytelli, "Zawahri urges Iraq Sunnis to wage guerilla war as IS loses more land," *Reuters*, Aug. 25, 2016.

2. Jabhat al-Nusra, then a branch of ISI, began its operations in rural areas in eastern Syria and near Damascus and focused on establishing roots among eastern tribes and local communities in the countryside of Damascus. Rania Abouzeid, "The Jihad Next Door," *Politico*, Jun. 23, 2014.

3. "Hiwar maa shaikhena abi qatada hawl tawaquatihi lima sayahduth fi asham wa shakhl adawla almumkin qiyamuha" (a conversation with Sheikh Abu Qatadah, may God preserve him, about his expectations for Syria, and the form of state that is possible to create), *Justpaste.it*, Sept. 9, 2016.

4. Josh Rogin, "Team Obama scuttles the term 'Afpak'," *Foreign Policy*, Jan. 20, 2010.

5. "Q&A: Iraq's Awakening Councils," *BBC*, July 18, 2010.

6. Joby Warrick and Souad Mekhennet, "Inside ISIS: Quietly preparing for the loss of the 'caliphate'," *Washington Post*, July 12, 2016.

7. "ISIS Spokesman Al-'Adnani Urges 'Caliphate Soldiers,' ISIS Supporters To Target Civilians in Europe, U.S. During Ramadan," *MEMRI*, May 20, 2016.

8. Al-Naba, Edition 43, "And lie in wait for them at every place of ambush," Aug. 18, 2016, p. 3.

9. Murad Batal al-Shishani, "The Islamic State's Strategic and Tactical Plan for Iraq," *Jamestown Foundation*, Aug. 8, 2014.

10. Citations in the context of the document should henceforth be assumed to be from the document, as translated by the author, unless otherwise indicated.

11. See discussion of these units later in the paper. These units have been a central component of ISIS's operations since its early days in Iraq, and the group often boasts about the clandestine networks' lethal abilities to hunt its enemies.

12. Gayle Tzemach Lemmon, "Is Obama's 'Iraq First' Strategy Working Against ISIS?" *Defense One*, Dec. 18, 2014.

13. Aron Lund, "Origins of the Syrian Democratic Forces: A Primer," *News Deeply*, Jan. 22, 2016.

14. "ISIS Lost 40 Percent of Territory in Iraq, 20 Percent in Syria: Coalition Spokesman" *NBC News*, Jan. 5, 2016.

15. Haid Haid, "Why Ahrar al-Sham couldn't stand up to HTS's attack in Idlib," *Chatham House*, Aug. 2017.

16. "Turkey sends tanks into Syria in operation aimed at Isis and Kurds," *The Guardian*, Aug. 24, 2016.

17. Aron Lund, "How Assad's Enemies Gave Up on the Syrian Opposition," *The Century Foundation*, Oct. 7, 2017.

18. Hassan Hassan, "What ISIL's rise in 2014 tells us about Al-Qaeda's potential in Syria today," *The National*, Aug. 23, 2017.

19. Interview with State Department officials, Jan. 2018.

20. "Final military defeat of ISIS will come in Euphrates River valley: coalition," *Rudaw*, Aug. 24, 2017.

21. "Syria war: Stranded IS convoy reaches Deir al-Zour," *BBC*, Sept. 14, 2017.

22. "Raqqa's dirty secret," *BBC*, Nov. 13, 2017.

23. Mohamed Mostafa, "Iraqi army recaptures first area in push for ISIS havens in Anbar," *Iraqi News*, Sept. 19, 2017.

24. Author interviews, local sources, Oct. 2017.

25. "Iraqi security forces retake al-Qaim from Islamic State: PM," *Reuters*, Nov. 3, 2017.

26. Tom O'Conner, "Syria and Russia say ISIS is dead, now U.S. must go," *Newsweek*, Nov. 14, 2017

27. Al-Naba, Editions 97 and 98, series entitled "Ways to evade crusader airstrikes," Sept. 14 and Sept. 21, 2017, respectively.

28. Al-Naba, Edition 94, "An interview with the military commander of Raqqa," Aug. 7, 2017, pp. 8-9.

29. Ibid.

30. Al-Naba, Edition 101, "Explosive Devices," Oct. 12, 2017, pp. 8-9.

31. Ibid.

32. Robert Burns, "US commander: Islamic State trying to regain initiative," *Associated Press*,

May 18, 2016.

33. Ibid.

34. Hassan Hassan, "Decoding the changing nature of ISIL's insurgency," *The National*, March 6, 2016.

35. John Davison, "Bombs kill nearly 150 in Syrian government-held cities: monitor," *Reuters*, May 23, 2016.

36. Author interview, U.S. Department of State official, May 2017.

37. Ibid.

38. "Islamic State attacks Kurdish-held town on Turkish border," *Reuters*, Feb. 27, 2016.

39. "New fears about the return of liberated areas to the control of ISIS," *Al Sumaria TV*, Oct. 18, 2016.

40. Martin Chulov, "Iraq says Balad suicide blast is Isis attempt to stir up sectarian war," *The Guardian*, July 8, 2016.

41. Michael Knights and Alexander Mello, "Losing Mosul, Regenerating in Diyala: How the Islamic State could exploit Iraq's Sectarian Tinderbox," *Combating Terrorism Center Sentinel*, Oct. 2016.

42. Michael Knights, "Predicting the shape of Iraq's next Sunni insurgents," *Combating Terrorism Center Sentinel*, Aug. 2017.

43. "Senior Iranian Commander Reportedly Killed Battling ISIS in Syria," *Haaretz*, Nov. 19, 2017.

44. "'Highest Ranking' Russian General Killed in ISIS Attack in Syria," *Haaretz*, Sept. 25, 2017.

45. Kyle Orton, "The Man Who Planned the Islamic State's Takeover of Mosul," Kyle Orton's Blog, Jan. 31, 2017.

46. Hassan Hassan, "ISIL has evolved into something more dangerous," *The National*, Jan. 29, 2017.

47. Aymenn Jawad Al-Tamimi, "Eye on the Battle: In Deir Ezzor, Nusra Maintains Upper Hand over ISIS," aymennjawad.org, Feb. 17, 2014.

48. Hassan Hassan, "A jihadi blueprint for hearts and minds is gaining traction," *The National*, March 4, 2014.

49. "Al-Qaeda leader in Syria speaks to Al Jazeera," *Al Jazeera*, Dec. 18, 2013.

50. Hassan Hassan, "Is it possible that Al Nusra and ISIL will join forces?" *The National*, April 17, 2016.

51. Pamela Engel, "This is the name ISIS hates being called more than 'Daesh'," *Business Insider*, Sept. 17, 2016.

52. Fabrice Balanche, "The Kurds may be winning against ISIS, but they could end up making tensions in the region worse," *Business Insider*, Jan. 6, 2016.

53. Interview with the author, December 2016.

54. Interview with the author, January 2017.

CHAPTER SIX

CONTEMPORARY JIHADI MILITANCY IN YEMEN:

HOW IS THE THREAT EVOLVING?

ELISABETH KENDALL

INTRODUCTION

Yemen's rugged topography of mountains, wadis, and deserts, coupled with a lack of robust government institutions, rampant political corruption, regional marginalization, and simmering tribal conflicts have long made it both an ideal refuge for terrorists and breeding ground for terrorism. More recently, even more favorable conditions for terrorism flourished due to the chaos and sectarian polarization brought about by the current war. Houthi rebels swept into the capital in late 2014, prompting a Saudi-led coalition of Sunni Arab countries to intervene militarily in 2015. Both al-Qaeda in the Arabian Peninsula (AQAP), which formed in 2009, and Islamic State in Yemen (ISY), which formally declared its Yemen province in 2014, benefited from the resulting security vacuum. Various developments from mid-2016 onwards, however, have placed unprecedented pressure on both groups. The gradual decentralization and/or fragmentation of Yemen's jihad movements have made the labels AQAP and ISY no longer as relevant. This does not mean the terrorist threat is diminishing, but rather that it is evolving. This paper traces the threads of this evolution using primary sources, including the jihadist groups' operational claims, formal statements, videos, speeches, lectures, poems, and *nashids*, or anthems, as well as informal communications on encrypted messaging applications, such as Telegram, and author interviews in Yemen with local communities.

The paper begins with a brief overview of the formation and evolution of jihadi militancy in Yemen. It then outlines AQAP's goals and governance strategies, focusing on four key areas that help to explain how AQAP succeeded in running a de facto state for an entire year, and why it was not usurped by the arrival of ISY. These areas of AQAP strength are local integration and branding, tribal relations, community development, and youth engagement. Next, this paper offers evidence of a recent decline in AQAP as a group, following the peak of its strength, influence, and power in 2015-16. It identifies five challenges and pressures that are symptoms of and/or reasons for this decline: Increasing counterterrorism strikes, dwindling support, weak leadership, poor communications, and decentralization and fragmentation. ISY has faced similar pressures and these are explored in the following section, which traces ISY's rise and decline in Yemen and assesses where it is currently. Finally, this paper looks ahead to the future of jihadi militancy in Yemen. The operational and organizational capacities of AQAP and ISY as centralized groups look to be in decline, and the distinction between them is becoming more blurred, despite the first instance of reported clashes between them in July 2018. Nevertheless, this paper explains why the terror threat in Yemen remains serious at both international and domestic levels. It explains why conditions on the ground in south Yemen may be setting the scene for a resurgence of militant jihad, even if a peace deal is finally concluded between the Houthis and the Saudi-led coalition backing the Yemeni government. The paper concludes by suggesting how the short-term opportunity that currently exists, as jihadi groups reel under recent pressures, might be used most effectively to cut off Yemen's persistent jihadi militancy problem at the grassroots level.

FORMATION AND EVOLUTION

Militant jihad in Yemen, as elsewhere in the Middle East, is fueled by war and civil unrest. Former President Ali Abdullah Saleh, who was in power for over three decades until 2012, eagerly allied with radical clerics in the '80s and '90s to further his political agenda. He framed southern socialists as godless infidels and enlisted Islamic extremists to wage a "jihad" against them. By the mid-1990s, a significant group calling itself the Aden-Abyan Islamic Army had formed around a local Yemeni veteran of the Afghan jihad, Zayn al-'Abidin al-

Mihdar. It operated with support from a high-ranking military commander, 'Ali Muhsin al-Ahmar. This is the same 'Ali Muhsin who in 2016 became Yemen's vice president and commander of the armed forces. This is significant because it hints at possible tacit alliances between AQAP and parts of the Saudi-backed Yemeni military fighting in the current war against Houthi rebels from Yemen's north.

Since 2000, al-Qaeda has been the dominant militant jihadist group in Yemen. The Aden-Abyan Islamic Army was terminated, in theory at least, after it kidnapped 16 Western tourists in 1998 and Mihdar was executed. In practice, however, the group was subsequently linked to several al-Qaeda attacks, including the suicide boat bombing of the U.S.S. Cole in 2000, which killed 17 U.S. sailors. Most likely, the group simply melted into al-Qaeda. Al-Qaeda's growth in Yemen was assisted by a groundswell of anger at the U.S. invasion of Iraq. This coincided with many jihadists being released from jail in the early 2000s to attend an incompetent re-education program which effectively let them loose on society.[1] Those who remained in jail, including both future AQAP leaders, Nasir al-Wuhayshi and Qasim al-Raymi, exploited their captivity to recruit fellow prisoners and build a strong jihad network. As opposition to the U.S. invasion of Iraq grew, Saleh agreed to arrest young Yemenis attempting to travel to Iraq or its neighbors without government permission. Once locked up in Yemen, they were easy pickings for the jihad networks forming in prisons.[2] So while it looked on the surface like al-Qaeda in Yemen was declining in the early to mid-2000s, beneath the surface it was building.

The resurgence of al-Qaeda in Yemen followed a grand jailbreak in 2006, in which 23 jihadists escaped from a high-security prison in Sanaa, taking the international community by surprise. Among the escapees was Nasir al-Wuhayshi, who quickly became al-Qaeda's leader in Yemen. He was the ideal choice owing to his tribal origins, religious schooling, and solid jihadist experience. Like many in his generation of Yemeni militants, he honed his jihadist credentials in Afghanistan, where he became Osama bin Laden's personal secretary. Several high-profile attacks followed in the wake of the jailbreak. Most notable among these were a suicide bomb attack on a Spanish tour group in 2007 and an ambitious double car bombing against the U.S. Embassy in Sanaa in 2008.

Perversely, al-Qaeda in Yemen was actually bolstered by the Saudi crackdown on Islamist extremism. Saudi jihadists fled across the border into Yemen and in January 2009, the Saudi and Yemeni branches of al-Qaeda merged to form AQAP. Attacks continued expeditiously, focusing on military and international targets inside Yemen, but also a handful outside Yemen. Key to such operations was AQAP bomb-maker Ibrahim al-'Asiri, whose creativity and devotion is perhaps best exemplified by his construction of a suicide bomb to insert in the rectum of his own brother to assassinate Saudi Prince Muhammad bin Nayif in 2009. The bomb succeeded in blowing up his brother but barely scratched the prince. 'Asiri is also thought to have been the brains behind the underwear bomb that an AQAP-trained Nigerian man tried to detonate in a plane over Detroit on Christmas Day of 2009, as well as two bombs hidden in printer cartridges and found on cargo planes in 2010. 'Asiri is likely still active, and in September 2017 authored a triumphant article celebrating 16 years since the destruction of New York's twin towers.[3]

Over the past decade, AQAP has taken advantage of war and instability to launch state-building enterprises on two occasions. The first was in 2011-12, when it capitalized on unrest following Yemen's Arab Spring uprising to declare small Islamic emirates in parts of Abyan and Shabwa. The second was in 2015-16, when AQAP resurged to run a de facto state out of Hadramawt in Yemen's east. AQAP took advantage of the security and governance vacuum that followed the intervention of a Saudi-led military coalition in Yemen in March 2015. As the coalition campaign against Houthi rebels began, AQAP was able to swell both its numbers and its coffers by staging another jailbreak, this time of an estimated 300 jihadists, seizing military hardware and robbing the central bank of an estimated $100 million USD.[4] It ran its de facto state for an entire year until United Arab Emirates Special Forces, with help from the U.S., forced it to withdraw in April 2016. This marked the high point of AQAP's influence and power in Yemen.

AQAP GOALS AND GOVERNANCE

The two core goals of AQAP can be summarized as expelling infidels from Muslim lands and introducing an Islamic regime to rule by Islamic law. While these goals have remained constant, circumstances and experience have refined AQAP's approaches to engaging local populations and achieving these goals.

To reach its recent zenith in 2015-16, AQAP employed a number of parallel strategies that were at once practical, tactical, and ideological. It is important to note that populations in Yemen's east, particularly in tribal areas, are well armed and would be difficult to terrorize into submission. The key to AQAP's success was not recruitment; even at its peak, its core fighters likely numbered no more than 4,000. Rather, AQAP worked to secure buy-in from key city and tribal leaders and to win passive toleration from local populations. It did this by focusing on four key areas: Local integration and branding, tribal relations, community development, and youth engagement.

LOCAL INTEGRATION AND BRANDING

First, regarding local integration and branding, AQAP had learned from its short period of rule in the small Islamic emirates it declared in 2011-12. At that time it had launched charitable projects and rebranded itself as Ansar al-Shari'a (the Partisans of Islamic Law) to distance itself from any negative associations with al-Qaeda. However, its unrelenting implementation of Islamic law and overbearing governance style alienated local communities and tribal leaders. Hence, the next time around in 2015-16, AQAP consciously relaxed its dictatorial approach and instead struck power-sharing deals with local governance structures. It again rebranded itself, this time as Abna' Hadramawt (the Sons of Hadramawt) for even greater local appeal.

It is significant that only three percent of tweets from AQAP's governance feed during 2016 were about the implementation of the harsh *hudud* punishments of Islamic law. This apparent laxity earned AQAP the contempt of ISIS. After three separate provinces of ISIS released videos specifically criticizing AQAP's weak implementation of Islamic law, AQAP released a full-length feature film, which it screened publicly in eastern coastal towns and also released online. "Hurras al-Shari'a," or "The Guardians of Islamic Law," released in December 2015, reaffirmed AQAP's commitment to global jihad and positioned its seemingly light touch as part of a smart long-term strategy for achieving an ultimately hardcore Islamic regime.

AQAP has since returned to favoring the Ansar al-Shari'a label, having dropped the Sons of Hadramawt label after being ousted from Mukalla in April 2016. There is no doubt that Ansar al-Shari'a is one and the same as AQAP. Ansar al-Shari'a correspondents' reports from the provinces are posted on the formal AQAP Telegram wire as official AQAP announcements. Moreover, AQAP Sheikh Abu al-Bara' in 2018 issued a call for tribesmen to join Ansar al-Shari'a on the Houthi battlefronts. He specifically identified Ansar al-Shari'a as al-Qaeda by describing it as such in brackets on the opening page.[5]

TRIBAL RELATIONS

Second, getting along with tribes has always been key to the survival of militant jihadists in Yemen.[6] The ability to reach some kind of understanding with local tribes — although not necessarily creating formal alliances and certainly not requiring *bay'a*, or an oath of allegiance — has been as central to al-Qaeda's success as it has to ISIS's relative failure in Yemen. AQAP achieved this through nurturing kinship ties through marriage and recruitment. When asked in late 2015 why AQAP was tolerated, one Hadrami told this author: "We don't support them. But they are our kinsfolk. We let them go about their business and we go about ours."[7] On occasions when innocent tribesmen were accidentally killed in operations designed to target the Yemeni military, AQAP published formal apologies and negotiated with the relevant tribes to pay blood money.[8]

This arrangement of mutual, if at times grudging, toleration in tribal areas is reflected in the results of a survey conducted by the Yemen Polling Center and the Center for Applied Research in Partnership with the Orient. Overall, Yemenis are more afraid of air strikes by the Saudi-led coalition or drones than of terrorism. The results obviously vary according to governorate. But even in al-Bayda', where AQAP has been the most consistently active since December 2016, 23 percent of respondents listed air strikes as one of "the three biggest security threats" in their area, while only 14 percent listed "terrorism/al-Qaeda Organization/ISIS (Daesh)."[9]

AQAP was also mindful to invoke and praise the glorious history and courage of various tribes in statements, videos, poems, and nashids, or anthems. It positioned its contemporary jihad as a simple continuation of the warlike prowess of tribal forefathers who fought independence battles against British colonialists in the 1960s. But perhaps most helpful to AQAP was the eruption of war in 2015, which gave it the opportunity to align itself with the anti-Houthi war effort. AQAP recast southerners' historical fears of a takeover by northerners as a sectarian battle of Sunnis versus Shi'a. Thus, disputes that were essentially political were reframed as religious, and endowed with a narrative of apocalyptic jihad. In short, AQAP did and does not control tribes. Rather, it has been able to make common cause with some tribes. [10]

COMMUNITY DEVELOPMENT

Third, AQAP courted local populations by fronting an impressive program of community development projects, such as improving electricity, water and sewage infrastructure, building roads, renovating schools, and stocking hospitals. Fifty-six percent of tweets from AQAP's governance Twitter feed during 2016 were about its hands-on development activities. In contrast to the war raging in Yemen's west, where coalition bombs rained down on civilian as well as Houthi military targets, AQAP's territory looked like a haven of stability. AQAP was able to finance such projects through oil imports and smuggling operations along Yemen's porous eastern coastline. Ironically, AQAP actually benefited from the Saudi naval blockade, which was focused on the west of Yemen, since this gave it a virtual monopoly over imports and generated an estimated $2 million USD per day.[11] AQAP also posed as a kind of modern-day Robin Hood by imposing windfall taxes on local companies with the stated aim of improving services and utilities for local people.

Youth Engagement

Fourth, AQAP spent considerable effort on youth engagement, understanding full well that founding a caliphate was still a faraway prospect and that re-education of the next generation was key to preparing for a caliphate and the full implementation of Islamic law. U.S. drone strikes, air strikes, and raids were exploited to the maximum by AQAP, particularly when poorly targeted strikes resulted in the deaths of women and children or the destruction of village housing. Several AQAP videos feature interviews with grieving villagers pasted alongside footage explaining the global jihadist agenda.[12] Following U.S. Navy SEAL raids in 2017, which killed villagers, AQAP issued statements designed to plug into tribal anger, positioning itself as the conduit for revenge; jihadist poems lamenting the dead are still appearing.[13] In March 2016, AQAP even held a "Festival of Martyrs of the American Bombing" in Hadramawt, which included a competition for schoolboys to design anti-U.S. and anti-drone posters. This kind of youth outreach nurtures the next generation of angry young men for potential recruitment.

While AQAP ran its state out of Mukalla, it held several festivals which included games, such as boys eating ice cream blindfolded, and Qur'an recitation competitions with weapons and motorbikes as prizes. Thirteen percent of its governance tweets were about celebrations. Even after being driven out of Mukalla, AQAP continued its youth engagement by exploiting battlefronts. Photos have emerged of AQAP openly driving a proselytization truck around the streets of Taiz. The side of the truck advertises CDs, films, nashids, lectures, books, and Qur'ans. One way to get boys interested in jihad was to entice them to read AQAP material. In Taiz, any youth who wrote a summary of AQAP's jihad booklet, "This is Our Mission," was entered to win a Kalashnikov as first prize, followed by a motorbike, laptop, revolver, or money. This focus on young hearts and minds indicates that the battle against AQAP will be a long one, even though it no longer runs a state or holds significant territory.

Signs of Decline in AQAP

AQAP activity — formally as a group — has declined dramatically over the past year and particularly since February 2018. AQAP had remained very active domestically despite being pushed out of Mukalla and losing its de facto state in April 2016. During 2017, it formally claimed a total of 273 domestic operations, which is roughly ten times as many as ISY during the same period. However, the frequency of formally claimed AQAP operations has declined steadily: From 145 during the first six months of 2017 to 128 during the second six months of 2017, then to just 62 during the first six months of 2018.

Throughout, AQAP's most operationally active location has been al-Bayda', where around half of all attacks have occurred: 55 percent during the first half of 2017, 47 percent during the second half of 2017, and 50 percent during the first half of 2018. The next ranking AQAP hotspot during both 2017 and 2018 is Abyan. AQAP activity has decreased significantly in Ibb and al-Dali' since mid-2017, but remained relatively steady in Hadramawt at around ten percent. The only area in which AQAP activity has continued to grow from mid-2017 and into 2018 is Shabwa. Ironically, the start of this uptick coincided with the launch of a major counterterrorism operation in Shabwa in August 2017; prior to this, AQAP had conducted no attacks in Shabwa during 2017. Although the numbers remain small, the Shabwa experience suggests that U.A.E.-led operations risk attracting opposition and may prove counterproductive over time. In summary, AQAP in 2018 is currently less than half as active as it was during 2017, but its core locations of activity have remained relatively constant. This indicates how difficult it is to uproot AQAP from an area once it has gained a hold.

The frequency of operations is of course only one measure by which to assess AQAP vitality. Another measure is AQAP's release of formal statements; this too has declined dramatically. During 2017, AQAP formally released at least 17 statements. This includes three joint statements with al-Qaeda in the Islamic Maghreb (AQIM)[14] but excludes statements that were never disseminated via the official wire, most notably two from Ansar al-Shari'a in Taiz and one from Abyan, and/or formally denied as fake.[15] By contrast, no formal AQAP statements bearing the official black flag header were released during the first six months of 2018. AQAP did issue a formal statement prohibiting jihadist communications via mobile phone and internet in January 2018, but it was dated 2017.

Therefore, it is reasonable to conclude that AQAP, as a centralized group concept, is currently in decline in terms of its operational and organizational abilities. This does not mean it cannot resurge again under more favorable circumstances. There are a number of current challenges and pressures that can be considered either symptoms of or reasons for this recent decline.

Current AQAP Challenges and Pressures

The main challenges and pressures facing AQAP, some of which are shared by ISY, might be summed up as increasing counterterrorism strikes, dwindling support, weak leadership, poor communications, and decentralization and/or fragmentation.

Increasing Counterterrorism Strikes

The U.S. has acknowledged carrying out over 120 airstrikes on AQAP and ISY targets during 2017 as well as multiple ground operations. This is more than three times as many as during 2016. Both terror groups have therefore suffered severe losses, including of key commanders.[16] AQAP's own media releases suggest it is feeling these losses keenly, both practically and emotionally.

In practical terms, AQAP released a film in early 2018 designed to expose the methods and catastrophic consequences of internal spies.[17] It features several interviews with AQAP traitors, often boasting of how easy it was to collect fatal intelligence. AQAP presents its statistics for the number of jihadist deaths arising from each type of information leak, resulting in a total of 410 jihadist deaths.[18] It claims that 30 jihadist deaths arose simply from telling a secret to just one person. AQAP's leader, Qasim al-Raymi, is featured doing an impression of a woman gossiping on the phone, and he chastises jihadists for sharing information with their chatty wives. The film ends by circulating an official statement, which describes conversation, mobiles, and social media as "out of control … reckless … and a grave danger to the jihad." It imposes a complete ban on communications via mobile phones and the internet and warns jihadists that anyone who contravenes this will be punished.[19] It is also significant that the first publication by AQAP's Al-Badr Media Organization, which relaunched in May 2018, was a booklet on how to avoid drone assassination. Ironically, it was written by Muhannad Ghallab, who was killed by a drone strike in 2015 on his very first night in Mukalla after the city was seized by AQAP.[20] AQAP's Abu al-Bara' also dedicated a lesson in his series on jihadist corruption specifically to the need to keep secrets, chastising "impatient" or "stupid" jihadists whose chat "causes damage and danger, the consequences of which he does not know."[21]

In emotional terms, the flood of dead jihadists has necessitated a reaffirmation of the benefits of martyrdom. To help one another cope psychologically, pro-AQAP wires on Telegram circulated a video clip from an old speech by Harith al-Nazari: "Don't think of those who are killed in the path of Allah as dead … don't worry about them. They are alive with their Lord and are receiving sustenance. And that's not all … they are rejoicing in what Allah's bounty has bestowed on them. Yes, the martyr is in good condition. He is happy. All is well."[22] Naturally, a recruitment drive was necessary to replenish numbers. Poster series like al-Mujahid Media's "Join the Caravan [of martyrs]" circulated on pro-AQAP wires in late January 2018, posing questions like "What's making you hang back from this great noble deed?"[23]

Dwindling Support

Second, there are several signs that support for AQAP is in decline. Drone strikes can increase local support for AQAP, which has positioned itself as a useful ally through which to avenge the deaths of innocents. Conversely, they can also arouse local hostility towards AQAP for attracting danger to an area in the first place.[24] Moreover, AQAP is now competing directly with the U.A.E. for recruits. Since driving AQAP from Mukalla, the U.A.E. has embarked on an ambitious recruitment program across Yemen's south to enlist locals into new security forces aimed, in part at least, at countering AQAP itself. This has elicited strong reactions from AQAP that express both anger and concern. AQAP released at least three formal statements during 2017 that specifically addressed tribes through a combination of advice, flattery, and threats. In Hadramawt, AQAP reassured tribes that "the sons of the noble Hadrami tribes are neither our opponents nor targets. Rather, we are of them, and they of us." But it follows with a warning: "But if he sells his religion for a worldly offer and agrees to become a soldier in the elite forces implementing and protecting the policy of the Emirates' statelet to combat the shari'a and its partisans, then he has chosen to become an enemy of the mujahidin and he must carry the responsibility for his actions."[25] Similarly, in Abyan, AQAP wrote: "We call on our honorable tribes to withdraw those sons who have enlisted with these forces ..."[26] Again in Shabwa, AQAP warns U.A.E.'s newly minted forces: "They will use you as cannon fodder [lit. firewood and fuel] to defend them and their bases from which they bomb Muslims. They steal your country's assets ..." It follows with a threat: "We will not refrain from targeting you."[27] During 2017, AQAP evolved its targeting from being overwhelmingly focused against Houthis to being almost equal between Houthis and U.A.E.-backed forces.[28]

Internal publications by the former judge of AQAP's shari'a court in Taiz, Abu al-Bara', also point to waning tribal support. In October 2017, Abu al-Bara' referred to a "setback" in the jihad movement, implying one problem may be a lack of enthusiasm for jihad. He quotes al-Rabbani to encourage men to join the jihad, reminding them of their choice: "Either the fire of this world or the fire of the next" and "the fire of hell is hotter."[29] Abu al-Bara' also issued a scathing call in early 2018 to tribes in al-Bayda' to join forces with AQAP in a lengthy essay entitled "Where are You? We are Here." He insults their manhood and tries to play on anger against the Americans. "Haven't you heard of the raid on Yakla by the Americans? Or have you blocked your ears, have you covered your eyes, have you buried your head in your clothes, have you vehemently insisted on distorting the facts?"[30] Moreover, in April 2018, a nashid began to circulate entitled "Of the Wrongdoing of the Tribes," chanting insults to tribesmen for abandoning their Muslim brothers by enlisting with U.A.E. forces.[31]

WEAK LEADERSHIP

Third, AQAP is also suffering from weak leadership. Its current leader, Qasim al-Raymi, is less popular and charismatic than his predecessor, Nasir al-Wuhayshi, who died in 2015 in a drone strike. Wuhayshi still features more prominently than Raymi in general AQAP media products — i.e. those that are not specifically by Raymi. AQAP's new Madad bulletin, launched by al-Malahim Media in 2018, has not yet featured Raymi at all, even in its editorial-like "Word of Truth" section. Likewise, the AQAP Partisans' Al-Badr Media Organization, relaunched in May 2018, has disseminated photos of Wuhayshi and extracts from his speeches, but nothing by or about Raymi. Moreover, at the time of writing, the latest AQAP video — which showcased operations in Hadramawt — included several sections featuring Wuhayshi but no footage, new or old, of Raymi.[32]

AQAP's current leadership has gone to ground. This can be dated roughly to late 2017, shortly before AQAP media instructed its ban on mobile and internet communications and released its spy video. This is clearly linked to a need to preserve the leadership in the face of unprecedented threats. As of June 2018, there has been no media release by Raymi since his stultifying 40-episode lecture series on al-Harthimi's medieval war treatise ended in February 2018. Even this was clearly prerecorded since Raymi's clothing and surroundings were exactly the same at the end of the series as at the start in November 2017. Khalid Batarfi too has all but fallen off the AQAP radar since the end of his 20-episode "Moments with the Prophets" video series in October 2017. He has resurfaced only twice, first prompted by Trump's recognition of Jerusalem as the capital of Israel, to deliver a fiery incitement to Muslims globally to kill Jews.[33] The second time was six months later in a lengthy written interview with al-Malahim Media that was clearly borne of the need to justify AQAP's decline in visibility. Batarfi insists that AQAP is lying low while it tackles its infiltration by spies, but that it is "improving and developing" in the background and will return to full action "at the appropriate time."[34] It appears that not all AQAP agree with the need for a leadership in hiding. AQAP Sheikh Abu al-Bara' has implied that all true Muslims should stay and fight "until Allah grants victory or martyrdom" rather than play it safe.[35] He also blames weak leadership for failing to attend sufficiently to the religious education of young recruits and to instill discipline, complaining of "jihadist youth being more hooked on nashids than on the Qur'an."[36]

COMMUNICATIONS CHALLENGES

Fourth, AQAP is clearly facing major communications challenges. Some of these, such as the need for the jihadists to self-impose a mobile phone and internet ban, have been referred to above. There is also a noticeably longer delay, often two months, between the production date stamped on a statement or video and its eventual release online. AQAP has also suffered various media production setbacks. July 2017 saw the abrupt cessation of the AQAP-linked *Al-Masra* newspaper, although AQAP later denied any link. It is possible that this was linked to the droning of an unnamed media star who was lamented in nashid a week later. A further setback was the droning of one of AQAP's most celebrated media activists, Shakim al-Khurasani, in December 2017, which generated many laments on jihadist social media. AQAP's normally reliable official wire on the encrypted Telegram service fell silent for over two weeks in November 2017 and again for nearly two weeks in December 2017 to January 2018. This was not owing to a lack of operational claims to post because AQAP supporters' wires continued to post such claims. A more likely explanation, therefore, is that the person(s) maintaining these communications was killed or captured. What is interesting is that when AQAP's wire caught up on posting missed claims, it omitted several operations that pro-AQAP wires had claimed for "the mujahidin." This may be a simple oversight, but it may also be another sign — in addition to those outlined below — that AQAP is fragmenting as it decentralizes.

DECENTRALIZATION AND/OR FRAGMENTATION

Given the pressures mentioned above, in particular weak leadership, decimation by drones, and poor communications, some decentralization of AQAP seems inevitable. During 2018, the frequency of operational claims made by AQAP on its formal Telegram wire is less than half that of the preceding year. Yet the number of "extra" claims made locally on pro-AQAP wires has risen. This implies the emergence of breakaway factions or like-minded jihadist groups who have not been or are no longer embraced by the AQAP leadership.

A clear case of fragmentation can be found in the frontline city of Taiz, which has become a hotspot for rival Salafi-jihadi groups. The main rivalry appears to be between militant Salafi brigades led by Abu al-'Abbas, aligned with the U.A.E., and Islah factions initially led by Col. Sadiq Sarhan. The latter is considered to be linked to elements in Saudi Arabia, as well as being aligned with some who self-identify as AQAP, such as judge and Sheikh Abu al-Bara'. An early hint that AQAP in Taiz was fracturing came in June 2016 when AQAP issued a formal statement expelling two prominent Salafis from

Ansar al-Shari'a in Taiz, Harith al-'Izzi and Humam al-San'ani, "owing to their many violations."[37] Local press sources identified these two figures as blowing up the shrine of Sufi Sheikh 'Abd al-Hadi al-Sudi in July 2017 but continued to describe them as AQAP despite, or in ignorance of, their expulsion from the group.[38]

Salafi-jihadi fighting flared up in Taiz at various points from August 2016[39] onwards, resulting in a rash of tit for tat assassinations.[40] The proxy nature of Salafi fighting in Taiz was well demonstrated by an incident in early May 2017. AQAP's Abu al-Bara' was to deliver a mosque lecture entitled "Who are the Terrorists?" which intended to point the finger at U.A.E. and its Salafi brigades. He was prevented by Abu al-'Abbas.[41] Abu al-Bara' responded by issuing an AQAP statement positioning AQAP as the good guys and Abu al-'Abbas' Salafis as guns for hire. But he also hinted at splits within AQAP's own ranks: "We have been pleased to deliver our mission to our brothers in Taiz through da'wa, lectures and publications, not guns and rifles. We show the true face of Ansar al-Shari'a contrary to the image portrayed by the press and detractors among our own." The statement ends ominously with a slight but significant shift in AQAP's mission; jihad is no longer a means to achieve a goal, but rather a goal in itself: "America and its lackeys continuously interfere with us and with the communication of our message, which is: Ruling by Islamic Law, spreading justice, and revitalizing the practice of jihad."[42]

Significantly, this AQAP statement by Ansar al-Shari'a in Taiz was neither acknowledged by nor disseminated on the official AQAP wires. The group issued a further statement in October 2017, also using the formal black-flag header of AQAP. It announced the closure of AQAP's shari'a court in Taiz over which Abu al-Bara' had presided: "We no longer have any court or judge who represents Ansar al-Shari'a in Taiz." [43] Likewise, this statement was never acknowledged by nor disseminated on AQAP's official wires. Finally, in May 2018, the newly relaunched pro-AQAP Al-Badr Media Organization published a damning essay on Abu al-'Abbas and his Salafis in Taiz whom it blamed for manipulating jihadi-minded youth into branding the Islah Party apostates in order to serve U.A.E. interests.[44] Again, AQAP formal wires ignored this.

During 2017, AQAP's official wires only ever issued one statement from Wilayat Taiz and it categorically denied any link to the assassinations taking place there, stressing, "We have no private agenda."[45] Moreover, of the 273 operations formally claimed by AQAP during 2017, only three were in Taiz. The fact that only one percent of AQAP's claimed activities centered on Taiz suggests the highly active self-identified AQAP group there was "rogue" and/or powered and assisted by external forces.

The various ills besetting the jihad movement in Yemen, or parts of it, are revealed in general terms in the writings of "rogue" Sheikh Abu al-Bara'.

Although these are not disseminated on AQAP's formal wires, they are enthusiastically forwarded on many of the staunchly pro-AQAP supporters' wires. In his 2018 series on jihadist corruption, he writes: "Wrongdoings are the cause of the split among the brothers." He lists the major problems as financial dealings, neglect of duty, moral flaws, loose talk, interference, and condescension.[46] As the series progresses, Abu al-Bara' appears to become more personal in his criticism, blaming jihadist woes on insufferable personalities, egotism, and self-aggrandizement.[47]

There is some broader evidence of criminality inside AQAP. The group formally expelled three members of AQAP's Ansar al-Shari'a in Abyan in June 2017 "owing to their many violations of legitimate organizational orders and their procurement of prohibited money."[48] In addition, locals in east Yemen's Mahra region are able to identify specific AQAP individuals involved in the smuggling networks that bring in weapons and drugs via the vast and porous coastline.[49] The overall impression is of a broad Salafi-jihadi melting pot now beset with organizational difficulties, in-fighting, and controversial links to organized crime.

ISLAMIC STATE IN YEMEN

ISY is also suffering from challenges similar to those of AQAP but its starting point was always weaker. Unlike AQAP, ISY never held territory and found it hard to integrate in Yemen. ISIS officially announced its expansion into Yemen on Nov. 13, 2014, following Caliph Abu Bakr al-Baghdadi's acceptance of an oath of allegiance sworn to him by "Yemen's mujahidin" in an audio recording. For a brief period, ISY expanded. Its key youth recruiter and coordinator for Hadramawt, Abu Karam al-Hadrami, opened hostels and managed the accommodation, everyday needs, and movements of new recruits. As ISY grew, he took on responsibility for logistics between ISY's provinces.[50] However, despite some early defections from AQAP to ISY, the self-proclamation of various ISY provinces around Yemen and several high casualty headline-grabbing attacks in 2015 and 2016, ISY was unable to usurp AQAP as Yemen's primary jihad group.

There are several possible reasons for ISY's inability to gain traction in Yemen. First, AQAP's launch of a successful state in 2015-16, with lucrative income from smuggling, windfall taxes, and bank robbery, likely made it a more attractive option than ISY for jihad-minded men. There is a hint in Abu Karam's eulogy that ISY jihadists may have missed the infrastructure and funding that controlling a "state" brings.[51] Meanwhile, AQAP was able to flourish and grow in its Yemen backwater while international attention was distracted away from Yemen to Iraq and Syria, and away from al-Qaeda to ISIS.

Second, the excessive brutality of ISY gave AQAP the opportunity to look like the "acceptable" face of jihad. AQAP criticized ISY's indiscriminate bombings in Yemen and pledged that, unlike ISY, it would not target "mosques, markets, and crowded places."[52] It apologized for its own previous excesses, such as the storming of a military hospital in Sanaa in 2013[53] and the beheading of 14 soldiers in Hadramawt in August 2014, which it implicitly blamed on the negative influence of ISY propaganda.[54]

Third, ISY did not engage well with local communities and tribes. It failed to carry out AQAP-style community development projects in Yemen, despite early efforts in this regard in Syria and Iraq. Moreover, its leaders gained a reputation for being overbearing and bossy. In mid-2016, copies of 15 shari'a court documents allegedly filed by ISY fighters against their then leader, Abu Bilal al-Harbi, circulated inside jihadist groups on Telegram. There are also reports of some ISY fighters defecting back to AQAP and lambasting the bulldozer tactics of ISY. One defector has recounted how ISY's emirs fought over money and girls, aligned with drug lords, and deceived audiences by filming videos in Hadramawt but pretending they were in Sanaa or Shabwa.[55] Finally, unilke AQAP, ISY produced little narrative that was culturally specific to Yemen aside from virulent disparagement of the Houthis as infidel agents of "Rejectionist" or Shi'i, Iran.[56] Hence, ISY's ability to entrench and spread in Yemen has been very limited.

Eventually, ISY withdrew to the Qayfa area of al-Bayda', presumably circa October 2016 since this is when its operational claims indicate it started to become active here. The Hadramawt branch of ISY must have decamped to Qayfa by June 2017 at the latest because ISY's eulogy for Abu Karam mentions that he participated in the Hammat Laqah raid. An indication of ISY's diminished circumstances lies in the changed role of Abu Karam himself — he went from being ISY's cross-Yemen logistics coordinator to being a water-carrier at the Qayfa front.[57]

ISY has tried to consolidate and expand from its location in Qayfa, al-Bayda'. As a major frontline against the Houthis, ISY has been tolerated by some local tribes as long as it focuses on fighting Houthi invaders. In early 2017, ISY set up two training camps in al-Bayda'. The first, the Abu Muhammad al-'Adnani camp, was specifically designed to graduate *inghimasiyyun*, or suicide fighters. This was quickly followed by the Abu Muhammad al-Furqan camp, which, as well as training suicide fighters, provided more sophisticated weapons training including for heavy weapons and night operations. Naturally, suicide fighters require indoctrination, and this was provided via 50-day shari'a courses.[59]

It is, of course, possible that ISY exaggerated the extent of its training capabilities. But the U.S. did locate and obliterate two ISY training camps in al-Bayda' in airstrikes in October 2017, killing dozens of jihadists. Thereafter, the frequency of ISY reports from al-Bayda' diminished significantly for several months, which indicates that its operational capacity was severely impacted by the U.S. strikes. However, ISY appeared to have regrouped to a limited extent after March 2018 if the uptick in its martyr claims is a measure.[60] Nevertheless, the names of its martyrs indicate that it is still struggling to harness local tribes. Of the 26 ISY martyrs named for Wilayat al-Bayda' during the first five months of 2018, less than a handful were local to al-Bayda'. The largest source of martyrs, 20 percent, was the battlefront city of Taiz.

In short, ISY has never succeeded in holding territory in Yemen and is now largely confined to the Qayfa front in al-Bayda'. While some operations further afield continued to be attributed to ISY, particularly around Aden, these appeared to be politically motivated and false flagged to ISY, likely by Saleh-Houthi forces targeting southern separatists. It may be no coincidence that, after a flurry of ISY attacks in Aden during November 2017, there was a total hiatus for almost three months following Saleh's death on Dec. 4, 2017.

Conclusion: Looking Ahead

ISY and AQAP are becoming less distinguishable. When ISY first showed up in force in Qayfa, AQAP was dismissive. Pro-AQAP wires accused ISY fighters of being lazy, not getting up before lunchtime, and only going to the battlefront for photo opportunities rather than to help fight. AQAP took the trouble to refute ISY claims in the initial months following ISY's arrival in al-Bayda'. For example, it roundly rejected ISY's claim, prominently placed in the main ISY weekly "*Al-Naba*'" bulletin, that it had repelled the "largest" Houthi advance in Qayfa to date.[61] AQAP claimed it was they, not ISY, who had pushed back the Houthis and immediately released a video "Elite Attack" to prove it.[62] Meanwhile, pro-AQAP wires angrily mocked ISY using an Arabic hashtag meaning "Exposing the Deceit of Yemen's Da'ish."

However, such open rivalry between ISY and AQAP declined significantly from 2017. There are likely several reasons for this. First, the two groups now have more in common. AQAP no longer needs to criticize ISY for indiscriminate mass casualty attacks as it is now focused mainly on the Houthi frontline. Batarfi stated in June 2018 that AQAP's relations with other Islamist groups is "generally at its best yet" and that they are cooperating on the Houthi battlefronts.[63] Similarly, ISY no longer needs to criticize AQAP for failing to implement shari'a law since AQAP no longer runs a "state." Second, an uptick in shared pressure from mutual enemies, especially the U.A.E. and U.S. Special Forces and drones, has likely created a grudging solidarity in adversity. Third, a vacuum of strong leadership and organized training, owing to deaths — and the need to go to ground — from increased drone strikes and ground operations, is likely driving the rank and file to become more fluid in their loyalties.

One apparently major exception to this occurred in July 2018 when a pro-AQAP wire on Telegram reported that AQAP had killed 25 ISY fighters in retaliation for ISY killing 13 AQAP fighters.[64] For several days, some pro-AQAP wires urged the annihilation of ISY fighters on the Qayfa front in al-Bayda' where the clashes allegedly took place. A two-minute video was then released bearing the logo of the central ISY news agency, A'maq, claiming to show that ISY had simply captured the AQAP fighters, not executed them.[66] There are several puzzling elements to these claimed clashes. Only half of the captives depicted in the alleged A'maq video wore beards, suggesting that they were not all AQAP. Meanwhile, the main ISIS weekly bulletin made no mention of any activities in Yemen, not even in its weekly roundup of ISIS operations in all its various provinces globally. Likewise, AQAP's formal wire has to date made no mention of any AQAP-ISY clashes, and some pro-AQAP wires have urged caution, reminding jihadists not to be distracted from the real battle. Possible explanations for these seemingly inconsistent elements are that: The clashes were essentially tribal in nature and not specifically related to jihadist rivalry; or they were a blip — possibly stoked by agents provocateurs — and are being dealt with; or they are just another indication of the lack of central control over fragmenting groups. One pro-AQAP wire cautioned jihadists not to speak about the events "as it fans flames that the wise are trying to extinguish."

The decentralization of Yemen's jihadists should not be mistaken for a lessening of the long-term threat. The overall Salafi-jihadi melting pot remains. Often, even when coalition forces declare an area free of AQAP following a ground offensive, this simply means that the jihadists move location, not that they suffer crippling losses. The threat, therefore, remains alive, both at the international and domestic levels.

As for the international threat, there are several reasons why AQAP still harbors ambitions to conduct an attack. First, the pressure it is under means it needs to reassert and prove itself. Second, it needs to avenge the large number of deaths by U.S. drones. Third, any détente that it may have once agreed to with local tribes to refrain from international attacks in order to avoid attracting retaliation is now off.[67] Fourth, Trump's decision to move the U.S. embassy in Israel to Jerusalem has sharpened the focus on hitting back, particularly given that AQAP's slogan has long been "Jerusalem, We're Coming." AQAP's Khaled Batarfi briefly broke his long silence to issue a bloodthirsty call to Muslims globally to "kill every Jew by driving over him, stabbing him, using a weapon or setting fire to their houses." He also called for revenge on America as well as those deemed historically responsible for the Palestinian issue including Britain, France, and the Arab states.[68]

AQAP has also continued to incite so-called lone wolf attacks in the West through its "Inspire" range of media products. AQAP leader Qasim al-Raymi in May 2017 released an "Inspire Address" calling on Muslims in the West to kill Americans at home, assuring them that Allah would bestow on them a higher grade in Paradise for a suicide attack. He advised them to "keep it easy and simple" like Omar Mateen who opened fire in an Orlando nightclub in 2016. To ensure the message reached its target audience, Raymi's Arabic was subtitled in English and the background soundtrack was the popular nashid in English "The Battle for the Hearts and Minds."[69] AQAP's bulky English language "Inspire" (2010-ongoing) magazine has become increasingly infrequent but no less virulent. Its latest issue in August 2017 consisted of 96 pages of rationale, advice, and instructions for conducting train derailment operations. The magazine has been supplemented since 2016 with a series of occasional "Inspire Guides" that offer lessons learned from various terror attacks in the West, including the Orlando gun massacre in 2016, the Nice truck massacre in 2016, and the Westminster attack in 2017.

There is ample evidence that AQAP has inspired international attacks without the need for direct operational links. Online sermons by Yemeni-American AQAP ideologue Anwar al-'Awlaqi, who helped found "Inspire," before being killed in a drone strike in 2011, have been linked to numerous international acts of terror. These include the 2013 murder of a British soldier in London, the 2013 Boston marathon bombing, and the 2015 *Charlie Hebdo* massacre in Paris. Such attacks highlight an important strength of AQAP media in recent years: It endows its most charismatic figureheads with an enduring ability to inspire long after they have been droned. This occurs in three ways. First, much AQAP material remains readily available online, particularly as security agencies were heavily focused on stemming the flow of propaganda from ISIS rather than al-Qaeda. Second, AQAP sermons and films are reposted frequently online, with entire channels on encrypted applications devoted to reposting archival material. Third, old footage of AQAP figureheads is reworked into new videos, giving the impression that "martyred" heroes continue to address the faithful from Paradise.

The international threat is not limited to the West. Arab regimes are considered agents of the West and therefore legitimate targets too. The threat has intensified against members of the Saudi-led coalition intervening in Yemen, particularly following the U.A.E.'s recruitment of local forces in the south and the resultant increase in counterterror operations. In June 2017, AQAP issued a nashid containing lyrics that directly threatened the U.A.E.: "Your time has come, O nest of clientelism and crime, Like explosive thunder, We're coming to blow up your towers, We'll leave them in heaps."[70]

At the domestic level, there is a risk that the recent successes of U.A.E.-backed forces in countering terrorist activity will be short-lived if the methods they use generate long-term popular resentment. Local anger has already erupted over U.A.E.-backed forces' involvement in forced disappearances, arbitrary arrests, torture, and the establishment of several "secret" prisons.[71] Anger has occurred at all levels, from inside the government down to the grassroots level where it ranges from women's demonstrations to young men's sung poetry like "O Elite [Forces] of Shame."[72] U.A.E.-backed forces are also widely held responsible for the assassination of over 25 imams and preachers across South Yemen, particularly in Aden, over the last two years.[73] AQAP Sheikh Abu al-Bara' has tried to exploit this for recruitment, publishing an essay in which he suggested that clerics should die on the battlefield of jihad rather than wait around to be assassinated.[74] Such practices play directly into the hands of terrorist propaganda that frames U.A.E. violations as part of a war on Islam, which can only be countered by jihad.

AQAP has also tried to exploit suspicions and anger over the U.A.E.'s potential commercial and political ambitions in Yemen. U.A.E.-backed forces have fought terrorism, but they have also helped to consolidate U.A.E. control of key ports and oil and gas producing areas, and the U.A.E. has been the main backer of the Southern Transitional Council (STC), which seeks secession from the north. This is problematic for three reasons. First, there are significant regions inside the former south that object to secession. Second, it is unclear how representative the STC is, even of those who favor secession — and there is a risk that the new power brokers and security forces are awakening age-old tribal/political fault-lines. Third, the U.A.E.'s alignment with militarized Salafism, where religious ideology is married to a political agenda for southern secession, is a recipe for further conflict beyond the current main war with the Houthis. AQAP has already latched onto such concerns and its framing of local suspicion and anger at the U.A.E. to fit its narrative of global jihad is likely to increase, even if, or when, the Houthi threat recedes.

However, there is some cause for hope. Current jihadi decentralization does provide a short-term window of opportunity for preventive initiatives to capitalize on the jihadists' disarray, internal suspicion over informers, poor communications, trauma at the relentless loss of "brother martyrs," dwindling tribal support, and the challenges of regrouping and rebuilding camps.

This window of opportunity should be used to address the underlying reasons behind the persistent phenomenon of militant jihad in Yemen. This needs to happen at two levels: First, at the level of actual recruits — often disillusioned young men, hardened by war, with few aspirations and opportunities, seeking a higher purpose, sense of belonging, and both mental and physical sustenance; and second, at the level of local populations and tribes, who often put up with such groups because they address their grievances after long years of marginalization by government. Any preventive initiatives will require careful, thoughtful, non-military strategies that are locally led. They should build on ideas and activities that have been locally generated rather than cooked up intuitively by well-meaning stabilization outfits in the West or simply lifted wholesale from what may have worked elsewhere like Libya or Afghanistan. For this, highly localized knowledge is invaluable. It might be gained through training grassroots organizations to gather data in simple surveys that use robust sampling methods.[75] For long-term success beyond the obvious need to build genuinely representative institutions, an immediate focus on educational peace-building initiatives and enterprise-generating programs is key. It is Yemen's young people who will ultimately need to rebuild Yemen if the country that emerges is to function.

Above all, ending the current war is imperative. This means increasing the pressure on the various actors, including the Saudi-led coalition, to make concessions that go beyond the unrealistic framework of U.N. Resolution 2216.[76] Leaving aside the obvious humanitarian toll, the continuation of the war fuels militant jihad. The war economy enables seriously organized crime networks to flourish, often in collaboration with terror groups. Famine, cholera, and air strikes in Yemen's west encourage migration east towards regions that are currently mainly held together by tribal law. A large influx of outsiders puts pressures on this system which groups like AQAP can exploit. Lastly, war makes it impossible to tackle other urgent problems, such as Yemen's rapidly depleting water resources, which if not addressed, will trigger future instability.[77] These are precisely the conditions that allow terror groups to thrive.

Endnotes

1. Gregory Johnsen, *The Last Refuge: Yemen, Al-Qaeda and the Battle for Arabia*, New York: Oneworld, 2012, Kindle Loc 2158.

2. Johnsen, o.c., Kindle Loc 2466-8.

3. Ibrahim Hassan al-'Asiri, "Fi Dhikra 11 September al-Mubaraka: Masirat al-Intisar wa-Hazimat Amrika" (On the Anniversary of the Blessed Attacks of 11 September: The Path of Victory and the Defeat of America), Al-Malahim Media, Sept. 2017.

4. Yara Bayoumy, Noah Browning, and Mohammed Ghobari, "How Saudi Arabia's war in Yemen has made al-Qaeda stronger — and richer," *Reuters Special Report*, Apr. 8, 2016.

5. Abu al-Bara' al-Ibbi, "Ayna Antum? Nahnu Huna" (Where are You? We are Here), Jan. 22, 2018, 1.

6. The difficulty of integrating among Yemen's tribes was a source of disappointment to Ayman al-Zawahiri's Islamic Jihad group in the mid-90s, who had anticipated that Yemen with its turmoil and rugged topography would be an ideal place to regroup after a crackdown in Egypt. Many ended up returning to Egypt.

7. Author interviews with community leaders from Mukalla, al-Ghayda, Nov. 7, 2015.

8. See, for example: AQAP Statement "Tawdih Hawla Qadiyat Qutla Qabilat Al Bu Bakr bin Daha wa-Ibn al-Hayj" (Clarification about the Issue of Killings of the Al Bu Bakr bin Daha Tribe and Ibn al-Hayj), Oct. 20, 2016; AQAP Statement "Bayan Nafy al-'Alaqa bi-'Amaliyyat Qatl fi 'Ubar Laslum" (Denial of Link to Killings in 'Ubar Laslum [al-Aslum]), Jun. 24, 2017. This is in addition to circumstantial evidence in the form of local accounts on Telegram.

9. Marie-Christine Heinze and Hafez Albukari, "Yemen's War as seen from the local level," Politics, Governance, and Reconstruction in Yemen, POMEPS 29, January 2018, 34-8: 37. The area in which terrorism was mentioned most as one of the three biggest security threats was Abyan (34 percent), followed by al-Bayda' (14 percent) and Shabwa (11 percent). The survey data was gathered in February and March 2017.

10. Nadwa al-Dawsari has written convincingly on the pragmatic and at times volatile relationship between AQAP and tribes in al-Bayda'. Nadwa al-Dawsari, "Our Common Enemy: Ambiguous Ties between al-Qaeda and Yemen's Tribes," *Carnegie Endowment for International Peace*, Jan. 10, 2018.

11. Yara Bayoumy, Noah Browning, and Mohammed Ghobari, "How Saudi Arabia's war in Yemen has made al-Qaeda stronger — and richer," *Reuters Special Report*, Apr. 8, 2016.

12. A good example is "Rad' al-'Udwan 6" (Repelling Aggression 6), November 2016, a 30 minute film produced by AQAP's Al-Malahim Media.

13. AQAP Statement "Bayan Hawla al-Majzara al-Amrikiyya fi Mintaqat Qayfa" (Statement on the Recent American Massacre in the Qayfa Region), Jan. 29, 2017. AQAP Statement "Bayan Hawla al-Inzal al-Amriki 'Ala Qabilat Murad" (Statement on the American Raid on the Murad Tribe), May 26, 2017.

14. The joint AQAP-AQIM statements were all on international matters: "Condolences of the Islamic Umma on the death of Sheikh 'Umar 'Abd al-Rahman in the Jails of Crusader America, Feb. 19, 2017, "Letter from al-Aqsa," Jul. 16, 2017, "Warning of Doom on Saudi Rulers," Sept. 28, 2017.

15. For example, AQAP firmly denied that it had issued an official looking statement dated May 21, 2017, about targeting Hadramawt University.

16. CENTCOM, "Update on recent counterterrorism strikes in Yemen," No. 20171220-01, Dec. 20, 2017.

17. Al-Malahim Media, "Asrar wa-Akhtar wa-Rahil Akhyar" (Secrets, Dangers and the Departure of the Best), December 2017 (released Jan. 27, 2018).

18. AQAP claims its statistics are based on direct spy confessions over the past nine years.

19. AQAP Statement, "Ta'mim li-l-Ikhwa al-Mujahidin fi Jazirat al-'Arab" (General Announcement to Jihadist Brothers on the Arabian Peninsula), Dec. 3, 2017.

20. Muhannad Ghallab, "al-Nasa'ih al-Yamaniyya li-Tajannub Qasf al-Drunz al-Amrikiyya", republished by Al-Badr Media Organization on Telegram, May 24, 2018.

21. Abu al-Bara' al-Ibbi, "Ifsha' al-Sirr" (Divulging Secrets), lesson 4 in the series "al-Ma'a fi Mufsidat al-Ikhwa" (100 Corruptions of the Brothers), Mar. 20, 2018, 3.

22. Untitled video clip of speech by Nazari, published on various jihad support wires

including that of Abu al-Bara' al-Ibbi, Jan. 4, 2018.

23. Al-Mujahid Media, "Hal Ta'lam?" (Do You Know?) poster, "Join the Caravan" Series, published on various jihad support wires including that of Layth al-Mukalla, Jan. 19, 2018.

24. Nadwa al-Dawsari has laid out several reasons why tribes might wish to dissociate with AQAP in "Foe not Friend: Yemeni Tribes and al-Qaeda in the Arabian Peninsula," POMED (February 2018), 21-7.

25. AQAP Statement, "Risala ila Ahli-na fi Hadramawt" (Message to Our People in Hadramawt), Mar. 16, 2017.

26. AQAP Statement, "Bayan Nasiha wa-I'dhar" (Declaration of Advice and Absolution), Aug. 17, 2017.

27. AQAP Statement, "Ila Ahli-na fi Shabwa" (To Our People in Shabwa), Aug. 22, 2017.

28. During the first six months of 2017, 75 percent of AQAP operations targeted Houthis and 25 percent U.A.E.-backed forces. During the second six months of 2017, 49 percent of AQAP operations targeted Houthis and 51 percent U.A.E.-backed forces.

29. Abu al-Bara' al-Ibbi, "al-Irjaf" (Spreading Lies), no.3 in the series "Asbab al-Intikasa" (Reasons for the Setback), Oct. 25, 2017, 1.

30. Abu al-Bara' al-Ibbi, "Ayna Antum? Nahnu Huna" (Where are You? We are Here), Jan. 22, 2018, 6.

31. Abu Muhammad al-'Awlaqi (words) & Mus'ab al-'Adani (singer), "Min Zulm al-Qaba'il" (Of the Wrongdoing of the Tribes), Apr. 4, 2018.

32. "'Ala Darbi-him Sa'irun" (On Their Path We Proceed), March 2018 (released May 27, 2018).

33. Al-Malahim Media, "Wajibu-na Tujaha Qudsi-na" (Our Duty Towards Our Jerusalem), December 2017 (released Jan. 21, 2018).

34. Al-Malahim Media, "Liqa' Suhufi ma' al-Shaykh Khalid bin 'Umar Batarfi", June 2018.

35. Abu al-Bara' does not specify which leader(s) are being targeted by his criticism. He may be targeting Salafi commander Abu al-'Abbas in Taiz or ISY leaders rather than AQAP's Qasim al-Raymi. Abu al-Bara' al-Ibbi, "al-Irjaf" (Spreading Lies), no.3 in the series "Asbab al-Intikasa" (Reasons for the Setback), Oct. 25, 2017, 3.

36. Abu al-Bara' al-Ibbi, "Saw' al-Tarbiya min Qibal al-Murabbin" (Poor Education from Their Educators), no.5 in the series "Asbab al-Intikasa" (Reasons for the Setback), Nov. 5, 2017, 1.

37. AQAP Statement, "Bayan Bara'a" (Declaration of Disavowal), Jun. 18, 2016.

38. "Tanzim al-Qaeda fi Ta'izz yufajjir Qubbat al-Hadi al-Athariyya", Barakish online, Jul. 30, 2016, and "al-Qaeda tufajjir Qubbat al-Shaykh 'Abd al-Hadi al-Sudi bi-Ta'izz", News Yemen online, Jul. 30, 2016,

39. "Ba'da Sa'at 'Ala 'Awdat Abu al-'Abbas min al-Sa'udiyya.. Ma'arik Bayna al-Salafiyyin wa-l-Islah Wasta Madinat Ta'izz", al-Yemen al-Yawm, Aug. 15, 2016.

40. 'Adil Bashar, "Fasa'il al-'Umala' ta'bathu bi-Ta'izz" (Proxy Factions to Mess with Taiz), al-Yaman al-Yawm, Feb. 20, 2017.

41. 'Adil Bashar, "Ta'izz taghraqu fi Wahl Fasa'il al-'Umala'" (Taiz Drowns in the Mud of Proxy Factions), al-Yaman al-Yawm, May 9, 2017

42. Statement by Ansar al-Shari'a in Taiz, 3 May 2017 (never disseminated on AQAP's formal wire)

43. Statement by Ansar al-Shari'a in Taiz, 7 Oct. 2017 (never disseminated on AQAP's formal wire)

44. Abu 'Abd Allah al-Ma'arifi, "Haqiqat al-Manhaj al-Jihadi: Nasiha li-Jihadiyyi Wilayat Ta'izz" (The Truth of the Jihadi Way: Advice for the Jihadists of Wilayat Taiz), al-Badr Media, 31 May 2018.

45. AQAP Statement , "Ila Ikhwani-na wa-Ahli-na fi Ta'izz" (To Our Brothers and Our People in Taiz), 25 Apr. 2017.

46. Abu al-Bara' al-Ibbi, "al-Dhunub wa-l-Ma'asi" (Sins and Wrongs), lesson 1 in the series "al-Ma'a fi Mufsidat al-Ikhwa" (100 Corruptions of the Brothers), 15 Feb. 2018, p.2

47. Abu al-Bara' al-Ibbi, "An Yakun Thaqil-an" (Being Unpleasant) and "al-Ananiyya wa-Tafkhim al-Nafs" (Egotism and Self-Aggrandizement), lessons 7 and 8 in the series "al-Ma'a fi Mufsidat al-Ikhwa" (100 Corruptions of the Brothers), 22 and 26 Apr. 2018.

48. AQAP Statement, "Bayan Bara'a" (Announcement of Disavowal), Jun. 17, 2017. The statement is signed by Ansar al-Shari'a in Wilayat Abyan and carries AQAP's black-flag header. However, it did not appear on official AQAP channels. This may simply be to avoid airing internal problems in public.

49. Author interviews with Mahri locals in al-Ghayda, Mahayfif and the northern deserts, Aug. 5-8, 2017.

50. "Abu Karam al-Hadrami", al-Naba' 133 (24 May 2018): 9.

51. Abu Karam had asked to leave Yemen to join IS in Syria since this would be more "prosperous" for him. "Abu Karam al-Hadrami", al-Naba' 133 (May 24, 2018): 9.

52. AQAP "Bayan Nafy al-'Alaqa bi-Tafjirat Masajid al-Huthiyyin fi San'a'" (Statement Denying Links to the Bombings of Houthi Mosques in Sana'a), Mar. 20, 2015.

53. Al-Malahim Media, "Ta'liq 'ala Istihdaf Wizarat al-Difa' bi-San'a' li-l-Qa'id Qasim al-Raymi" (Commentary on the Targeting of the Ministry of Defence in Sana'a, by Commander Qasim al-Raymi), December 2013.

54. Al-Malahim Media, "al-Mu'tamar al-Suhufi al-Duwali al-Awwal, ma' al-Shaykh Nasr bin 'Ali al-Anisi" (First International Press Conference, with Sheikh Nasr bin 'Ali al-Anisi), December 2014.

55. On Nov. 1, 2017, messages started circulating on pro-AQAP Telegram wires celebrating the "repentance" (i.e. defection) of ISY fighters. The reasons given for defection were ISY's irreligious approach, mistreatment and its leaders' behavior. See also al-Sarim al-Battar, "Shahada li-Ahad al-Munshaqqin 'an Far' Tanzim al-Dawla fi al-Yaman" (Testimony of an ISY Defector), al-Badr Media, Jul. 24, 2018.

56. For a fuller comparison of AQAP and IS local engagement strategies in Yemen, see Elisabeth Kendall "Al-Qaeda and Islamic State in Yemen: A battle for local audiences," in Simon Staffell and Akil Awan (eds), *Jihadism Transformed: Al-Qaeda and Islamic State's Global Battle of Ideas* (London: Hurst, 2016), 89-122: 103-08.

57. "Abu Karam al-Hadrami", al-Naba' 133 (May 24, 2018): 9.

58. "Mu'askar al-Shaykh Abi Muhammad al-Furqan" (Sheikh Abu Muhammad al-Furqan Camp), al-Naba' 76 (Apr. 13, 2017): 15.

59. "al-Dawrat al-Shar'iyya fi Wilayat al-Bayda'" (Sharia Courses in Wilayat al-Bayda'), al-Naba' 77 (Apr. 20, 2017): 14.

60. During 2018, ISY's Wilayat al-Bayda' released no martyr claims during January and February, but during March, April, and May it announced 26 martyrs. In reaching this total I have been careful to avoid double-counting (owing to name variations in photo releases and galleries of martyrs on video) by cross-checking martyr headshots.

61. "Junud al-Khilafa yusdiruna Akbar Hujum li-l-Hutha 'Ala Mawaqi'i-him fi Mintaqat Qayfa" (Caliphate Soldiers launch the Biggest Attack against Houthi Positions in the Qayfa Region), Al-Naba' 51(Oct. 20, 2016): 3.

62. AQAP video, "Sawlat al-Akhyar: Sadd al-Mujahidin li-Taqaddum al-Huthiyyin 'Ala 'Iddat Mawaqi' bi-Wilayat Rada'"(Elite Attack: The Mujahidin Resist Houthi Advances on a Number of Fronts in Wilayat Rada'), Oct. 26, 2016.

63. Al-Malahim Media, "Liqa' Suhufi ma' al-Shaykh Khalid bin 'Umar Batarfi", June 2018, p.1.

64. Guardians of Tawheed Media, Telegram post, Jul. 12, 2018.

65. IS video, "Anasir min Tanzim 'Qa'idat al-Yemen' Asara-hum Muqatilu al-Dawla al-Islamiyya fi Qayfa Shimal Gharbi al-Bayda'", Jul. 15, 2018.

66. AQAP's account of U.A.E.-led Operation al-Faysal to clear it from Wadi al-Masini in Hadramawt in February 2018 was obviously very different from the coalition account. It claims it killed over 40 soldiers before withdrawing to "a nearby area." Abu Suhayb al-Hadrami, "Hal Khasara al-Mujahidun Ma'rakat Wadi al-Masini bi-Sahil Hadramawt?!" (Did the Mujahidun lose the Battle of of Wadi al-Masini in Coastal Hadramawt?!), released on Telegram by Ansar Qa'idat al-Jihad fi Jazirat al-'Arab, Feb. 26, 2018.

67. Erlend Ofte Arntsen, "Yemen's al-Qaida: Entered agreement with tribal leaders not to attack the West", VG, April 16, 2017, and unpublished correspondence with the Yemen representative of al-Qaeda-linked Al-Masra newspaper, Apr. 18-24, 2017.

68. Khalid Batarfi, "Wajibu-na Tujaha Qudsi-na" (Our Duty Towards Our Jerusalem), December 2017 (released Jan. 23, 2018).

69. Qasim al-Raymi, "Mujahid Munfarid Am Jaysh fi Mujahid" (A Lone Mujahid or an Army in [One] Mujahid) (video), al-Malahim Media, May 2017.

70. Al-Basha'ir Audio Productions, "Khabbaru-hu al-Tahaluf" (Tell it to the Coalition), Jun. 30, 2017.

71. These practices were listed in the U.N. Security

Council "Final Report of the Panel of Experts on Yemen", Jan. 26, 2018, 48-9. However, it is possible that the true extent of the violations may be greater. As early as May 2017, locals had compiled a list of 560 violations perpetrated by U.A.E.-backed forces in the governorate of Lahj alone (circulated on Telegram, May 4, 2017) although these cannot obviously not be verified. Regarding women's protests, see for example "Waqfa Ihtijajiyya li-Ummahat al-Makhfiyyin Qasriyy-an fi 'Adan Januba al-Yaman" (Protest by Mothers of Those Forcibly Disappeared in Aden in South Yemen), Dec. 20, 2017,

72. "Ya Nukhbat al-Dhull" (O Elite of Shame), a sung poem which includes the refrain "We are Hadrami and free," circulated on Telegram during April 2018.

73. "Killing Spree of Clerics Spreads Fear in Yemen's Aden," *The New Arab* online, Apr. 5, 2018.

74. Abu al-Bara' al-Ibbi, "Waqafat ma' Ightiyalat al-Mashayikh wa-l-Du'ah" (Positions on the Assassinations of Sheikhs and Preachers), Oct. 31, 2017.

75. This is labor intensive but it can be done. This author partnered with a grassroots youth NGO in east Yemen's Mahra region in 2012-13 to organize the training of around 70 fieldworkers to conduct a scientifically sampled face-to-face survey of over 2,000 tribesmen and women.

76. For a good summary of what is wrong with U.N. Resolution 2216, read Stephen A. Seche, "Give Peace a Real Chance in Yemen: The time is now to redraw outdated UN plans to end the war," *IRIN online*, Apr. 18, 2018.

77. See Helen Lackner, "Water scarcity: Why doesn't it get the attention it deserves?" in Helen Lackner (ed), *Why Yemen Matters* (London: Saqi, 2014), 161-82.

CHAPTER SEVEN

LIBYA'S TERRORISM CHALLENGE:

ASSESSING THE SALAFI-JIHADI THREAT

LYDIA SIZER

INTRODUCTION

One day after the Salafi-jihadi attack on the U.S. Special Mission in Benghazi in mid-September 2012, local residents crowded squares condemning the incident. Within the week, they had expelled one of the groups responsible for the attack, Ansar al-Shariah's Benghazi branch, from the city.[1] Despite this popular rejection of Salafi-jihadi movements in Benghazi, Ansar al-Shariah and other groups gradually made their way back into the city, initiating an assassination campaign targeting police and military officials by early 2013.

Libya is a conservative society in which Islam plays an important role. This is true across the political spectrum from hardline Islamists to self-proclaimed secularists. Salafi-jihadis make up only a small minority of the Libyan population, yet they have wielded disproportionate influence since 2011.

Salafi-jihadi movements fall within a highly diversified and competitive militia landscape, including allies of the anti-Islamist general, Khalifa Hifter, as well as Islamist militias, tribes, and criminal gangs. Hifter has tried to tie rival militia groups to Salafi-jihadi movements to discredit them. For example, the Benghazi Defense Brigades contained anti-Hifter police and army personnel as well as hardline Islamists and anti-Hifter Benghazi residents.[2]

Mapping the Salafi-Jihadi Landscape in Libya

Libyan Islamic Fighting Group

Current Status: Formally disbanded (1995-2010)

Area of Operation: Predominantly eastern Libya, around Derna and Benghazi. Many former leaders are based in Tripoli today

Leaders: Abdel Hakim Belhadj (also known as Abu Abdullah al-Sadiq), Sami al-Saadi

Fighter Size: Always limited to only a few hundred members[4]

Capabilities: Many received training in Afghanistan during the Soviet-Afghan war and in Sudan from the Taliban and al-Qaeda; specialized in clashes with police forces and assassination attempts on Muammar al-Qaddafi

The Libyan Islamic Fighting Group (L.I.F.G.) was a Salafi-jihadi movement that posed the most formidable threat to Qaddafi during his dictatorship. The L.I.F.G. contained many "Afghan Arabs" who fought alongside other global Salafi-jihadis in Afghanistan in the 1980s.[5] The group attempted to assassinate Qaddafi multiple times in the 1990s before a regime crackdown that imprisoned many and forced others to flee to Britain.
Since 2007, however, many L.I.F.G. leaders have backed away from jihadism, even forming political parties, running in elections, and serving in government positions after 2011.[6] From 2007-2009, Qaddafi's son, Saif al-Islam, engaged in talks with L.I.F.G. leaders; the result of which was the release of some 250 L.I.F.G. members after the group renounced violent jihad, and apologized to the Qaddafi regime.[7]

The L.I.F.G. officially disbanded shortly thereafter, but following the 2011 uprisings, some former L.I.F.G. leaders sought larger roles in Libyan politics and society. For example, the emir of the L.I.F.G., Abdel Hakim Belhadj, formed the al-Watan Party and unsuccessfully ran for office in the 2012 parliamentary elections.[8] The L.I.F.G.'s spiritual leader, Sami al-Saadi, separately formed the Umma Party, alongside fellow L.I.F.G. members Abdel wahad Qaid.[9] Qaid is the brother of the late senior al-Qaeda official Abu Yahya al-Libi, who was killed in a U.S. airstrike in Pakistan in 2012. He also served as a member of the General National Congress after 2012.[10] Other former members remained closely connected to Salafi-jihadi groups like Ansar al-Shariah.

Jama'at Nasr al-Islam wal Muslimin

Current Status: Active since March 2017 as face of al-Qaeda in the Maghreb (AQIM) in Libya, made up of Ansar Dine, al-Mourabitoun, Macina Liberation Front, and the Saharan branch of AQIM. Many of these groups have been active in Libya since at least 2011

Area of Operation: Predominantly in Mali, but also southwest Libya

Leader: Iyad Ag Ghali

Fighter Size: Over 5,000[11][12]

Capabilities: Have used Libya as a base from which to launch attacks in neighboring countries, and as a source of arms and ammunition. Attacks on critical energy infrastructure, hotels, local and foreign security presences, including the U.N.; kidnap for ransom operations; infiltration of local smuggling routes

Al-Qaeda has had an influence on Libya since the 1990s. Although the L.I.F.G. never fully subscribed to the al-Qaeda ideology, there were individuals within Libyan society who did. Some of these individuals traveled to Iraq after 2003 to fight alongside al-Qaeda in Iraq. Umbrella groups for al-Qaeda affiliates in Libya have been constantly shifting since 2011 — working flexibly with some of the militias that proliferated after that time to tailor their approach to the Libyan context and advance their goals.

AQIM's evolution since 2011 reflects the flexibility with which it operates in the ever-changing Libyan context. The regional al-Qaeda affiliate, AQIM, had been represented in Libya since late 2011 by Ansar Dine and al-Mourabitoun. Ansar Dine followed the leadership of AQIM Emir Abdelmalek Droukdal. Mokhtar Belmokhtar led al-Mourabitoun, created from the merger of Belmokhtar's al-Mulathamoun (the Masked Men Brigade) and the Movement for Oneness and Jihad in West Africa (MOJWA) in 2013. Al-Mourabitoun also maintained a presence in Libya from which to launch regional attacks. Al-Mulathamoun — itself created as an offshoot of AQIM in late 2012 — was responsible for regional attacks on foreigners, including the In Amenas attack in January 2013. After 2015, AQIM re-merged with al-Mourabitoun. Reports that Belmokhtar was killed in an airstrike in Ajdabiya have not been confirmed.

Finally, in early March 2017, representatives from Ansar Dine, al-Mourabitoun, the Macina Liberation Front, and the Saharan branch of AQIM released a video announcing their merger into the Jama'at Nasr al-Islam wal Muslimin under the leadership of former Ansar Dine leader Iyad Ag Ghali.
These groups have integrated themselves in local communities including some components of the Tuareg minority group, although their persistent existence in southwestern Libya is mostly due to the security vacuum there. They have more recently participated in fighting in Benghazi since 2014. Most of their attacks, however, have occurred further south in the Sahel, sometimes using southwestern Libya as a staging ground.

Ansar al-Shariah

Current Status: Active since 2011; Benghazi branch formally dissolved in May 2017.

Area of Operation: Benghazi, Derna, Sirte, Ajdabiya

Leaders: Abu Khalid al-Madani (since January 2015)

Fighter Size: Over 5,000 members in 2012

Capabilities: Assassination campaigns targeting local police and military officers, as well as infrastructure; targeting foreign nationals; bank robberies; destruction of Sufi shrines; social service provision to local communities; imposition of sharia law in areas under their control; threatening democratic institutions and processes.

Newer groups like Ansar al-Shariah affiliates in Benghazi, Derna, Sirte, and Ajdabiya have sought to carve out areas of influence since 2011. Ansar al-Shariah emerged from the consolidation of hardline Islamist militias in the 2011 uprisings, and sought to prevent Libyan participation in parliamentary elections in 2012. It has had connections to the Ansar al-Shariah branch in Tunisia. The leader of the Tunisian branch, Seifallah Ben Hassine, was the target of a U.S. airstrike in June 2015.[17] Ansar al-Shariah's Benghazi and Derna branches were listed as terrorist organizations subject to sanctions under U.N. Security Council Resolution 2253 (2015).[18] Since its establishment, Ansar al-Shariah has received support from AQIM. In return Ansar al-Shariah in Libya has provided AQIM affiliates with fighters in Mali and training for al-Moulathamoun fighters in 2013.[19] Members of Ansar al-Shariah, including Ahmed Abu Khattala in Benghazi and Sufian Bin Qumu in Derna, also have been implicated in the attack on the U.S. special mission in Benghazi.

After the death of the group's leader, Mohamed el-Zahawi, in late 2014, Ansar al-Shariah began losing members to the new ISIS state in Libya. These defections were especially widespread within the Derna branch. Many senior leaders were also killed in fighting in Benghazi against Hifter from 2014-2017. Consequently, in late May 2017, Ansar al-Shariah's most active branch in Benghazi announced its dissolution.[20] But these defections do not mean that the Salafi-jihadi fighters have been defeated. In fact, many of those fighters who defected to ISIS when Ansar al-Shariah was under pressure in the east are now returning to al-Qaeda affiliation.[21]

Benghazi Revolutionaries Shura Council

Current Status: Active since June 2014

Area of Operation: Benghazi

Leaders: Ismail Sallabi, Mohamed el-Dresi, Wissam bin Hamid (deceased), Jalal Makhzoum (deceased)

Fighter Size: Around 4,000-5,000 in 2014

Capabilities: Assassination campaigns targeting local police and military officers, as well as infrastructure; urban warfare including setting landmine boobytraps, occupying residential complexes, and reliance on snipers, car bombs, and suicide attacks; anti-aircraft equipment; attacks on critical infrastructure, such as airports.

Some groups have had independent success, but there has been a tendency to form Salafi-jihadi umbrella organizations with some connections to al-Qaeda. One of the predominant organizations is the B.R.S.C., which has contained once-powerful militias like Ansar al-Shariah-Benghazi, as well as the Omar Mokhtar Brigade, the February 17th Brigade, Libya Shield 1 Brigade, and the Rafallah al-Sahati Brigade. The B.R.S.C. was created in response to Hifter's Operation Dignity, which was launched in May 2014 to rid Benghazi of these groups. The groups within the B.R.S.C. have varying degrees of affiliation with AQIM, however their primary goal has been to resist Hifter.

The B.R.S.C. has at different times cooperated with ISIS on the shared goal of fighting Hifter, but has strived to distance itself from the Islamic State. The group has been more closely aligned with the Benghazi Defense Brigades (B.D.B.), an umbrella group with connections to Ansar al-Shariah that existed from June 2016-June 2017 to support the B.R.S.C. mission. Elements from the B.D.B. are still active since Hifter's forces removed them from their base in Jufra in mid-2017. The B.R.S.C. reportedly lost a number of important commanders in 2017, including Jalal Makhzoum and Wissam bin Hamid, as Hifter's forces sought complete control of Benghazi. By the summer, the B.R.S.C. controlled very little territory within Benghazi itself and its fighters were attempting to flee the city.

Derna Mujahideen Shura Council

Current Status: Active since December 2014

Area of Operation: Derna and its environs

Leaders: Salim Derby (deceased), Abdul-Hakim el-Hasidi

Fighter Size: Around 1,000-3,000

Capabilities: Provision of public services and city administration, urban warfare, anti-tank and antiaircraft equipment, summary executions, other human rights violations on the local population

In Derna, the Derna Mujahideen Shura Council (D.M.S.C.) is the other predominant Salafi-jihadi umbrella organization, and includes the Abu Salim Martyrs' Brigade (A.S.M.B.). Some members of the A.S.M.B. have sought to participate in democratic processes, putting them at odds with other hardliners, including Ansar al-Shariah's Derna branch, which has worked with the D.M.S.C. in the past. AQIM has supported the B.R.S.C., D.M.S.C., and other, smaller shura councils, including through providing advice on how to resist ISIS expansion.[22] Elements of the D.M.S.C. have controlled Derna — supplanting any central government control from Tripoli — since 2012. Unlike the B.R.S.C., the D.M.S.C. has more consistently been at odds with ISIS, with the latter using Derna as its first Libyan headquarters from late-2014 until the D.M.S.C. expelled it from the city in mid-2015 during a temporary period of cooperation with Hifter.

The D.M.S.C. has opposed Hifter and the L.N.A. since mid-2014, only briefly working together in 2015 to expel ISIS from Derna. But Hifter has attempted to blockade Derna to weaken the D.S.M.C. since shortly after the group re-assumed control of the city from ISIS later in 2015. This blockade intensified in late-2016/early-2017. Under increasing pressure from Hifter's forces, the D.M.S.C.'s mission has expanded from implementing a strict interpretation of shari'a law within Derna to resisting L.N.A. advances. The group has also pledged allegiance to the hardline Islamist Grand Mufti Sadiq el-Ghariani, who has expressed broad support for Ansar al-Shariah.

ISIS in Libya

CURRENT STATUS: ACTIVE SINCE NOVEMBER 2014, NO MEANINGFUL TERRITORIAL CONTROL SINCE DECEMBER 2016

AREA OF OPERATION: NO CURRENT HEADQUARTERS, BUT SCATTERED ACROSS LIBYA INCLUDING IN BANI WALID, SABRATHA, BENGHAZI, THE SIRTE ENVIRONS TO THE SOUTH, AND POSSIBLY IN THE SOUTH AROUND UBARI AND SEBHA

LEADERS: JALAL EL-DINE EL-TUNISI, ABU HADHIFA AL-MUHAJIR, ABU TALAHA EL-TUNISI

FIGHTER SIZE: SEVERAL HUNDRED IN 2017 (POSSIBLY UP TO 5,000 AT ITS PEAK)[23]

CAPABILITIES: URBAN WARFARE INCLUDING SNIPER ATTACKS, LANDMINE BOOBY TRAPS, CAR BOMBS; PUBLIC ADMINISTRATION INCLUDING POLICING AND TAXATION; ACCESS TO FOREIGN FIGHTERS; ATTACKS ON CRITICAL ENERGY INFRASTRUCTURE, HIGH VALUE TARGETS FREQUENTED BY FOREIGN NATIONALS, LIKE HOTELS, AS WELL AS LIBYANS AND EXPATRIATE WORKERS IN LIBYA

LIBYA'S PERMISSIVE ENVIRONMENT ALLOWED ISIS TO ESTABLISH ITS STRONGEST EMIRATE OUTSIDE IRAQ AND SYRIA IN LATE 2014.[24] UNLIKE MOST OTHER SALAFI-JIHADI MOVEMENTS IN LIBYA, ISIS HAD TERRITORIAL ASPIRATIONS TO BUILD AN ISLAMIC STATE WITHIN LIBYA'S BORDERS. BY JANUARY 2015, ISIS WAS ABLE TO ATTACK THE CORINTHIA HOTEL, A POPULAR DESTINATION FOR FOREIGNERS VISITING TRIPOLI, IN ONE OF ITS FIRST ATTEMPTS TO COMMUNICATE ITS POWER IN LIBYA.[25] OVER THE NEXT YEAR, ISIS CLAIMED DERNA AS ITS HEADQUARTERS, FOLLOWED BY SIRTE AFTER THEY WERE EXPELLED BY THE D.M.S.C. IN MID-2015. IT ALSO BEGAN ATTACKING EASTERN OIL INSTALLATIONS FROM ITS NEARBY HEADQUARTERS IN SIRTE IN AN ATTEMPT TO DISRUPT REVENUES TO ANY GOVERNING BODY THAT COULD RESIST THEM. THE INTENT WAS NEVER TO CONTROL LIBYA'S OIL.

MILITIAS MOSTLY FROM NEARBY MISRATA, NOMINALLY ALIGNED WITH THE INTERNATIONALLY RECOGNIZED GOVERNMENT OF NATIONAL ACCORD (G.N.A.), LAUNCHED AN OFFENSIVE IN APRIL 2016 THAT EVENTUALLY ROUTED ISIS FROM SIRTE EIGHT MONTHS LATER. U.S. AIR SUPPORT THROUGH OPERATION ODYSSEY LIGHTNING WAS CRITICAL TO THIS SUCCESS. SINCE DECEMBER 2016, ISIS IN LIBYA HAS BEEN DEBATED AS A FALL-BACK POSITION FOR ISIS FORCES UNDER PRESSURE IN IRAQ AND SYRIA, BUT ISIS NO LONGER HOLDS TERRITORY THERE.[26]

Yet, Hifter and his allies have justified targeting this group by accusing them of working closely with Salafi-jihadi organizations, including the Benghazi Revolutionaries Shura Council (B.R.S.C.) and Ansar al-Shariah.[3] The Benghazi Defense Brigades officially disbanded in June 2017 after Hifter removed them from their base in the Jufra region.

The absence of functioning state institutions or an accountable military with a monopoly on the use of force has allowed Salafi-jihadi groups to exist in parts of Libya for decades. Other groups have flourished since the 2011 revolution.

There is collaboration and competition within and among the Salafi-jihadi groups themselves, underscoring the fluid nature of Salafi-jihadi allegiances. ISIS and Ansar al-Shariah members fought side-by-side against Hifter in Benghazi, with the B.R.S.C. only recently distancing itself publicly from ISIS.[27] Ansar al-Shariah Libya branches have also maintained connections to transnational Salafi-jihadi groups like Ansar al-Shariah's Tunisia branch and AQIM.[28]

But ISIS officials regularly cited the complex Salafi-jihadi competition in Libya as one of the main challenges to expansion.[29] After Ansar al-Shariah's leader, Mohammed el-Zahawi, died in Benghazi in late 2014, ISIS benefited from defections of Ansar al-Shariah to its camp.[30] After devastating setbacks for ISIS in Sirte, Benghazi, and Sabratha since 2016, Ansar al-Shariah's remaining branches may already be benefiting from ISIS defectors in turn. The D.M.S.C. was also critical to expelling ISIS from its initial headquarters in Derna in 2015.[31] AQIM has also tried to undermine ISIS as a group encroaching on its area of operations.[32] The formation of the Jama'at Nasr Al-Islam wal Muslimin in March 2017 may also have been a way for al-Qaeda affiliates to compete with ISIS.[33] In addition, there are tensions between the three generations of Salafi-jihadis: The "Afghan Arabs" who fought Qaddafi in the 1990s, those who fought alongside al-Qaeda in Iraq after 2003, and those who fought in Syria after 2011 (which include some individuals from the second generation).[34]

Although all these groups ascribe to strict interpretations of shari'a, their operational, strategic, and spiritual objectives differ. Ansar al-Shariah and ISIS have attempted to fill the institutional vacuum with their own police and courts. To fulfill their objectives of local or territorial control, these groups undermine central and local government authority, often through assassination campaigns. ISIS has employed particularly brutal techniques to impose its views, while Ansar al-Shariah and components of the Jama'at Nasr al-Islam wal Muslimin have emphasized outreach to local communities. Some Salafi-jihadi movements in Libya have also rallied against Hifter, who poses an existential threat. Other groups like AQIM and al-Mourabitoun seek to undermine insufficiently Islamic governments and attack foreigners while maintaining safe havens from which they can launch such attacks in neighboring countries.[35]

DRIVERS OF SALAFI-JIHADI MOVEMENTS: PUSH AND PULL FACTORS

Despite the complex and competitive militia landscape, Salafi-jihadi movements have sustained themselves due to a number of push and pull factors incentivizing membership and support. No one push or pull factor can be the sole driver of Salafi-jihadi movements. For example, socioeconomic drivers alone cannot explain radicalization since most Libyans experience socioeconomic hardships, but eschew violent extremism. There are also very personal reasons why individuals would be driven to join these movements. Taken together, however, the factors below illustrate why these movements have thrived and may help policymakers develop effective tools to combat them.

PUSH FACTORS

Factors that push individuals toward Salafi-jihadi movements in Libya include a history of participation in such groups, the cult of victimhood pervading Libyan society, marginalization of specific groups, and socioeconomic hardships. Libyans made up a significant proportion of the "Afghan Arabs" in the 1980s. In late 2007, the Sinjar records also revealed that disproportionate numbers of al-Qaeda in Iraq fighters were Libyan.[36] In 2016, an ISIS defector leaked around 3,600 foreign fighter records, revealing that Derna and its environs had the single highest per capita rate of foreign fighters joining ISIS of global provinces recorded.[37] Over three generations, jihadi activity has become a profession in some communities.

Salafi-jihadi activity also provides a way for individuals to reclaim their dignity and respect after decades of repression during the Qaddafi regime. This cult of victimhood is likely to continue, especially if Hifter gains more power and employs repressive tactics against moderate political Islamists and other enemies. It will also persist if the Libyan people feel abandoned by global partners and a persistently corrupt government.[38]

Some groups are more prone to being subsumed by this cult of victimhood, especially minority communities like the Tuareg and Amazigh, as well as some Islamist groups. All these groups have experienced marginalization during and after the Qaddafi regime. Tuareg and Amazigh communities, for example, felt that their rights were not protected by Qaddafi, by subsequent governments, or through post-2011 draft constitutions.

Tribes seen as complicit in Qaddafi-era crimes are also vulnerable to radicalization due to neglect and/or persecution since 2011. Elements within the Warfalla tribe, for example, have complained in the past about disenfranchisement as retribution for their favored status during the Qaddafi regime. ISIS tried to exploit that marginalization and built cells near the Warfalla stronghold of Bani Walid beginning in late 2016.[39]

The decline in standards of living in Libya since 2011 and the lack of economic opportunity may also drive individuals toward Salafi-jihadi movements. Public services including electricity, telecommunications, water, sanitation, and local security are weak, especially in the west and south. Libya's bloated energy sector and state policies inhibit the privatization and economic diversification needed to create attractive jobs for young people. Despite recent improvements in the oil sector, oil production is volatile in the absence of state control over oil infrastructure. Libya risks complete economic collapse by 2019, preventing any government from paying state salaries or coping with the security vacuum these groups exploit.[40][41]

Pull Factors

There are also factors that pull individuals to Salafi-jihadi groups, many of which relate to the security vacuum: Access to weapons, money, foreign fighters, and the lack of organized resistance to these movements. The presence of key Salafi-jihadi leaders and perceived support for Salafi-jihadi movemen among key Libyan spiritual leaders like Grand Mufti Ghariani also attra individuals. Local affinity for Salafi-jihadi ideology is less of a pull factor. Mc Libyans adhere to the Maliki madhab, a moderate school of Islamic thought.

Salafi-jihadi movements have had access to loose weapons and foreign fighters due to the massive weapons stockpiles and porous borders that have characterized Libya in the absence of strong governing institutions. After the 2011 revolution, Libya had one of the largest uncontrolled stockpiles of man-portable air defense systems (MANPADS) in the world, as well as around 250,000-700,000 less sophisticated conventional weapons and associated equipment.[43] Successive Libyan governments have been unable to secure these weapons, which have easily made their way into the hands of Salafi-jihadi organizations and weapons traffickers.[44][45] Libya's vast desert borders have stymied government efforts, as well as Libya's neighbor's efforts to contain threats from Salafi-jihadi movements.

Salafi-jihadi organizations also have had a wide variety of potential financing mechanisms, including through connections to smuggling networks, kidnap for ransom (K.F.R.) operations, access to state salaries, taxation of local populations, bank robberies, foreign funds from Libyans overseas, or wayward Qatari support.[46][47][48][49] With this funding, groups including ISIS and Ansar al-Shariah have been able to pay fighters monthly salaries of $100 or more, which is more than many individuals could make working legitimate jobs.[50]

Trafficking in drugs, weapons, other commodities, and people earn non-state actors including Salafi-jihadi organizations millions of dollars per year.[51] Mokhtar Belmokhtar in particular has been able to take advantage of the lucrative cigarette smuggling business in the region, which is worth around $1 billion per year. After unifying with MOJWA, al-Mourabitoun also began benefitting financially from the regional cocaine trade.[52] The burgeoning coastal migrant trafficking economy separately contributes up to $371 million per year to the black economy in which these groups participate.[53] Salafi-jihadi organizations often launder money from these trades through charity front organizations.[54]

K.F.R. operations are on the rise in Libya in 2017, including in Tripoli. Ransom demands for local residents can net groups around $150,000.[55] By contrast, these groups tend to demand millions of dollars in ransom payments from governments when they kidnap foreign nationals.[56]

More recently, militias in Libya, likely including Salafi-jihadist groups, have begun kidnapping migrants making their way to the coast and demanding ransom payments from their families. Migrants have claimed these militias have demanded between $8,000 to $10,000, and threatened to kill them if they were not paid.[57] ISIS has also taxed criminal gangs involved in the smuggling trade.[58] Interpol and Europol have suggested that there are currently 800,000 migrants in Libya waiting to travel to Europe, making K.F.R. operations targeting migrants a potentially large source of income for militias, including those affiliated with Salafi-jihadist movements.[59]

During its occupation of Sirte, ISIS was able to impose religious *zakat*, "taxes" on the local population, which could cost business owners around $3,500 per year.[60] Since ISIS lost a territorial foothold in Libya, however, other sources of financing have become more important. There have also been allegations that ISIS loots antiquities from Libya's many world heritage sites to sell in Europe.[61] It has also been suggested that extremist groups in the Sirte area were able to benefit significantly after an October 2013 bank robbery in the city that netted the perpetrators $54 million in local and foreign currency.[62]

Yet none of these groups has been able to significantly exploit Libya's oil. Many of them remain only modestly financed, but Libyan authorities cannot police any of these funding sources.

Libya's security and political vacuum is the greatest pull factor driving Salafi-jihadi movements. Then-U.N. Special Envoy to Libya Martin Kobler quipped at the height of ISIS's power that the group had the strongest governance model among competing power centers.[63] Other groups like Ansar al-Shariah have sought to provide public services where the central government could not to build local support. Libya remains attractive to foreign fighters as a refuge where they can interact with senior leaders and transit between fronts.[64] ISIS emir Abu Bakr al-Baghdadi even encouraged fighters to fall back to Libya amid international pressure on Raqqa and Mosul in 2016.[65]

Even when there was only one government in Libya from 2011-14, it was too weak to counter threats from these groups. Since the political crisis beginning in late 2013 and accelerating into civil unrest in 2014-15, multiple, parallel governments have been preoccupied fighting among themselves instead of unifying against common threats from Salafi-jihadi movements.

The Outlook for Salafi-Jihadi Movements in Libya

Without widespread support from locals, most Salafi-jihadi movements have not been able to expand rapidly. Yet they have been able to maintain safe havens, even under significant pressure like ISIS was in late 2016 and into 2017. Competing poles of power — Hifter in the east and militias nominally aligned with the G.N.A. in the west — have fought ISIS in Benghazi and Sirte, respectively, to gain international support as primary counterterrorism partners. But after pro-G.N.A. forces worked with U.S. Africa Command (AFRICOM) to successfully dislodge ISIS from its Sirte headquarters, denying it territorial control in Libya, factions have competed for power instead of uniting to eliminate common enemies.[66]

This infighting has allowed ISIS and other Salafi-jihadi groups to evolve and grow in late 2016 and 2017. ISIS could turn into a group with similar attributes to al-Qaeda affiliates in the area. Unification under the Jama'at Nasr al-Islam wal Muslimin in March 2017 will undoubtedly strengthen future coordination among al-Qaeda groups, leading to new attacks through the Maghreb and Sahel.[67] Al-Qaeda affiliates also remain in a strong financial position, especially compared with ISIS today, because of their relationships with Libya's black market economy, institutionalized over decades.

Political opposition to Salafi-jihadi movements is also weak. The defunct government in Tripoli that still attempts to undermine the G.N.A. has defended Ansar al-Shariah, protesting its designation as an international terrorist organization in 2014.[68] Hifter's supporters have accused rivals of providing material support to these groups in Benghazi, particularly by sea via Misrata.[69] They have also tried to link powerful rivals from Misrata to terrorist activity. Hifter's campaigns in Benghazi and Derna led to the deaths and capture of many al-Qaeda-affiliated leaders, but disunity has prevented total expulsion of these groups after over three years of fighting.

The drivers of Salafi-jihadi movements in Libya are unlikely to change markedly in the next one to four years. These movements will, therefore, continue to cooperate and compete with each other in the persistent vacuum.

It will take years for Libyan institutions to have the capacity necessary to support rule of law, control loose weapons, manage borders, counter terrorist financing, and provide public services and security throughout Libya. These efforts can only take place in the absence of the civil unrest that currently plagues Libya. These are key capacities needed to counter some of the push and pull factors mentioned above, underscoring the deep importance of the faltering political dialogue to end the crisis and combat the power of Salafi-jihadi movements.

Hifter's role in Libya's future will also have an impact on the future of Salafi-jihadi activity. It is likely that he will have a leading role in a reunified government when it can be formed. The U.N. mediator and other world leaders have accepted this eventuality, as have some political Islamists including Muslim Brotherhood-affiliated groups.[70] Hifter, however, is an enabler of future Salafi-jihadi activity as much as he claims to be its chief threat. He has been largely unwilling to participate in political dialogue, believing he can take over the country without compromising. As a result, Hifter would marginalize parts of the population most vulnerable to recruitment by Salafi-jihadi movements. At the same time, Hifter does not have the capacity to cope with the magnitude of the Salafi-jihadi threat alone.

In the near future, some anti-Hifter and nominally pro-G.N.A. forces could be tempted to align with some groups with Salafi-jihadi ties to form a viable counterweight to Hifter's expansion. Hifter and his allies will seize the opportunity to cast them as terrorists as well — particularly in the context of increased hostility toward all Islamists in Libya following the fall-out between Qatar and other Gulf states in June 2017. This portrayal would leave these groups vulnerable to discreditation, marginalization, and physical attack. Already Hifter's forces have targeted military members of the Misratan military council with connections to the controversial B.D.B.[71] If pro-G.N.A. forces surrender to this temptation, there is a risk that foreign security assistance to the internationally-recognized government could end up in the hands of Salafi-jihadi movements.

Concurrently, it is also unlikely that Libya will experience enough economic growth and development in the next one to four years to overcome the socioeconomic factors that push individuals toward Salafi-jihadi movements. Post-revolution budgets have prioritized large allocations to subsidies and the bloated public sector, which employs around 77 percent of the workforce.[72] Development spending that would help increase economic diversification and educational and employment opportunities for vulnerable communities is negligible. This lack of development could exacerbate the cult of victimhood among vulnerable populations, especially if scarce investments are not distributed throughout Libya.

CONSEQUENCES OF SALAFI-JIHADI PERSISTENCE

Although ISIS and Ansar al-Shariah have faced setbacks since late 2016, they have not significantly diminished the Salafi-jihadi influence in Libya. The chaotic environment will continue to make Libya attractive to these groups, including reconstituted ISIS cells.[73]

In this context, terrorist attacks — including targeting foreigners — will likely continue and possibly intensify in Libya, the region, and Europe. These attacks could fuel instability in vulnerable neighboring countries, including Tunisia, Egypt, Mali, and Niger. Libyan cells have been implicated in terrorist attacks since 2015 in Paris, Berlin and, more recently, Manchester and London.[74][75] Libya's persistent status as a Salafi-jihadi safe haven would provide these groups with an escape valve and limit the effectiveness of regional counterterrorism policies. Airstrikes and drone strikes will not be able to reliably prevent such attacks as long as Libya's porous borders, loose weapons, and security vacuum persist.

In Libya itself, hotels popular with foreign diplomats and businessmen are particularly vulnerable, as are oil and gas facilities, government and security institutions, and foreign missions. The economic impact of such attacks could be staggering, especially attacks that halt oil production and disrupt electricity.

These attacks could intensify as more foreign diplomats attempt to reopen embassies in Tripoli, as the Italians and Turks have already done.[76][77] International oil corporations would also have to take this increased threat into account when deciding how to reengage now that oil production has risen since September 2016 — reaching 900,000 barrels per day as of late June 2017, according to the Libyan National Oil Corporation.[78][79] As ISIS reconstitutes itself and competes with other Salafi-jihadi movements for recruits and influence, these groups may also resort to high-profile attacks as part of recruitment strategies.

These attacks would not only prolong Libya's global isolation, but they would also undermine much-needed capacity-building in state institutions. These interferences have been a clear motivation behind ISIS's probing attacks on oil installations in Libya since 2015.[80] There is also a chance that more al-Qaeda affiliates could form a temporary alliance to combat any increased ability of the central government to threaten them — building off of the new Jama'at Nasr al-Islam wal Muslimin group. In the continued vacuum, transnational Salafi-jihadi movements under pressure in other countries will be able to retreat to Libya, where they will continue to provide services the government cannot to win over local recruits and supporters.

Weak government institutions have also begun to rely on foreign airstrikes to augment their own counterterrorism capabilities. Four months of U.S.

AFRICOM airstrikes against ISIS targets in Sirte were critical to expelling the group from its headquarters by December 2016. Hifter separately relies on support from Egypt and the U.A.E. for its airstrikes targeting these groups, among other opponents.[81] [82] But these airstrikes have been unable to prevent ISIS cells from proliferating on the outskirts of Sirte, Tripoli, and Bani Walid as well as in Sabratha and in the restive southwest. Dependence on international counterterrorism support, including through special forces operators in Libya, could also lead to local resentment of international actors and their own, weak government, especially if civilian casualties can be tied to this support.

Responding to the Persistent Salafi-Jihadi Threat

Libya's stability is a generational project. Reversing the drivers of Salafi-jihadi movements requires long-term, diverse, and expensive programs. Support to unofficial factions in the conflict that claim to be fighting these groups in conjunction with airstrike campaigns will not effectively mitigate this threat. At the same time, Libya is not a foreign policy priority for most international powers, and Libya lacks the funds, institutional capacity, and unified will to reverse these drivers itself.

Given these realities, Libya and its international partners must focus on both short- and long-term programs that will directly impact these drivers, suggestions for which are provided below. Some of these programs may already be underway but should be assessed for adequate funding and appropriate long-term focus.

Addressing Push Factors

To impede the generational cycle of Salafi-jihadi membership as a professional choice, Libya's international partners could work with vetted Libyan and regional intelligence to identify and target recruiters and foreign fighter facilitators. The ISIS documents leaked by an ISIS defector in 2016 often identify facilitators for specific individuals, which could be a starting point for developing recruitment network maps.

International organizations dedicated to religious freedom could work with Libyan lawmakers to draft legislation protecting religious freedom while discouraging extreme rhetoric, especially in mosques in vulnerable communities. Current laws on these issues are very weak and compete with more extreme fatwas from Grand Mufti Ghariani's influential Dar al-Ifta.[83] To the degree possible, educational N.G.O.s could work with Western governments to expand scholarship opportunities for at-risk, young Libyans to go abroad, independent of Libyan government funding.

Addressing the cult of victimhood that drives frustrated Libyans to Salafi-jihadi movements will require Libyan and international dedication to a long-term national reconciliation process to overcome grievances of the Qaddafi era and post-revolution period. Previous attempts have failed, in part because these processes themselves became mired in the political crisis.

Concurrently, interested global actors should help prevent further marginalization of vulnerable communities. For example, timely and comprehensive assistance reconstructing Sirte is critical. As a favored city under Qaddafi, Sirte residents had been marginalized in the post-revolution context, making them vulnerable to ISIS takeover. The U.N. Development Programme administers millions of dollars in the Stabilization Fund for Libya allocated to cities including Sirte for this purpose. Yet, the $7.6 million allocated to Sirte is not enough to help the city recover from damage both from the anti-ISIS fight and from the 2011 revolution.[84] Investment in Libya's long-neglected south is also of critical importance in this respect.

Influential international actors should also press Libyan leaders, especially Hifter, to avoid ostracizing whole segments of the population — whether they are political Islamists, former Qaddafi-era bureaucrats, or minority groups. International actors could tie coveted counterterrorism assistance to such conditions.

There are also many tactics Libya and its supporters could employ to address declining standards of living. Job creation and economic diversification will take time, but investments can begin now, including through corporate social responsibility programs of large international oil companies. The private sector has an important role to play, and companies should strengthen existing coordination with international assistance organizations to ensure programs meet both corporate and Libyan interests.[85] Programs could create educational, entrepreneurial, and internship opportunities linked to universities and youth civil society organizations that naturally lend themselves to viable job prospects.

Because financial institutions will not reform themselves overnight — especially if there is deliberate obstruction by participants in the political crisis — the United States and/or United Kingdom should continue to take the lead supporting negotiations between the G.N.A., the central bank, the audit bureau, the National Oil Corporation, and the House of Representatives to ensure all Libyan citizens have access to adequate public services and salaries.

Attacks on critical infrastructure also have a direct effect on Libyans on the state payroll. Countries with significant commercial interests involving critical infrastructure, including the United States, Britain, Italy, Spain, France, Austria, Greece, and Turkey, should consider commissioning feasible technological and operational solutions to some of these threats. These countries should tie this assistance to more long-term efforts to create security institutions loyal to a unity government, not individual militias.

ADDRESSING PULL FACTORS

To curb Salafi-jihadi and other militia access to loose weapons, international governments could resume site surveys of ammunition storage areas as part of broader demobilization, demilitarization and reintegration, and national reconciliation efforts. By sharing survey information with reunified Libyan defense institutions, international security partners could help craft a strategy to support government efforts to control loose weapons.

Tunisian authorities began construction on a 125-mile border barrier with Libya shortly after Salafi-jihadi groups launched the Bardo Museum and Sousse attacks from Libyan soil in 2015.[86] But the barrier has not been effective. ISIS was notably able to launch an attack on the border town of Ben Gardane in Tunisia in March 2016.[87] The Algerian and Chadian governments have also placed more troops along their vast borders with Libya to prevent free-flowing Salafi-jihadi fighters.[88][89]

But manpower alone cannot combat vulnerabilities along thousands of miles of unclear border markings in the harsh desert. For example, AQIM affiliates in Algeria are still able to coordinate with affiliates like Jama'at Nasr al-Islam wal Muslimin in Libya.[90] Because of weak governance and porous borders, ISIS in Libya has even been able to plot operations in Europe.[91]

Improved border management is also critical to addressing Salafi-jihadi access to weapons, funding, and foreign fighters. It would also deter Salafi-jihadi leaders from using Libya as a safe haven. Instead of futilely stationing hundreds of troops along Libya's long, desert borders, the E.U., Libya, Algeria, Tunisia, Mali, Niger, Chad, Sudan, and Egypt could establish an intelligence sharing mechanism. Through such a mechanism border management officials globally can share intelligence voluntarily and regularly about Salafi-jihadi movements, foreign fighter movements, and other smuggling activities. One focus of this new mechanism would be on flows through transit hubs like Sebha, rather than through the borders themselves.

From its Tunis headquarters, the E.U. Border Assistance Mission to Libya could narrow its broad mandate to devote its limited resources to leading these efforts.[92] The curators of this new mechanism could also encourage anti-ISIS coalition entities monitoring foreign fighter flows, vetted elements of the Libyan Coast Guard, and even security services from oil companies to share diverse signals, human, and open source intelligence. This arrangement would give neighboring states and regional actors a better understanding of the nature, location, and usage of smuggling networks. This mechanism could even reveal planned K.F.R. operations.

To counter funding for Salafi-jihadi movements, Western countries should also diversify their financial intelligence assistance, moving from a historical focus on asset recovery to countering terrorist financing.[93] They should also more aggressively pursue Libyan financiers of Salafi-jihadi movements in their own territories — expanding E.U. sanctions to include actors like Grand Mufti Ghariani. Libya could revive efforts to establish a Financial Intelligence Unit (FIU) and draft money laundering and terrorist financing legislation to cooperate with regional and global partners through the Egmont Group.[94] International donors could link assistance related to public financial management to such efforts, which could be monitored by the Middle East and North Africa Financial Action Task Force (MENAFATF). MENAFATF has been planning a site visit to Libya in 2017.[95]

FUTURE SCENARIOS

Libya can make little progress addressing the drivers of Salafi-jihadi movements until the political and security vacuum ends.[96] Ultimately, many of the suggestions above depend on political reunification and the emergence of empowered official interlocutors. Finally, addressing the challenge of destabilizing militias is critical to this effort; however these militias will not surrender their weapons or join weak security institutions voluntarily. It will take years to develop institutions capable of compelling this behavior. In the meantime, the best option to combat the political vacuum and begin to address the security vacuum is to support a reunified government capable of working with international partners ready to help Libya strengthen security institutions.

There are two realistic scenarios where one government emerges in the next one to four years: A government resulting from a political dialogue process or a government controlled by Hifter. The first scenario requires significantly more international commitment than the second. Such commitment may not be forthcoming for Libya as a second-tier foreign policy priority among world powers like the United States.

Powerful factions in the conflict, especially those aligned with Hifter, have discredited the U.N.-facilitated political dialogue process. After one year in Tripoli, the G.N.A. and the Presidency Council have not been able to address worsening standards of living in areas under their authority. The House of Representatives has deliberately delayed recognizing the G.N.A., as pro-Hifter House leaders seek revisions to the political agreement signed in 2015 to empower the field marshal. External interference from Egypt, Russia, and the U.A.E. further undermines the G.N.A.'s authority.

The G.N.A. could prevail if political dialogue efforts succeed in finding revisions to the political agreement acceptable to the House and if Hifter's international patrons convince him that he lacks the capacity to take over all of Libya. The political agreement would require provisions to prevent manipulation by Hifter or other factional leaders. In this scenario, international partners could rely on relatively weak but clear interlocutors with whom they could cooperate on short- and long-term measures countering Salafi-jihadi movements. Hifter's acceptance of the G.N.A. would also make it easier for assistance to reach all of Libya, including potentially marginalized communities under his control. A unified government would create space to complete important, delayed processes like drafting the constitution and pursuing national reconciliation. In this scenario, the Salafi-jihadi threat would likely diminish in the long run.

Alternatively, if Hifter eventually deposes the G.N.A. or prevails in presidential elections — currently planned for March 2018 — international partners would find a military ruler with a keen interest in fighting a continuous battle against a broadly defined group of "terrorists." As in the previous scenario, there would be clear interlocutors for international donors.

But Hifter not only lacks the capabilities to enforce rule of law and fight terrorism throughout Libya, he would use severe counterterrorism methods and political tactics that would marginalize vulnerable communities, while assisting Salafi-jihadi movements. Despite the illusion that Hifter controls an army, he enjoys weak alliances with many of his supporters and exercises little control over many of their actions. Powerful militias refusing to reconcile with Hifter, including from Misrata, would retreat to the margins, potentially cooperating with Salafi-jihadi groups to undermine his weak authority. International actors may still be able to implement some effective measures to counter some of the drivers of Salafi-jihadi movements, especially through institutionalizing counterterrorism cooperation among Libya's neighbors. But in this scenario, international partners would find a suboptimal partner in combating Salafi-jihadi activity in Libya, which is likely to become a greater challenge in the long run.

A third possible scenario which becomes more likely with international neglect is continued chaos and possible formal division of Libya. Parallel governing institutions already exist in the east and west. Factions supporting parallel institutions fight sporadically for control of the south. It is possible that no reunification could occur — either under the G.N.A. or Hifter — leading to continued uncertainty about interlocutors and delayed international assistance. If the country splits, it would also leave international partners with multiple sets of unstable interlocutors. This scenario is ideal for Salafi-jihadi movements, both in the short and long run, as they maintain the conditions in which drivers of Salafi-jihadi movements flourish.

Conclusion

Many different local and transnational Salafi-jihadi movements have taken advantage of Libya's governed spaces to establish safe havens, impose their ideologies on local populations, and even attempt to re-establish a caliphate. Libyans tend to be religiously conservative, but they have not broadly supported these movements. Yet Salafi-jihadi groups have been able to attract some recruits and maintain operations to meet their objectives in Libya because of six main drivers: 1) Membership as a traditional profession in certain communities; 2) the cult of victimhood; 3) declining standards of living; 4) easy access to weapons, money, and foreign fighters; 5) the presence of Salafi-jihadi leaders and support from local spiritual leaders; and above all; 6) the persistent security and political vacuum.

Because of the ongoing political and security vacuum, it is unlikely that these drivers will be eliminated in the next one to four years, exposing Libya, its neighbors, and other U.S. allies in Europe to terrorist attacks and other destabilizing activities. There are a number of ways Libya's international partners, including the United States, could combat these drivers. Honed assistance could include: 1) Advanced targeting of Salafi-jihadi recruitment networks; 2) smart investments in expanding educational and economic opportunities for vulnerable youth; 3) increasing focus on national reconciliation; 4) providing assistance to protect critical infrastructure; and 5) developing and sharing intelligence on weapons caches, illicit financial transactions, and transborder smuggling networks.

Few of these responses will be effective in the persistent political and security vacuum. It will take years for Libya to develop institutions strong enough to work with international partners to address these drivers adequately. Ending the political crisis is a critical initial step for countering Salafi-jihadi movements. The two apparent options for reunifying the country — consolidating international and domestic support for the flagging G.N.A. or lending support to Field Marshal Hifter — have very different long-term implications for Salafi-jihadi movements. Although both scenarios create clear interlocutors for international donors, Hifter's intentions and leadership style would empower Salafi-jihadi movements in the long run.

ENDNOTES

1. Sulaiman Ali Zwai and Kareem Fahim, "Angry Libyans Target Militias, Force Flight," *The New York Times*, September 21, 2012, accessed February 1, 2017.

2. Mary Fitzgerald and Mattia Toaldo, "A Quick Guide to Libya's Main Players," *European Council on Foreign Relations*, December 2016, accessed February 1, 2017, http://www.ecfr.eu/mena/mapping_libya_conflict.

3. "East Libyan Forces Launch Air Strike against Rivals in Central Desert," *Reuters*, December 26, 2016, accessed February 1, 2017.

4. "Libyan Islamic Fighting Group (L.I.F.G.)," Global Security, accessed June 26, 2017.

5. Camille Tawil, *Brothers in Arms: The Story of al-Qaeda and the Arab jihadis* (London: Saqi Books, 2011), 13.

6. Omar Ashour, "Post-Jihadism: Libya and the Global Transformations of Armed Islamist Movements," *Terrorism and Political Violence* 23 (2011): 383-384.

7. "International Religious Freedom Report 2010: Libya," *U.S. Department of State*, November 17, 2010.

8. "Profile: Libyan Rebel Commander Abdelhakim Belhadj," *BBC*, July 4, 2012.

9. Omar Ashour, "Libya's Jihadist Minority,'" *Brookings*, September 15, 2012.

10. Marhta Raddaz and Muhammad Lila, "Drone Strike Targets Top al-Qaeda Leader," *ABC News*, June 4, 2012.

11. "Profile: al-Qaeda in the Islamic Maghreb," *BBC News*, January 17, 2013, accessed June 26,2017.

12. Conor Gaffney, "Mali Hotel Attack: What is the Macina Liberation Front, Mali's Boko Haram?" *Newsweek*, November 14, 2015.

13. Andrew Lebovich, "AQIM's Formalized Flexibility," *How Al-Qaeda Survived Drones, Uprisings, and the Islamic State*, Aaron Zelin, ed., (Washington, DC: *Washington Institute for Near East Policy*, 2017), 57.

14. Angelique Chrisafis, Julian Borger, Justin McCurry, and Terry Macalister, "Algerian Hostage Crisis: The Full Story of the Kidnapping in the Desert," *The Guardian*, January 25, 2013.

15. Andrew Lebovich, "The Hotel Attacks and Militant Re-alignment in the Sahara-Sahel Region," *Combating Terrorism Center*, January 19, 2016.

16. William Burns, Frederic Wehrey, and Jonathan Winer, "Libya Beyond ISIS: Prospects for Unity and Stability," *Carnegie Endowment for International Peace*, January 25, 2017.

17. Carlotta Gall and Eric Schmitt, "Jihadist From Tunisian Died in Strike in Libya, U.S. Official Says," *The New York Times*, July 2, 2015.

18. "U.N. Security Council Resolution 2253: 2015)," *U.N. Security Council*, December 17, 2015.

19. Frederic Wehrey, "Insecurity and Governance Challenges in Southern Libya," *Carnegie Endowment for International Peace*, March 30, 2017.

20. Mostafa Hashem and Eric Knecht, "Libyan Islamist group Ansar al-Sharia says it is dissolving," *Reuters*, May 27, 2017.

21. Frederic Wehrey, "Insecurity and Governance Challenges in Southern Libya," *Carnegie Endowment for International Peace*, March 30, 2017.

22. Thomas Jocelyn, "Libya's Terrorist Descent: Causes and Solutions," *Long War Journal*, September 27, 2016, accessed February 7, 2017.

23. Eric Schmitt, "Warnings of a 'Powder Keg' in Libya as ISIS Regroups," *The New York Times*, March 21, 2017.

24. "Libya: Extremists Terrorizing Derna Residents," *Human Rights Watch*, November 27, 2014, accessed February 1, 2017.

25. Suliman Ali Zway and David Kirkpatrick, "Group Linked to ISIS Says It's Behind Assault on Libyan Hotel," *The New York Times*, January 27, 2015.

26. Frederic Wehrey and Wolfram Lacher, "Libya After ISIS: How Trump Can Prevent the Next War," *Foreign Affairs*, February 22, 2017.

27. Mohamed Eljarh, Twitter post, January 6, 2017, 5:41 p.m..

28. "Ansar al-Shariah in Tunisia (AST)," *Counter Extremism Project*, 2017.

29. Abdul-Mughirah al-Qahtani, "Interview with Abdul-Mughirah al-Qahtani," Dabiq No. 11, September 9, 2015, 60-63.

30. Ulf Laessing, "Leader of Libyan Islamists Ansar al-Shariah Dies of Wounds," *Reuters*, January 23, 2015, accessed February 8, 2017.

31. Frederic Wehrey and Ala al-Rababah, "Splitting the Islamists: The Islamic State's Creeping Advance in Libya," *Carnegie Middle East Center*, June 19, 2015, accessed February 1, 2017.

32. Anouar Boukhars, "How West Africa Became Fertile Ground for al-Qaeda and ISIS," *World Politics Review*, November 29, 2016, accessed February 8, 2017.

33. Lebovich, "AQIM's Flexibility," 61.

34. Fitzgerald and Toaldo, "A Quick Guide to Libya's Main Players."

35. Geoff Porter, "AQIM Objectives in North Africa," *Combating Terrorism Center*, February 1, 2011, accessed February 7, 2017.

36. Joseph Felter and Brian Fishman, "al-Qa'ida's Foreign Fighters in Iraq: A First Look at the Sinjar Records," *Combatting Terror Center at West Point*, June 2010, accessed February 3, 2017.

37. Nathaniel Rosenblatt, "All Jihad Is Local: What ISIS's Files Tell US About Its Fighters," *New America Foundation*, July 2016, accessed February 2, 2017.

38. Transparency International. "Corruption Perceptions Index 2016." www.transparency.org. January 25, 2017. Accessed September 14, 2017.

39. Maria Abi-Habib and Hassan Morajea, "Islamic State Fighters in Libya Flee South as Stronghold Crumbles," *The Washington Post*, August 14, 2016, accessed February 2, 2017.

40. John Hamilton, Lydia Sizer, Mary Fitzgerald, and Michael Willis. "The Conflict in Libya". *Middle East Centre*. Podcast audio, January 27, 2017.

41. Guilian Denoeux and Lynn Carter, "Guide to the Drivers of Violent Extremism," *USAID*, February 2009, accessed February 1, 2017.

42. Youssef Sawani, "Post-Qaddafi Libya: Interactive Dynamics and the Political Future," *Contemporary Arab Affairs* 5, no. 1 (January-March 2012): 2.

43. C.J. Chivers, "How to Control Libya Missiles? Buy them up," *The New York Times*, December 22, 2011.

44. Mark Shaw and Fiona Mangan, "Illicit Trafficking and Libya's Transition: Profits and Losses," *United States Institute of Peace*, February 2014, accessed January 13, 2017.

45. C.J. Chivers, "Facebook Groups Act As Weapons Bazaars for Militias," *The New York Times*, April 6, 2016.

46. Geoff Porter, "How Realistic is Libya As an Islamic State 'Fallback'?" *Combatting Terrorism Center at West Point*, March 17, 2016, accessed February 2, 2017.

47. Faisal Irshaid, "Profile: Libya's Ansar al-Shariah," *BBC News*, June 13, 2014, accessed February 2, 2017.

48. Christopher S. Chivvis and Andrew Liepman, "North Africa's Menace: AQIM's Evolution and the U.S. Policy Response," *RAND Corporation*, January 2013, accessed February 3, 2017, 6.

49. James Risen, Mark Mazzetti, and Michael S. Schmidt, "U.S.-Approved Arms for Libya Rebels Fell Into Jihadis' Hands," *The New York Times*, December 5, 2012.

50. Letta Tayler and Brahim Elansari, "'We Feel We Are Cursed': Life under ISIS in Sirte, Libya," *Human Rights Watch*, May 2016.

51. "Libya: A Growing Hub for Criminal Economies and Terrorist Financing in the Trans-Sahara," *The Global Initiative Against Transnational Organized Crime*, May 11, 2015.

52. Ibid, 7.

53. Samuel Osborne, "Libya's Coastal Cities Are 'Making Millions from People Smuggling,'" *The Independent*, December 1, 2016.

54. "Terrorist Financing in West and Central Africa," *Financial Action Task Force*, October 2016.

55. Moutaz Ali, "Second Kidnapped Washefana Boy Murdered When Ransom Unpaid," *Libya Herald*, May 9, 2016.

56. "Kidnapped Italian Engineer Freed in Libya," *Agence France Presse*, November 13, 2014.

57. "Facebook Video Circulates Showing 260 Somali and Ethiopian Migrants and Refugees Abused, Held Against Their Will by Gangs in Libya," *International Organization for Migration*, June 15, 2017.

58. "Smuggled Futures: The Dangerous Path of a Migrant from Africa to Europe," *Global Initiative Against Transnational Organized Crime*, May 2016, accessed June 29, 2017.

59. "Some 800,000 Ready to Leave Libya for E.U. says Europol-Interpol Report," *ANSA*, May 17, 2017.

60. Letta Tayler and Brahim Elansari, "'We Feel We Are Cursed': Life under ISIS in Sirte, Libya," *Human Rights Watch*, May 2016.

61. Christina Schori Liang, "The Criminal-Jihadist: Insights into Modern Terrorist Financing," *Geneva Centre for Security Policy*, August 2016, accessed June 29, 2017.

62. "Libya Robbery: Sirte Gunmen Snatch $54 million from bank van," *BBC News*, October 28, 2013.

63. Rod Nordland and Nour Youssef, "Libya: Unified against ISIS, Fragmented After," *The New York Times*, September 3, 2016.

64. Savannah de Tessiéres, Naji Abou-Khalil, Jan Barend Coetzee, Simon Dilloway, Juan Alberto Pintos Servia, and Steven Spittaels, "Final Report of the Panel of Experts Established Pursuant to Resolution 1973 (2011)," *U.N. Security Council*, March 9, 2016, accessed February 8, 2017.

65. "ISIS Leader Abu Bakr al-Baghdadi Urges Fight to Death in Iraq, Audio Claims," *The Guardian*, November 3, 2016.

66. Sami Zaptia, "U.S. Releases Video Footage of Airstrikes against ISIS in Sirte," *Libya Herald*, August 6, 2016.

67. Caleb Weiss, "Analysis: Merger of al-Qaeda Groups Threats Security in West Africa," FDD *Long War Journal*, March 18, 2017.

68. Carole Landry, "U.N. Security Council Adds Libya Islamists to Terror List," *Agence France Presse*, November 20, 2014.

69. Moutaz Mathi, "Benghazi Militants Admit It Was Their Supply Ships Sunk in Misrata on Sunday," *Libya Herald*, October 27, 2016.

70. Catherine Philip, "Back Libyan Strongman, Says Johnson," *The Times*, February 7, 2017, accessed February 8, 2017.

71. "L.N.A. Aircraft Targets Misrata Delegation Visiting Jufra Airbase; Misrata Military Council Head among Injured," *Libya Herald*, January 3, 2017, accessed February 14, 2017.

72. "Public-Private Partnerships for Jobs in Libya Are Key for Youth and Women, Now More Than Ever," *World Bank*, May 3, 2016, accessed February 8, 2017.

73. Frederic Wehrey and Wolfram Lacher, "Libya After ISIS: How Trump Can Prevent the Next War," *Foreign Affairs*, February 22, 2017, accessed June 28, 2017.

74. Vikram Dodd, "More Arrests as Police Tell How Terrorists Wanted to Use Truck," *The Guardian*, June 10, 2017, accessed June 29, 2017.

75. Jamie Doward, Ian Cobain, Chris Stephen, and Ben Quinn, "How Manchester Bomber Salman Abedi Was Radicalized by His Links to Libya," *The Guardian*, May 28, 2017, accessed June 29, 2017.

76. Tulay Karadeniz and Aiden Lewis, "Turkey Reopens Embassy in Libya, Vows to Support Unity Efforts," *Reuters*, January 30, 2017, accessed February 8, 2017.

77. John Irish, "France Says Security Conditions Not Right to Reopen Libya Embassy," *Reuters*, June 2, 2017, accessed June 29, 2017.

78. Saleh Sarrar and Hatem Mohareb, "Libya's Crude Output Rises as Oil Fields Restart, Ports Reopen," *Bloomberg*, September 20, 2016, accessed February 8, 2017.

79. "Oil Output Passess 900,000 bpd Says NOC," *Libya Herald*, June 20, 2017, accessed June 29, 2017.

80. Matthew Reed, "Libya's Oil in ISIS's Crosshairs," *The Fuse*, January 20, 2016, accessed February 8, 2017.

81. Savannah de Tessiéres, Naji Abou-Khalil, Jan Barend Coetzee, Simon Dilloway, Juan Alberto Pintos Servia, and Steven Spittaels, "Final Report of the Panel of Experts Established Pursuant to Resolution 1973 (2011)," *U.N. Security Council*, March 9, 2016, accessed February 8, 2017.

82. Ahmed Aboulenein and Giles Elgood, "Is Egypt Bombing the Right Militants in Libya?" *Reuters*, June 1, 2017.

83. "International Religious Freedom Report 2015, Libya," *U.S. Department of State Bureau of Democracy, Human Rights, and Labor*, 2015, accessed February 6, 2017.

84. "Assistance Package of $US10 Million Dollars to Sirte, Sebha Approved," *U.N. Development Programme*, September 12, 2016.

85. Noura Hamladji, Twitter post, January 22, 2017, 1:45 p.m..

86. "Tunisia Builds Anti-Terror Barrier along Libyan Border," *BBC*, February 7, 2016.

87. Heba Saleh, "Tunisia Border Attack by Suspected ISIS Forces Kills 52," *Financial Times*, March 7, 2016.

88. Lamine Chikhi, "Algeria's Military Chief Calls Alert over Libyan Frontier," *Reuters*, March 14, 2016.

89. Madjiasra Nako, "Chad Shuts Border with Libya, Deploys Troops amid Security

Concerns," *Reuters*, January 5, 2017.

90. Morgan Winsor, "ISIS, al-Qaeda in Africa: U.S. Commander Warns of Increased Collaboration between AQIM and the Islamic State Group," *International Business Times*, February 12, 2016.

91. Spencer Ackerman and Chris Stephen, "U.S. Planes Strike ISIS Fighters in Libya 'planning attacks in Europe,'" *The Guardian*, January 19, 2017.

92. "EUBAM Libya: Mission Extended, Budget Approved," *European Council*, August 4, 2016.

93. "International Narcotics Control Strategy Report: Volume II, Money Laundering and Financial Crimes," *U.S. Department of State Bureau of International Narcotics and Law Enforcement Affairs*, March 2015, accessed February 7, 2017.

94. "Middle East and North Africa Region," last modified 2017.

95. "11th Annual Report of the Middle East and North Africa Financial Action Task Force for the Year 2015," *MENAFATF*, 2016, accessed February 7, 2017.

96. International actors and Libyans have rejected international intervention to impose order given local sensitivities about foreign interference and lack of international resources or will to make such a commitment.

Chapter Eight

Iran's Use of Shi'i Militant Proxies:

Ideological and Practical Expediency versus Uncertain Sustainability

Alex Vatanka

Introduction

The purpose of this chapter is to assess the central role of the Iranian state in mobilizing, deploying, and sustaining violent transnational groups across the Middle East, and in the Arab world in particular. As this chapter will outline, much evidence points to how key policymakers in Tehran consider the use of the armed non-state actor — or the proxy model — as an apt instrument to project Iranian power across multiple arenas in years to come. Such Iranian efforts have not gone unnoticed in the capitals of some of Iran's regional rivals such as Jerusalem, Riyadh, or Abu Dhabi. This is a worrying trend, as it elevates the risk of a cycle of retaliation or reciprocation with violent sectarianism becoming a primary instrument in the hands of regional states seeking to advance their geopolitical agendas and ambitions.

This chapter will be divided into four sections, beginning with a historical framework placing the non-state Shi'a proxy model within the context of modern Iranian history. In this opening section, the paper will also summarize and critique key findings from existing literature on the topic. Secondly, the utility of the non-state proxy model will be examined as a key component of Iran's ongoing military force restructuring. Thirdly, the ideological underpinnings of Iran's non-state militant model will be measured against Tehran's other international priorities and placed in the context of political competition inside the Iranian Shi'a Islamist regime. In this section, the ideological preferences of Ali Khamenei, the Iranian supreme leader, will receive closer attention. Fourth, and finally, the paper will summarize key findings and point to U.S. policy options that could potentially mitigate further Iranian investment in the militant Shi'a non-state proxy model.

HISTORICAL CONTEXT

The Iranian state's use of Islamist Arab proxies is almost entirely a post-1979 phenomenon. The former regime of Mohammad Reza Pahlavi very rarely adopted the use of foreign proxies, Arab or otherwise, as part of its foreign policy doctrine. When he did — best exemplified by the shah's support for Iraq's militant Kurds who stood in conflict with the central government in Baghdad through the 1960s and 1970s — he did so based on an approach that was devoid of any sectarian inclinations, even though he was the absolute monarch of the world's largest Shi'a Muslim country with plenty of resources at his disposal.

Put simply, the sectarian card was very rarely exploited by Iran before 1979. And yet, close personal and ideological ties between Arab and Iranian militants do date back to the reign of the shah. Mostafa Chamran, the first defense minister of the Islamic Republic, and many other anti-shah Iranian activists from that generation, were first exposed to the doctrines of irregular warfare among Arabs in Lebanon and Syria in the 1970s. This list of Iranians includes many that later became prominent commanders in the Islamic Revolutionary Guards Corps (IRGC) such as Yahya Safavi, IRGC's top leader from 1997 to 2007.[1]

After 1979, the founder of the Islamic Republic, Ayatollah Ruhollah Khomeini, swiftly added the sectarian layer to Tehran's quest for geopolitical influence. As a man who had lived over a decade in involuntary exile in Najaf, Iraq during the era of Saddam Hussein, Khomeini was, after seizing power in Tehran, quick to turn against his old — albeit reluctant — host by inciting Iraq's Shi'a to rise against the Sunni Baathist strongman.

As Vali Nasr noted, "Arab nationalism [as in Saddam's Iraq] holds an inherent bias against the Shi'a" and that itself presented an opportunity for Khomeinists.[2] As early as 1971, Khomeini had formulated his ideas for an "Islamic Government," which became the title of one of his influential books.[3]

In his mind, this notion of "Islamic Government" was to be transnational and Shi'a communities everywhere were principal intended audiences.

And unlike the shah, Khomeini promptly framed the struggle against Saddam in Islamist revolutionary terms with tailored messages aimed at mobilizing the Iraqi Shi'a masses. It was often far from subtle. On Apr. 19, 1980, the title of Iran's biggest paper, *Kayhan*, was "Imam [Khomeini] Invites the Iraqi Military to Rebel [against Saddam].[4] It is important to note that while he was in exile in Iraq, Khomeini's appeal to Shi'a political mobilization had already made considerable inroads.

As Patrick Cockburn observed, "For Khomeini, Islam [was] political" and he played a decisive role in the so-called Shi'a awakening among Iraqis.[5] He taunted traditionalist clerics: "You busy yourself with Islamic laws concerning menstruation and giving birth; I am leading a revolution."[6] Indeed, as Fuad Ajami put it, "The dominant Shi'a tradition [had historically] counseled distance from political power."[7] For Khomeini, however, religion and politics were inseparable. Within two years of the shah's fall, Iran's Islamist regime created the Office of Islamic Liberation Movements (OILM), placed under the auspices of the IRGC and tasked with exporting Iran's revolutionary model.[8]

Still, such radical religious interpretations or political meddling were not without direct consequences for the Iranian nation itself. From early on, this led to a debate inside the regime itself about the best way forward. Khomeini's incitement of the Iraqi Shi'a was undoubtedly a major factor in Saddam's decision to invade Iran in September of 1980. It is thus important to recognize and factor in Iranian Shi'a Islamists' historical links to their Iraqi counterparts when we set out to measure the depth of Tehran's present-day religious and political clout in post-Saddam Iraq.

It is also equally important to acknowledge that this relationship has had, and continues to have, unintended effects. For example, a few years after 1979, the more moderate voices in the Iranian regime successfully defanged the OILM. One of the key personalities in the OILM, Mehdi Hashemi, was executed in 1987 in a campaign led by the more moderate voices in the regime led by speaker of the parliament, Ayatollah Akbar Hashemi Rafsanjani.[9] Their argument was that Iran, as both a state and a regime that wanted to survive, needed to be selective in the battles it chose to wage.

By 1982, Iran had helped bring about the birth of the anti-Saddam Badr Corps in Iraq and Hezbollah in Lebanon, both comprised of Shi'a Islamist activists that embraced Khomeini's doctrine of sweeping political resistance. Both groups remain to this day the most successful Shi'a militant proxies aligned with Tehran. Throughout the 1980s, Iranian-inspired political radicalism and occasional acts of violence were witnessed in Bahrain, Kuwait, Pakistan, and Saudi Arabia.[10]

Pan-Islamist Utopia vs. Sectarian Allure

In a sense, as Emmanuel Sivan observed in 1989, the radical Shi'a militant strategy as espoused by the Islamic Republic was at the time very similar to that embraced by its Sunni counterparts, such as the Muslim Brotherhood. In both versions, the first step is to delegitimize the ruling power, followed by an armed uprising, and then a taking over of government to impose Islamist rule (shari'a) over society.[11] It was, of course, in Shi'a-majority Iran that this formula was first successfully executed following the toppling of the shah in 1979. A large and resourceful state had become the key staging ground for this revolutionary Shi'a creed. Once in power, Iran's Islamist rulers looked for ways to redefine Shi'a Islam and to export this brand to Shi'a communities beyond Iran's borders.

The Islamic Republic, as is enshrined in its constitution from 1979, ideologically committed itself to a mission of mobilizing the *mostazafeen*, so-called downtrodden Muslims, against what Tehran labeled unjust rulers. This refers to Muslims in general and did not distinguish between Shi'a and Sunnis. As Afshon Ostovar pointed out in his chapter in *Beyond Sunni and Shi'a*, critics of Iran have tended to see Iranian behavior since 1979 as "an expansive, transnational, pro-Iranian Shi'a polity." The track record, Ostovar maintains, shows something else. He claims that sectarian factors play a role in Iran's strategic calculations but "not in the single-minded, all-encompassing way that Iran's critics suggest."[12]

To make this point, Ostovar highlights moments when Tehran's actions ignored sectarian preferences. For example, during the Lebanese civil war in the early 1980s, Tehran backed Yasser Arafat's Sunni Fatah movement in its conflict with the Lebanese Shi'a movement Amal. For its political agenda at the time, Tehran prioritized Arafat's anti-Israel stance over Amal's narrow focus on Shi'a Lebanese interests. For Ostovar and many others, such examples embody the Islamic Republic's realpolitik.[13]

Though the presence of realpolitik in Iran's foreign policy behavior since 1979 is not in question, evidence of it does not negate the Islamic Republic's innate sectarian tendencies. The clearest proof is enshrined in the constitution of the Islamic Republic itself: Only a Shi'a Muslim can hold the office of supreme leader and the presidency in Iran, a rigid stipulation that Iran's Sunni minority — about ten percent of the country's population — find discriminatory.[14]

On the other hand, Tehran's outreach to the broader and less or non-Islamist-leaning Shi'a communities across the Middle East has not always been entirely successful either. In the case of the minority Shi'a Hazaras in Afghanistan, many in the beleaguered community had little choice but to accept Iranian assistance during the Afghan civil war (1989-2001) when under assault by anti-Shi'a Afghan militants. And yet, there is also a rich record of this community resisting Iranian attempts to impose its ideological preferences on them.[15]

Beyond the hardened Shi'a Islamist circles, the same lukewarm posture was evident in the largely dismissive reaction of Iraqi Shi'as to Khomeini's call for an uprising against Saddam throughout the 1980s. In Pakistan, where the state apparatus is relatively strong, Iran's initial outreach to the large Pakistani Shi'a minority in the 1980s at first created a newfound sense of militancy there. Still, Tehran pulled back from inciting on Pakistani soil when confronted with Islamabad's ire. In reference to the then potential dangers of sectarianism, President Pervez Musharraf said in 2003 that "the greatest danger to Pakistan is not external; it is internal."[16] The warning to Tehran, and other states such as Saudi Arabia that wanted to exploit sectarianism in Pakistan as part of a regional quest for power, was unmistakable.

And yet the successful inroads Tehran made on this front in the 1980s proved enduring and, as time would show, highly valuable to its geopolitical ambitions. Some of today's most powerful Iraqi Shi'a militia leaders, such as Hadi al-Ameri (Badr Corps) and Abu Mahdi al-Mohandes (Kata'ib Hezbollah), were not only early recruits and highly useful to Iran as collaborators during the Iran-Iraq War (1980-88), but they remain close allies of Tehran to this day.

By the time of Khomeini's death in 1989, an intra-regime debate in Tehran about the utility of the export of the Islamic revolution via the proxy model had led to an end to the more excessive Iranian behaviors. In comparison to the 1980s, which Iran's present-day Supreme Leader Ayatollah Ali Khamenei in his June 2017 speech touted as the "golden revolutionary age," the 1990s witnessed a retrenchment in Tehran's use of the proxy model.

This was partly due to a measure of policy reassessment in Tehran, but it was also due to a lack of opportunities; few security voids made themselves available for exploitation in the region that Tehran could seek to fill with its message of armed resistance. This lull, however, proved to be temporary. Following the U.S. invasion of Iraq in 2003 that catalyzed a sudden power vacuum in that country, Tehran hugely bolstered its use of the Arab proxy model.

IRAQI AND SYRIAN CHAOS: INCUBATORS FOR NON-STATE GROUPS

The 2003 U.S. invasion of Iraq was easily the single key moment that unleashed the phenomenon of violent non-state actors, beyond any other event before it. In other words, it was again a vacuum that others had created that paved the way for Iran and its Islamist message to be disseminated. What swiftly followed the toppling of Saddam Hussein was the rapid disintegration of Iraq along ethnic and sectarian lines. In the ensuing anarchy, competing Iraqi groups often looked to outside powers for patronage.

Among Iraq's many shades of Shi'a Islamist strands, many looked to their next-door neighbor, the Islamic Republic of Iran, for ideological sustenance and more importantly for arms and funding, as they set out to confront local rivals within post-Saddam Iraqi chaos. Tehran, fully sensitive to the fact that Saddam's fall had put the Middle East in the throes of historical change, was happy to oblige. It might have appeared as a marriage of convenience of sorts, but this was hardly a partnership of equals.

The Islamic Republic, born out of the 1979 revolution as the world's first modern-day theocracy, was the model to be emulated. With a unique revolutionary ideological agenda, often sectarian, deeply suspicious of the West and wholly antipathetic toward Israel, the ruling Islamist authorities in Tehran saw and continue to see themselves as the center of the "Axis of Resistance." Thus, for any militant non-state actor to fall under Iranian tutelage means mirroring the Islamic Republic's basic tenets.

With an expanding portfolio of experience in this field dating back to 1979, Tehran quickly expanded this model. After 2003, Iran's IRGC stepped quickly in to identify and cultivate what is in Persian referred to as the *Goro-haaye Vije*, or "special groups" — Arabs and other non-Iranians — who would become the Islamic Republic's foot soldiers. Additional proxies were created under Iranian auspices due to other regional upsets, such as the outbreak of the Syrian conflict in 2011 and the upsurge in ISIS with its capture of Mosul in June 2014. Iran decided to intervene by proxy in both countries to keep Bashar al-Assad in power in Syria and to prevent ISIS from taking Iraq's capital Baghdad. Among the most prominent groups within the two states are:

➢ Asa'ib Ahl Al-Haq (League of Righteous People): Iraq and Syria
➢ Saraya Khorassani (Khorasani Brigades): Iraq and Syria
➢ Saraya Al Zahra (Zahra's Brigades): Iraq
➢ Harakat Hezbollah Al Nujaba (The Movement of the Noble of Hezbollah): Iraq and Syria
➢ Kata'ib Imam Ali (Imam Ali Brigades): Iraq
➢ Zeynabiyoun Brigade (Pakistanis): Syria
➢ Fatemiyoun Division (Afghans)[17]: Syria

According to Nick Heras, 40 out of the estimated 67 Popular Mobilization Forces (PMF) militias in Iraq share close links with Iran's IRGC.[18] By late 2017, an estimated 50,000 PMF fighters had mobilized against ISIS within units under direct or indirect Iranian control. To put this number in perspective, the total number of PMF fighters was estimated at 110,000-122,000.[19]

In the years after 2011, Iran was instrumental in keeping Assad in power. A principal contributing factor that enabled Iran's successful military intervention in Syria was Tehran's ability to mobilize and deploy various transnational militant, and often sectarian, groups to Syria's battlefields. In that sense, at its core, Tehran's military intervention in the Syrian war was very similar to the Iranian modus operandi developed in Iraq in the 2000s, where Iran bolstered local non-state militant actors as its foot soldiers in the broader fight for influence. The major departure in Syria, when compared to the situation in Iraq, was the need for Iran to bring in droves of non-locals — such as Iraqis, Afghans, Pakistanis, and Hezbollah from Lebanon — to fight under Iranian leadership to keep the Assad regime from collapse.

This external focus was necessary due only to demographic realities — Syria's substantial Sunni majority and a general shortage of available Syrians willing to be recruited. Tehran did not engage in any large-scale recruitment of Iranians to be dispatched to Syria. The few thousand Iranians sent to Syria, ostensibly as military advisors, were overwhelmingly drawn from the ranks of the volunteer IRGC and not the conscripted Iranian army (Artesh).

Tehran's reluctance to commit manpower to the Syrian campaign has also been evident in casualty figures. According to available data for the January 2012-January 2018 period, more Lebanese (1,213) and Afghans (841) died in Syria than Iranians (535), despite the fact that Iran has the largest population of those three countries.[20]

Such realities suggest that despite Iran's rhetoric about its Syrian intervention being a defensive act necessary to protect national security interests, the authorities in Tehran evidently do not believe mainstream Iranian public opinion shares this view.

Accordingly, Tehran's mobilization effort in Syria has relied heavily on financial and other material incentives, plus the injection of a considerable dose of sectarian messaging to successfully recruit non-Syrians (and non-Iranians) for the pro-Assad military campaign. Afghans, Iraqis, and Pakistanis top the list among recruits to fill the ranks of pro-Iran militias in Syria. This has been a new phase in the evolution of Tehran's war-through-proxy approach and arguably the pinnacle of the internationalization of the Iranian proxy model.

Meanwhile, regional developments following the popular Arab revolts that began in 2011 played a decisive role in pushing the Islamic Republic down the path of more pronounced sectarian biases. One principal byproduct of these insurrections in mostly Sunni-majority Arab states was the rise of violent anti-Shi'a groups. While not necessarily of Iran's making, Tehran's actions supporting the Alawi-based Assad regime and other Arab Shi'a communities have played a significant role in fueling this phenomenon of Sunni extremism and militancy.

In 2014, when ISIS erupted throughout Iraq and Syria and threatened core Shi'a population centers in Iraq, the Iraqi Shi'a religious leadership led by Ayatollah Ali Sistani quickly sought to mobilize local Shi'a against ISIS's genocidal sectarian agenda. In this ideological but also considerable logistical effort, Iran and its Iraqi allies were fully on board to the point of becoming critical to the success of what became Iraq's PMF against ISIS. As Abu Mahdi al-Mohandis, the top de facto operational commander of the PMF, put it, without Ayatollah's Ali Sistani's *fatwa* [religious decree], the PMF would have never been born, and without Iranian technical support, it could have never been sustained.[21]

It was, however, also a moment when Iran became wholly associated with the Shi'a Islamist cause as never before. Put simply, the Islamic Republic's relationship with non-Iranian Shi'a militant Islamists has so far experienced three phases.

The first phase began in 1979 when the fledgling Islamic Republic prioritized Shi'a Islamist groups for two main reasons: Existing personal bonds and theological proximity — as evidenced by linkages between Iranian Islamists and Twelver Shi'a counterparts in Iraq and Lebanon — and opportunities to become a benefactor to groups such as the Badr Corps and Hezbollah, the most lasting groups set up in this timeframe.

What is also noticeable in this first phase is the focus on the U.S. and Israel as primary external ideological targets. At a minimum, this focus on the non-Muslim "other" meant sectarian differences with Sunnis were made secondary. In fact, the focus on non-Muslim adversaries became a basis for collaboration with Sunni groups such as Hamas. Iran cultivated its ties to Hamas from the early 1990s onward, in which the anti-Israel message was the central driving force.[22]

In the second phase, the U.S. invasion of Iraq in 2003 provided the Iranians with the opportunity to double down on this tested formula of mobilizing proxies. In this second phase, which played itself out mostly in the context of an internal Iraqi competition for power, Tehran began its progression toward becoming more of a protector of the Shi'a and less the pan-Islamic power that the 1979 revolution had stipulated it to be.

In this Iraqi theater, the Iranians backed Iraqi Shi'a militias that were engaged in a conflict with local Sunni Iraqis. The latter were often ideologically and financially backed by Iran's Sunni rivals such as Qatar, Turkey, Saudi Arabia, and the United Arab Emirates.

In the third phase, the role of sectarianism as a mobilizer was elevated and Sunni states to some extent replaced the U.S. and Israel as the principal external adversaries of Iran and its proxies. In this phase, the same modus operandi and largely the same calculations of maintaining maximum political influence at both the local and regional levels propelled Iran into replicating the Iraqi experience in the Syrian theater. Unlike in Iraq, which is the cradle of Shi'a

Islam,[23] religious justification for intervening in Syria — a country with only a tiny Shi'a population — was a steep hill to climb for Tehran.

Still, thanks to a quick mobilization campaign, the Iranian authorities swiftly turned the fate of a number of religious sites in Syria that some Shi'a revere — such as the Sayyidah Zaynab Mosque located in outer Damascus — into red lines that could not fall victim to ISIS's deadly anti-Shi'a worldview. Nonetheless, to paint the military campaign in support of the secular Baathist Assad regime as a religious obligation remained problematic for Tehran within its own population.

In fact, despite the Western press' tendency to classify the Assad regime as "Shi'a" and therefore naturally aligned with Iran, there is no strong sectarian connection between Iran's Twelver Shi'a Islam and Assad's Alawite sect, an offshoot of Shi'a Islam. In other words, the Iranian military intervention in Syria was more about Tehran's geopolitical agenda, driven by a fear of Gulf Arab encroachment in the Levant.

To a significantly lesser extent, this competition with the Arab States of the Persian Gulf has also unfolded in Yemen. As with Syria's Alawites, the Houthi rebels in Yemen quickly found a champion in Iran. Not because of close religious ties between Iran and the Houthis — who are Zayidi Muslims, a sect theologically closer to mainstream Sunni Islam than the Twelver Shi'a creed found in Iran — but because of shared common adversaries in the shape of Saudi Arabia, the United Arab Emirates, and the United States.[24]

The Yemeni civil war is a prime example of Islamists in Tehran opportunistically intervening when an occasion presents itself. As Joost Hiltermann of the International Crisis Group put it in 2004, "The Iranians are just brilliant. They play no [decisive] role whatsoever [in Yemen], but they get all the credit, and so they are capitalizing on it."[25] Iran's relations with the Houthis have since sharply increased, but overwhelmingly due to the onset of the Yemeni civil war in 2015 and the search of the Houthis for an outside benefactor. It is very doubtful that Iran would have been able to make inroads into Yemen in the same fashion had there been no Yemeni civil war.

As in the case of its relations with the Houthis, despite the awkward religious rationale for its military intervention in Syria, there is presently little reason to assume that Iran's political-military operational blueprint will cease to be relevant once the wars in Iraq and Syria come to a de facto end. A decade and a half after the U.S. invasion of Iraq, Iran's adaptation of the "militant proxy model" is considered by many in Tehran and beyond as a successful strategy worthy of further investment. Relevant officials in Iran never shy away from regularly reminding everyone that this non-state proxy model is here to stay.

From its own perspective, Iran would likely prefer for the Sunni-Shi'a divide to be downgraded in regional importance. That would allow the Islamic

Republic to once again present itself as the champion of the entire Islamic world. It is also amply clear that Tehran would prefer to reinstate the question of the future of Palestine into its main ideological mission, if not its casus belli, potentially as a way to bridge the sectarian divide.

THE PROXY MODEL IN IRAN'S MILITARY PLANNING

The non-state militant proxies that Iran recruited, indoctrinated, and helped arm have often had little option but to look to Iran for support. This is leverage that Supreme Leader Ayatollah Ali Khamenei and other hardliners in Tehran consider vindication of their support for the Arab proxy model.

General Qassem Soleimani, the head of the IRGC's expeditionary arm, the Quds Force, who is the public mastermind of the Iranian model, declared publicly on Nov. 21, 2017, that ISIS had been defeated in Syria. In his public response and in a clear signal of Tehran's future intentions, Supreme Leader Khamenei urged Soleimani to "maintain readiness for meeting future regional challenges."[26] Two days later, the head of the IRGC, General Mohammad Ali Jafari, explicitly reminded Assad that he was "indebted" to the "people's militias" and called on Assad to "institutionalize [the militias] so they will remain relevant in the face of future threats."[27]

It goes without saying that for Jafari, it is up to Tehran to determine the identity of such future threats, and it is a safe bet that the group's usual targets — notably the U.S., Israel, and the Saudis — will be on that list. Such a transition from armed militia to a formidable state-within-the-state reflects, in essence, the historical evolution of the IRGC itself. It began as a militia in 1979 and is today one of the three pillars of power in Tehran (the others being the Office of the Supreme Leader and the presidency). The IRGC is now envisaging that the non-Iranian proxies it supports in Iraq and Syria should undergo the same process.

The promotion of the proxy model combined with Tehran's eagerness to make sure armed victories are translated into political capital reflects Iran's own military limitations. While the Islamic Republic likes to present itself as a martyrdom-seeking cause and therefore an inherently anti-status quo power, in reality, Iran's conventional military strategy has mostly been cautious. Tehran has consistently been careful about the number of troops it has been willing to deploy to Syria and to this day, it does not dispatch conscripts to either Iraq or Syria. Doing so would risk generating awkward political questions within the Iranian public about the direction of the country.

However, as IRGC generals are keen to repeat, the shifting regional security environment requires Iran's military strategy to adapt and reinvent itself. In Tehran, this is increasingly referred to as "forward defense" and the idea that Iran should battle its opponents beyond its borders in order to prevent conflict from taking place on Iranian soil. When ISIS carried out its first attacks in Tehran in June 2017, the proponents of "forward defense" wasted no time to argue that had Iran not militarily intervened in Syria and Iraq, Iran would have had to confront a far greater ISIS threat inside its borders.[28]

The plan behind "forward defense" necessitates substantial readjustments, including the conversion of some of the existing regular military units. It is in the ranks of the conscripted Artesh where Iran has the most potential for a transformation.

The Artesh is in terms of size (about 350,000) approximately three times larger than the IRGC (about 120,000). Artesh ground force units are mostly organized in heavily armored infantry and mechanized units. These are a distinct legacy of defense planning from the days of the former pro-U.S. shah when America had helped Iran plan for major conventional ground battles against the likes of the Soviet Union and Saddam Hussein's Iraq.

Today, there is virtually no prospect for such ground-based military battles between Iran and its closest adversaries. As is currently evident, Iran's two most intense regional rivalries with Saudi Arabia and Israel are both happening overwhelmingly via proxy actions and not through direct conventional military confrontation.

Accordingly, some military planners in Tehran appear to consider the Artesh's present capabilities as ill fitting and inappropriate for Iran's foreign policy ambitions in the region in places like Syria. By converting some Artesh manpower for so-called "forward operations," the battle-hardened IRGC military units could be made more readily available for domestic security operations should circumstances require it. For example, another domestic opposition movement similar to Iran's Green Movement of 2009 would require a determined suppression.

In other words, if Iran opts for a major military makeover, it will be in the realm of the Artesh where it will find space for change and reform. Potentially in order to expedite this process, Khamenei appointed a former IRGC commander, Kiumars Heydari, as the new head of the Artesh Ground Forces in November 2016.

Again, Iran's latest declarations of a new "forward-defense" strategy are in fact only an extension of a process that has been in motion for many years. The main difference today is that Iran can now launch asymmetric efforts — mostly via the use of Arab proxies — on a scale unseen before, thanks to power vacuums found in so many conflict arenas in the broader Middle East. Iranian operations in Iraq and Syria since 2011 and 2014, respectively, are the best examples of this new reality.

In such a context, and given Tehran's ongoing ideological commitments, the use of the Arab proxy model plays an unquestionably important role.

Whether the IRGC can continue to succeed in such efforts depends largely on two factors: The willingness of Arab groups to continue to be subservient to the IRGC (Iranian) agenda, and the tolerance level of the Iranian public to see the IRGC continue its military adventurism in the region despite the risks and costs it entails.

In the meantime, the IRGC will continue to retain and perhaps even replicate more proxy groups in Iraq, Syria, and elsewhere whenever circumstances call and allow for it. There can be no doubt that Tehran will continue to look for ways to break its image as a "Shi'a power," which inherently limits its ability to maneuver; it is doing so by maintaining ties to Sunni organizations such as Hamas. However, Tehran's reliance on Shi'a militant groups is where it has found the most return on its investment.

To measure the commitment of hardliners inside the Iranian regime to this model of operation, one only has to listen to their public pledges. "The Islamic revolution in Iran [of 1979] is different from the French or the Russian revolutions as it is a religious and divine revolution … and its ultimate architect is God." This was a statement made by Ali Saeedi, Ayatollah Khamenei's personal representative at the IRGC. Saeedi uttered these words while speaking to the uniformed IRGC leadership, the more distinguishable mortal architects of Tehran's regional plans. These are the same men who today spearhead Iran's military interventions in Syria, Iraq, and elsewhere in the Middle East.

IDEOLOGY VS. INTERNATIONAL PRESSURES AND DOMESTIC POLITICAL REALITIES

Not everyone in Tehran, however, is as convinced as Khamenei, Soleimani, and other hardliners about the long-term utility of the proxy model as a sustainable way to project Iranian power. Social and political unrest in Iran erupted on Dec. 28, 2017, where the anger of the protesters was focused upon, among other things, the ruling elite in Tehran's prioritization of foreign ideological pursuits over the everyday needs of the Iranian population. In the aftermath of this event, the likelihood of the Iranian state having to reassess the cost of its proxy model has become stronger. Nor should rising international concerns be underestimated. President Trump's decision on May 8, 2018, to pull out of the 2015 nuclear agreement with Iran was strongly influenced by — among other things — Iran's unwillingness to curb its practice of fermenting Shi'a militancy in the Middle East. European countries such as France, Britain, and Germany share this American concern, which can only mean it will remain a topic of contention in the foreseeable future.

Fundamentally, this is a question about the political future of the Islamic Republic and whether it will remain dedicated to being a revolutionary Shi'a Islamist model. When Iran's relatively moderate President Hassan Rouhani was re-elected in a landslide on May 19, 2017, many in the West hoped it was an event that might herald a new era in Tehran's posture toward the outside world. Following Tehran's successful signing of a nuclear deal with world powers in 2015, Rouhani's continued statements in support of policies aimed at bringing about further détente were interpreted in the West as signifying a moment of Iranian introspection.

In this reading of possible Iranian transformation, Tehran might have expanded its capacity to compromise on non-nuclear issues such as its controversial support for militant Arab proxies in various theaters in the Middle East. In Iran's labyrinthine political setup, however, the highest elected office is not the pinnacle of power. That role belongs to the unelected supreme leader, Ayatollah Khamenei, and he acted swiftly to counter such expectations.

In his capacity as the voice that frames the overall trajectory of Iranian foreign policy, Khamenei was quick to move against unwarranted notions that Rouhani's re-election was somehow a harbinger of a new dawn. In a speech on June 4, 2017, Khamenei stressed the need for policy continuity and re-emphasized pillars of the Islamic Republic's foreign policy creed.[29]

In Khamenei's worldview, Tehran's ideological and financial investments in its Arab proxies cannot be separated from its long-standing conflict with the U.S. As he put it, compromising with America will not be possible because Washington's intrinsic objective is the overthrow of the Iranian political system. Instead, Khamenei urged, Tehran should remain a "revolutionary" state and challenge American supremacy in the Middle East and beyond.[30]

Iran's continued support for Arab proxies must be seen in this context. The Islamic Republic does not see its relations with smaller subordinate militant groups as an end in and of itself. Rather, they are a mechanism to advance Tehran's broader agenda in a zero-sum competition where Tehran faces multiple neighbors that are in the American orbit and seen as inherently hostile to Iran.

In the same spirit, Khamenei pointed to the 1980s as a good "revolutionary" decade. This was the period when Iran's then newly ascendant Shi'a Islamist leaders were at their peak ideological fervor and hell-bent on spreading the message of Iran's 1979 revolution that had created the modern world's first theocratic system.

Khamenei's speech was therefore not just a reminder to Rouhani and his supporters about the finite mandate they had reaped from the May 2017 election. With an eye on his legacy, it was also arguably a call to return to the basic principles of the revolution and an attempt by the 78-year-old Iranian supreme leader to map out a vision for the future. By ostensibly making himself into the ultimate arbiter, Khamenei stated that to be "revolutionary" is to be for "original Islam" versus so-called "American Islam." In his words, this perceived "American Islam" has two branches: "Reactionary Islam" and "secular Islam."[31]

In Khamenei's lexicon, the two labels are interchangeably applied to both his domestic opponents but also to many of Iran's neighboring states that have taken a different approach to the practice of Islam. No doubt, the energy-rich Arab States of the Persian Gulf that are aligned with the United States are considered by Khamenei to be deluded at best or complicit at worst in American policies aimed at subduing the Islamic world.

In that sense, Khamenei's full support for Iran's use of Arab proxies in battling it out for influence in conflict zones such as Syria against the U.S. and U.S.-allied states such as Saudi Arabia is a logical extension of his judgment and his preferred prescription for an Iranian triumph.

In his speech on Jun. 4, 2017, Khamenei said: "What we are saying is that America is the enemy of the [Iranian] Revolution. It is in the nature of global imperialism to show enmity towards a system such as the Islamic Republic. Their interests are 180 degrees different from [Iran's]. Global imperialism is after showing treachery, waging wars, creating and organizing terrorist groups, suppressing freedom-seeking groups, and exerting pressure over the oppressed — such as the oppressed in Palestine and countries like Palestine. This is in the nature of global imperialism."

One could explain away that speech as nothing but Khamenei pandering to his hardline domestic support base. The speech was given on the anniversary of the death of Ayatollah Ruhollah Khomeini, the founder of the Islamic Republic. It can also perhaps be dismissed as tokenism by a man who had just approved a historic nuclear compromise deal with the arch-enemy, the U.S. If, however, the speech is to be interpreted in its fullest possible meaning, Khamenei seemingly foresees Iran to be in an open-ended conflict with the United States.

The truth is probably somewhere between the two interpretations. Khamenei, a man who as the supreme leader since 1989 has carefully avoided any direct confrontation with the U.S., speaks loudly but appears unwilling or unable to ultimately carry a big stick vis-à-vis his American foe. And yet, his enunciations on the need to vie for power against the U.S. in the Islamic world are hardly empty words.

THE PROXY MODEL IN CONTEXT OF KHAMENEI'S FEARS ABOUT THE U.S.

In his first major post-Arab Spring speech on Feb. 21, 2011, Khamenei argued that two simple solutions are needed to solve the problems that trouble the Islamic world. According to Khamenei, "unity among Muslim [states]" and "the weakening of America" are the two necessary steps that all Muslims must take to secure a "bright" future for the *umma*, or the worldwide Muslim nation.

It is easy to dismiss such rhetoric as wishful thinking masquerading as strategy. A closer examination, however, shows that broader Iranian strategizing and investment is underway to at least become the indisputable vanguard of the global Shi'a community, with an appropriate capacity to engage in armed campaigns. In April 2018, following Israeli missile strikes against Iranian targets in Syria, and after American pronouncements that Iran should leave Syria and other Arab countries where it has a presence, Khamenei again focused on the role of the U.S. in the Middle East. Viewing the U.S. as the enabler of Israel, Khamenei said: "The one who must leave is the U.S., not the Islamic Republic. We are from this region: The Persian Gulf is our home; West Asia is our home."[32]

The militia model should, therefore, be viewed as an increasingly integral part of this broader Iranian blueprint that has been in use since 1979. There are different parts to this design, including an ostensibly theological campaign that amounts to ideological indoctrination. For example, in 2009, on the orders of Ayatollah Khamenei, the al-Mustapha International University was launched in the holy city of Qom. A brainchild of Khamenei, the university has two core objectives: To focus on "Islamic" propagation (as per the official ideology of the regime), and to train non-Iranians to become Shi'a clerics. The university is the result of the consolidation of a number of existing initiatives that had since 1979 engaged in educating non-Iranians to become Shi'a clerics.

However, as Khamenei matured politically and as older, senior ayatollahs died (who had historically been independent of the state), he set out to streamline, modernize, and impose central control over the activities of the seminaries in Qom and elsewhere in the country in cities such as Mashhad and Esfahan. This was both extremely sensitive — as many existing ayatollahs resented relinquishing their financial and theological independence to the Office of the Supreme Leader — but also of paramount importance to Khamenei's vision to cultivate a modern bureaucratic clerical class that could act as the political commissary of the regime. Today, al-Mustapha University has many dozens of seminaries and religious centers in Iran and outside of the country. It is perhaps not a surprise, therefore, that many non-Iranians who joined pro-Iran militias in Iraq and Syria reportedly came from the ranks of the student population from this same university system.[33]

Meanwhile, the man Khamenei appointed to head the university, Ali-Reza Arafi, shares Khamenei's key concerns: To combat anti-Shi'a militant Sunni Islam; to combat traditional [non-revolutionary] Shi'a Islam; and to take the fight to the U.S. and its Arab allies such as Saudi Arabia. The potential scope for such efforts should not be underestimated. Based on Arafi's statements, there are some 40,000 non-Iranian seminarians studying in Iran today, and a further 80,000 have graduated from al-Mustapha University in recent years. His political philosophy, as he put it, is that "Seminaries [in Iran] need to be from the people, in solidarity with the downtrodden, be political [Islamist], revolutionary, and international [in approach]."[34] This clearly amounts to the mindset of an ideologue and one who Khamenei handpicked. Meanwhile, even Iran's efforts to spread the religious Shi'a message have been bothersome for a number of Arab States. In 2009, Morocco broke diplomatic ties over alleged Iranian conversion attempts in the country. The issue has also been a bone of contention in Tehran's relations with Sudan, Comoros, and Egypt.

In other words, to fully understand Iran's present-day ideological and financial investment in the militant proxy model, one has to push deeper into the larger world outlook of the elite in the Islamic Republic, particularly of the hardline faction around Khamenei. Meanwhile, from the perspective of IRGC military planners, the use of foreign proxies is both relatively inexpensive but also provides considerable scope for deniability for their often controversial actions both in Iran and outside.

Still, there are potential drawbacks. There is always an inherent danger that proxy groups may act unilaterally or even against Tehran's wishes. The cases of Hezbollah's 2006 war with Israel (which Iran had initially opposed) or the decision by Hamas in 2011 to abandon Bashar al-Assad, are two good examples of Tehran being outmaneuvered by its proxy allies. While the Iranian state has demonstrated strategic patience in many of their regional military operations, there is always a danger of overreach by undertaking too much too fast, amid the multiple fronts that have opened up in the Middle East since 2011.

The winding down of the conflict in Iraq also raises difficult questions for the Iranian leadership. What, for example, will Iran-backed proxies do after their action in Iraq is concluded? What would Tehran like to see become of them? Among the local recruits, will they become part of a state-within-a-state, as is the case with Hezbollah in Lebanon? Among non-local recruits, is it plausible for Afghans, Pakistanis, and other non-locals under Iranian command in Syria to become a lasting feature in these countries? Alternatively, perhaps they can move back to native countries to continue the fight. In the case of Shi'a Afghan militias, there is already much talk in Iran about the need for them to transfer from Syria to Afghanistan to contain the rise of ISIS in that country. If not, how else can Iran politically preserve its military victories? Finally, pro-Iranian militant proxies are not monolithic and it is likely that Tehran may encounter unforeseen challenges to its control them over them in the longer term.

Despite such potential drawbacks, the Iranians are for now committed to this model of operation. Tehran's cultivation of Arab proxies is also a way of creating political leverage inside state institutions in targeted countries such as Iraq and Syria. These proxies have a proven record to eventually become mouthpieces for Iran's regional agenda and the implications of such political linkages will last much longer than Iran's present-day military agenda. The evolutionary path of Hezbollah in Lebanon is a prime example. Another recent trend is Tehran's forceful lobbying in Baghdad for Iraqi militias to be able to enter the formal legislative politics of the country.[35]

In short, there is no doubt that Iran has been, in the post-Arab Spring period, highly successful in internationalizing its "Axis of Resistance," its purported front against the U.S. and its regional allies in the Middle East. In the foreseeable future, as the region remains in flux, these armed militias will remain some of the most formidable and organized political-military entities to be reckoned with.

Policy Takeaways

As the above discussion about the Iranian policy-process makes clear, the creation of the militant proxy model has been long in the making and has been shaped as much by the Islamic Republic's ideological prerogatives as regional developments outside of Iran's control. As a trend, therefore, the model can hardly be said to be irreversible. It is evident that broader Iranian public opinion is disillusioned by the regime's pursuit of foreign policy adventurism under the guise of securing national interests. Meanwhile, Washington's May 2018 decision to pull out of the nuclear agreement with Iran, citing among its reasons Tehran's continued support for militants in the Middle East, can revive painful international economic isolation that Tehran has desperately sought to put behind it. Should the Iranian nation have to pay a greater price for Tehran's controversial regional interventions — for example, in the shape of more international pressure that in turn squeezes the already beleaguered economy and therefore the average Iranian — there is a real possibility for severe popular backlash inside Iran.

Such a scenario is bound to shape the calculations of Khamenei and the IRGC, the regime's armed custodian that has spearheaded the physical implementation of the proxy model across the Middle East. After all, as the Islamic Republic's ebbs and flows in commitment to exporting its ideology make clear, the utility of the proxy model is only advantageous to Iran while its benefits outweigh the costs. In order to roll back or weaken Tehran's appetite to deploy its proxy model going forward, it is imperative that a more systematic effort is put into probing the cost of maintaining the long list of proxies that are today linked to Tehran. On the home front, further information and publicity in this context will not favor the IRGC, which always prefers to downplay its operational costs. One of the notable causes of the December 2017 mass protests in Iran was the Rouhani government's intentional release of financial data showing the cost of maintaining various religious and ideological institutions.[36]

For the West, the United States in particular, and Iran's regional rivals, a number of key factors are critical to take into account as future policy toward Iran is devised. First, the Iranian nation as a whole is highly dubious about the Islamic Republic's costly commitment to its ideological mission to be the self-appointed vanguard of Shi'as in the world. In particular, Tehran's drive to become a dominant actor in the Arab world rests on fragile political and economic rationale. As Mahmoud Sariolghalam, a former foreign policy advisor to Rouhani, put it at the height of the power of ISIS, "for some [in Tehran] developments in Iraq are the most significant national security issue for Iran."[37]

The remark was intended to show the distance between the agenda of the ruling class in Tehran and the people of the country. The economic rationale is even less clear: Since 1979, Iran's key Arab partners — ranging from Lebanon's Hezbollah to Hamas to the Assad regime in Syria — have cost Iran countless of billions of dollars in financial support. It is questionable if such financial drain can be sustainable. With mounting problems in various fields on the home front, the average Iranian longs for policy re-prioritization in favor of tackling domestic challenges.

This, of course, does not mean that Iran does not have genuine defensive needs. Any Iranian government irrespective of its ideological makeup would have needed to prepare to stop the spread of ISIS given its genocidal anti-Shi'a agenda. Where the international community needs to push back is on the question of Tehran's methods to deal with threats to its national security. Above all, it is important to demonstrate to Tehran and the Iranian people that the Islamic Republic's ideology and tactics have often fueled extremism and violence in the region. Iran should not be prevented from sitting at the regional table as part of any political process to find solutions to the array of security challenges inflicting the Middle East, as long as it is prepared to act as a nation-state with defined interests and not in pursuit of an open-ended ideological agenda.

Finally, Iran's Sunni Arab neighbors, in particular Saudi Arabia and the United Arab Emirates, have to continue to appeal to non-Islamist Shi'a Arabs. The policy of treating all Shi'a, regardless of their political persuasions, as

Iranian proxies badly backfired and forced many from Arab Shi'a communities into Tehran's arms. Events since 1979 show elevated sectarianism in the Middle East makes Tehran's Islamist message — and hence its ability to form Arab surrogates and sustain its proxy model — far more alluring than would otherwise be the case.

ENDNOTES

1. Afshon Ostovar, "Vanguard of the Imam: Religion, Politics, and Iran's Revolutionary Guards," p.27.

2. Vali Nasr, *The Shi'a Revival*, W.W. Norton and Company, 2007, p. 92.

3. Vali Nasr, *The Shi'a Revival*, W.W. Norton and Company, 2007, p. 125.

4. Radio Zamaneh, "Why is Khomeini guilty in the making of the Iran-Iraq War," September 26, 2014 .

5. Patrick Cockburn and Scribner, "Muqtada Al Sadr: The Shi'a revival and the struggle for Iraq," p.38-39, New York, 2008.

6. Ibid.

7. Fuad Ajami, "The Vanished Imam," p.31, Cornell University Press, 1986.

8. Ed. John Horgan & Kurt Braddock, "Terrorism Studies: A Reader," p.158

9. John Kifner, "Aide to Khomeini Heir Apparent is Executed in Tehran," September 29, 1987, *New York Times*.

10. Some good existing scholarly studies on this topic include: "Iran's Security Policy in the Post-Revolutionary Era" (D. Byman, S. Chubin, and A. Ehteshami — 2001, RAND); "Militancy and Political Violence in Shi'ism" (A. Moghadam, 2012, Routledge).

11. Emmanuel Sivan, "Sunni Radicalism in the Middle East and the Iranian Revolution," pp.1-30, *International Journal of Middle East Studies*, Vol.21, No.1, Feb. 1989.

12. Afshon Ostovar, "Vanguard of the Imam: Religion, Politics, and Iran's Revolutionary Guards," p.113-115, Oxford University Press, 2016.

13. Ibid.

14. "Iran: Ethnic and Religious Minorities" (Congressional Research Report: November 25, 2008). The Iranian constitution stipulates that "The official religion of Iran is Islam and the Twelver Ja'fari school [in usual al-Din and fiqh], and this principle will remain eternally immutable." See "The Constitution of the Islamic Republic."

15. See for example Hafizullah Emadi's "Exporting Iran's Revolution: The Radicalization of the Shi'a Movement in Afghanistan," *Middle Eastern Studies*, Vo. 31. No. 1. 1995.

16. I.B. Tauris, "Iran and Pakistan: Security, Diplomacy and American Influence," p.239, London, 2015.

17. For an extensive background see: https://bit.ly/2KwPNaY (Tasnim News is a media outlet believed to be under the control of the IRGC).

18. Nick Heras, "Iraq's Fifth Column: Iran's Proxy Network."

19. Ibid.

20. Ali Alfoneh "Tehran's Shi'a Legions," January 30, 2018.

21. Al-Kawthar, "The role of Qassem Soleimani in the fight against Daesh according to Abu Mohandis," June 27, 2017.

22. The Islamic Republic has always publicly embraced Hamas but it denies being the ideological godfather of the organization, which it correctly presents as an offshoot of the Muslim Brotherhood. For example, see Elahe Rostami-Povey's "Iran's Influence: A religious-political state and Society in its region," London, 2013.

23. For a comprehensive account on how and why Iranian Shi'a Islamists in the 1970s moved to accept Alawites as "Shi'a" see Jubin Goodarziand I.B. Tauris' "Syria and Iran: Diplomatic Alliance and Power Politics in the Middle East," London, 2009.

24. Joost Hilterman and April L. Alley, "The Houthis are not Hezbollah," *Foreign Policy*, February 27, 2017.

25. Alex Vatanka, "Iran's Yemen Play," *Foreign Affairs*, March 4, 2015.

26. Qassem Soleimani's message to Supreme Leader: "I announce the end of Daesh," IRINN, November 21, 2017.

27. Tasnism News, Head of IRGC: "Iran provides Yemen with relief," November 23, 2017.

28. For closer look at the concept of "forward defense" see "Iran's Priorities in a Turbulent Middle East," *International Crisis Group*, April 12, 2018.

29. Speech by Ayatollah Khamenei: "Officials Should Not Set Themselves the Goal of Satisfying Arrogant Powers, They Should Satisfy the People," June 4, 2017.

30. Ibid.

31. Ayatollah Khamenei's views on "American Islam" are wide-ranging but center only on one key gripe: That some Muslim states have opted to have good relations with the United States.

Even worse, some Muslim states have de facto accepted the right of the State of Israel to exist.

32. *Sputnik International*, "If you hit, you will be hit back," May 5, 2018.

33. *BBC Persian*, "Afghan and Pakistani Shi'a part of the Iranian deployment to Syria," April 23, 2015.

34. Young Journalist Club, "Seminaries need to be from the people, revolutionary and international," September 23, 2017

35. *Foreign Policy*, "Iraq's Militias Set Their Sights on Political Power," January 30, 2018.

36. *Radio Farda*, "Clergy Secures Millions of Dollars in Iran Budget Bill," December 15, 2017.

37. *ISNA*, "Iran's biggest problems," October 1, 2014.

CHAPTER NINE

HEZBOLLAH'S EVOLUTION:

FROM LEBANESE MILITIA TO REGIONAL PLAYER

NICHOLAS BLANFORD

DRIVERS, DYNAMICS, AND IMPACTS

EXTERNAL INFLUENCES

Hezbollah's primary external patron is the Islamic Republic of Iran. The Islamic Revolution in Iran in 1979, and Israel's invasion of Lebanon three years later, paved the way for collaboration between Tehran and Lebanese Shi'a activists who followed the teachings of Ayatollah Ruhollah Khomeini. The Islamic Revolutionary Guard Corps (I.R.G.C.) deployed to Lebanon and helped build an anti-Israel resistance movement that became Hezbollah. Iran provides financing and weapons to Hezbollah as well as strategic guidance while often leaving tactical implementation to its Lebanese ally.

A second external influence on Hezbollah is Syria, although the dynamics of that relationship have changed significantly in the past 17 years. Hafez al-Assad, the former president of Syria, viewed Hezbollah as little more than a useful means to pressure Israel in south Lebanon during the on-off Middle East peace negotiations in the 1990s. Bashar al-Assad, who succeeded his father in July 2000, had a warmer relationship with Hezbollah, allowing the party to gain more influence in Lebanon. Syria also for the first time became an important source of armaments for Hezbollah. Hezbollah's military intervention in Syria from 2012 to assist the Assad regime against the armed opposition has placed the Lebanese party on a partnership footing with Damascus, a significant shift from the subordinate role it played under the rule of Hafez al-Assad.

IDEOLOGY

Hezbollah is a militant jihadist Islamist organization and follows three fundamental visions. The first is the establishment of an Islamic state in Lebanon, as called for in Hezbollah's "Open Letter" manifesto released in February 1985. However, Hezbollah's leaders have acknowledged that Lebanon's pluralistic nature weighs against this occurring in the near future and they have consistently said the party will not impose such a system of governance on the country. The second is the pursuit of jihad. This includes the "greater jihad," which is the daily spiritual struggle within the carnal soul to overcome the vices and temptations of the human condition to achieve divine knowledge, spiritual harmony, and love. Adhering to the "greater jihad" then paves the way for pursuing the "lesser jihad," which is split into "offensive" and "defensive" jihads. The former permits Muslims to invade other countries and subjugate their citizens with the justification that Islam is the one true religion. "Defensive jihad," as the name suggests, obliges Muslims to defend their homeland and people from external aggression. Hezbollah's resistance campaign in the 1980s and 1990s against the Israeli occupation of south Lebanon and its current posture toward the Jewish state are justified under the rubric of "defensive jihad." The third basic vision is submission to the *wilayat al-faqih*, or rule of the jurisprudent, a model of governance for an Islamic state that was articulated by Khomeini. In Shi'ism, senior clerics, known as *marjaa e-taqleed*, or sources of guidance and imitation, advise Muslims on how to accurately follow Islamic teachings, but they eschew roles in politics and governance. The concept of the *wilayat al-faqih*, however, maintains that a chosen ultimate source of religious learning should be responsible not only for administering Islamic behavior, but also for defining the general politics of a nation.

According to Khomeini, "If you were able to understand the essence of religion in this Islamic culture of ours, you would clearly see no distinction between religious and political leadership and moreover it would become apparent that political strife is an integral part of religious duty. Leading such political strife and steering it in the right direction is thus an element of a religious leader's functional responsibilities."[1]

Although the *wali al-faqih*, currently embodied by Ayatollah Ali Khameini, is the supreme leader of Iran, his authority extends to all Muslims that adhere to the *wilayat al-faqih*, which includes Hezbollah. For Hezbollah, the *wali al-faqih* is the party's overseer whose knowledge of Islam is unsurpassed and whose rulings must be obeyed. In practical terms, the *wali al-faqih* will set the strategy (e.g. resisting Israel's occupation of south Lebanon) while leaving Hezbollah to determine the tactics to achieve the strategic goal.

FINANCING

Iran is the principle external financial backer of Hezbollah, a long-understood fact that was confirmed for the first time by Hezbollah Secretary-General Hassan Nasrallah in June 2016.

"We are open about the fact that Hezbollah's budget, its income, its expenses, everything it eats and drinks, its weapons and rockets, are from the Islamic Republic of Iran," he said in a speech.

Estimates of Iranian funding of Hezbollah vary widely from $50 million a year,[2] to $100 million a year,[3] to $200 million a year,[4] to $60 million a month (with an additional $40 million a month coming from Hezbollah's own global sources of revenue[5]). Given the downturn in oil prices since 2014 and Hezbollah's own extensive sources of income, Tehran's contribution to Hezbollah's treasury could be at the lower end of the estimates.

Hezbollah long ago diversified its revenue streams so as not to be wholly reliant on Tehran. It takes advantage of the Lebanese diaspora, particularly in Africa and South America, to build both legitimate and illegitimate commercial enterprises as well as to receive Islamic charitable donations of *zakat* and *khoms* from its supporters. Hezbollah's reliance on its own global financial resources has steadily grown, particularly in recent years with a downturn in oil prices and a sanctions regime on Iran that has had a negative impact on the Iranian economy and led to a decrease in annual funding. Despite the adoption of the Joint Comprehensive Plan of Action (J.C.P.O.A.) agreed upon in 2015, there does not appear to have been a significant increase in funding from Iran to Hezbollah. Furthermore, in recent years the United States has tightened the financial screws on Hezbollah by sanctioning individuals or entities that have any financial dealings with the party.

RECRUITMENT AND TRAINING

Hezbollah aspires to be more than just a political party or a military organization. Since its inception in the early 1980s, Hezbollah has sought to build a "culture of resistance" within Lebanon's Shi'a community — a self-sustaining, generational mode of thought and behavior that embraces the notion of resistance and steadfastness against a predatory Israel and Western ambitions in the Middle East.

Young Shiites are raised in environments that venerate Hezbollah and are surrounded by the party's motifs of flags, banners, and pictures of martyrs' on neighborhood walls. Youths of five- or six-years-old are encouraged to join martial parades to commemorate the annual al-Yom al-Quds (Jerusalem Day) and join Hezbollah's Mahdi Scouts where they receive elementary religious lessons and an introduction to light military training at summer camps in south Lebanon. Having been raised in such an atmosphere, fully joining the party at 18 years old — the traditionally required age to engage in combat — is often a natural progression.

Hezbollah's recruitment process is an arduous and thorough undertaking often lasting months, blending religious education and military training along with an initial detailed security assessment of each recruit.

The first phase of recruitment involves extensive religious and doctrinal lessons known as *tahdirat* or "preparation," where candidates learn the ideological foundations of Hezbollah. They are taught the concept of the *wilayat al-faqih* and the importance of the "greater" and "lesser" jihads, and how they are channeled into enmity toward Israel. The students also learn the culture of martyrdom and its importance within Shi'a doctrine. They are taught that advances in understanding the "greater jihad" will bring the *mujahid*, or holy struggler, closer to God and remove the human fear of death. Martyrdom is considered by Hezbollah as the ultimate expression of self-sacrifice and demonstration of faith in God.

The basic military training usually takes place in camps in the Bekaa Valley in east Lebanon. Basic training includes improving fitness and endurance through forced marches across mountains with heavy backpacks, and often sleeping out in the open regardless of weather conditions. They learn navigation with compass, maps, G.P.S. systems, and reconnaissance and surveillance. The recruits are taught basic weapons drills with automatic rifles, light machine guns, and rocket-propelled grenades, as well as small unit tactics in keeping with traditional doctrine against the Israel Defense Force (I.D.F.). In the past decade, Hezbollah has also introduced urban warfare training. There are several small-scale urban warfare training facilities at camps in the Bekaa Valley, most of them consisting of two parallel rows of roofless single-story cinder block buildings emulating an Israeli-style street. The urban warfare training and at least one propaganda video from 2014 suggest that the facilities are intended to train combatants to stage cross-border raids into Israel in the event of another war.[6]

There is also at least one urban warfare site that features a collection of multi-floor buildings clustered around a "mosque" and a "water tower" that resembles an Arab-style village, and may be used with the Syrian theater in mind. Once basic training is complete, fighters can elect (or are sometimes encouraged) to pursue a specialized skill, such as artillery rockets, sniping, or anti-tank missiles. Iran is the main venue for advanced training, such as the 90-day course for recruits into Hezbollah special forces units, as well as training in amphibious warfare techniques and handling more sophisticated and larger weapons systems such as anti-tank missiles, air defense systems, and sub-ballistic artillery missiles.

Role and Dynamics in Lebanon

Hezbollah's core goal is to preserve the military component of the organization, which it calls its "resistance priority." All other facets of the organization — the socio-economic welfare programs, the parliamentary presence, the role in government — are designed to buttress and protect the "resistance priority." Prior to 2005, Hezbollah's armed status was guaranteed under Syrian fiat. While Hezbollah maintained a small presence in parliament, it had not sought — nor was it asked — to join any of the post-Lebanese Civil War governments. However, since Syria withdrew its troops in the wake of the assassination of former Prime Minister Rafik Hariri in February 2005, Hezbollah has had to play a more engaged role in domestic politics to safeguard its core interests. From 2005, the fate of Hezbollah's weapons lay at the heart of the schism between the Western- and Saudi-backed March 14 parliamentary coalition and the Syria- and Iran-backed March 8 coalition.

The climactic moment came in May 2008 when Hezbollah deployed its armed forces into the western half of Beirut in response to the then government's decision to shut down Hezbollah's private telecommunications network. Several days of fighting ended with Qatari intervention, which mediated a political agreement among the feuding parties.

The lesson of the May 2008 crisis was that Hezbollah indubitably holds the balance of political and military power in the country, and is prepared to use force if sufficiently threatened. The Lebanese Armed Forces (L.A.F.) stood on the sidelines as Hezbollah men and their allies overran west Beirut, unwilling to risk enflaming the situation further by tackling the powerful militia head on. And the government, humiliatingly, was forced to rescind its earlier decisions that had triggered Hezbollah's armed response in the first place. The domestic political process since 2008 has been beset by successive waves of paralysis and stalemate. Hezbollah's opponents have come to accept that they have little leverage against a party that carries with it an implicit threat of violence if its interests are challenged.

Hezbollah's grip on Lebanon is unlikely to change significantly for the foreseeable future, especially with Christian ally Michel Aoun as president and the effective collapse of the March 14-March 8 paradigm that shaped post-2005 politics.

However, the biggest evolution undergone by Hezbollah in recent years is in the military realm. Since the 2006 war, Hezbollah has grown enormously in terms of manpower, weaponry, and equipment. It has an army numbering in excess of 20,000 fully-trained combatants, many of them hardened by battle in Syria, along with tens of thousands more part-time reservists.

It reportedly possesses more than 100,000 rockets and missiles, including sub-ballistic guided missiles fitted with 1,100-pound warheads, as well as advanced air defense systems, anti-ship missiles, and a fleet of unmanned aerial vehicles (U.A.V.s), some of them possibly combat-capable. Hezbollah's military includes a large special forces unit, a signals intelligence (SIGINT) unit, and an amphibious warfare unit, potentially equipped with swimmer dispersal vehicles and semi-submersible craft. In Syria, it operates an armored "brigade" consisting of armored personnel carriers, tanks, and mobile anti-aircraft systems used in a ground support role.

Many of the lessons Hezbollah has learned in Syria will not be relevant in the context of a future war with Israel — Hezbollah will not be fielding armored vehicles against the I.D.F. nor calling in airstrikes. But Hezbollah has benefitted from combat experience in a multitude of geographical environments, and it has also learned improved fire and maneuver tactics as well as how to utilize reconnaissance and intelligence data to develop more complex operations.

Hezbollah's lessons learned in Syria sit uncomfortably with Israel. The Syria experience, as well as the acquisition of advanced weaponry over the past 10 years, has turned Hezbollah into "currently the gravest military threat facing Israel," according to Israel's influential Institute for National Security Studies in its annual strategic assessment for 2017.[7]

New Role and Future in Syria

Hezbollah's intervention in Syria is its greatest military undertaking, larger in scale than even its resistance campaign against Israeli troops occupying south Lebanon in the 1990s. An estimated average of 8,000 fighters serve in Syria at any one time with the numbers fluctuating according to operational needs. The party has played a key role in preserving the Assad regime. In general, Hezbollah is employed as the spearhead in new offensives because of its advanced training, cohesion, and discipline compared to other pro-regime forces in Syria. Beyond a direct combat role, Hezbollah engages in corseting operations with other units to stiffen their backbone and deploys non-commissioned officer (N.C.O.) equivalents to command other militia units such as those belonging to Liwa Fatemiyoun, the Afghani volunteer force, and Liwa Zeinabiyoun, the Pakistani volunteer force. Hezbollah also plays an important force-multiplier role by training new trainers as well as regular recruits. At a command level, Hezbollah officers work alongside senior I.R.G.C. and Syrian army staff to devise operational planning.

Hezbollah justifies its intervention on two basic levels. The first, according to Nasrallah, is that the war in Syria was a "political project" of the United States for the interests of Israel. Syria under Assad represents the "backbone of the resistance" and its fall would weaken the anti-Israel front and mark the loss of the Palestinian cause.

"The resistance cannot remain idly by while its back is exposed or its support broken," Nasrallah said on May 25, 2013, in which he first confirmed Hezbollah's presence in Syria.

The second reason is the threat posed by the rise of Sunni extremist groups in Syria such as ISIS and Hay'at Tahrir al-Sham to whom Hezbollah ascribes the term "*takfiri*," meaning radicals who view as apostates all those that do not share their austere interpretation of Islam.

As of mid-2017, with the war in Syria having entered its seventh year, the Assad regime appears to be gaining the upper hand in a conflict that has left more than 400,000 dead and much of the country in ruins. The seizure of eastern Aleppo from rebel hands in late 2016, and successive cease-fire arrangements between the regime and rebels has pacified much of western Syria, the main battleground for most of the war. Attention has turned to regaining eastern Syria from ISIS and denying U.S.-supported militia elements a toehold. As of October 2017, Hezbollah is playing a major role in the push to retake the Deir Ezzor region and the Euphrates River valley to Abu Kamal on the Syria-Iraq border. With these fierce battles ahead, there is little prospect of Hezbollah withdrawing its forces from Syria any time soon. Indeed, Hezbollah may well continue to play an important role in Syria, even if there is a resolution to the conflict.

Iran and Hezbollah have a strategic interest in maintaining a presence in the Golan Heights opposite Israeli lines. In 2014, Hezbollah began work on a defensive infrastructure in the northern Golan that had little to do with the current conflict against the anti-Assad opposition, and more to do with potential future operations against Israel. On Jan. 18, 2015, a team of Hezbollah operatives and an I.R.G.C. general were touring the completed facilities, according to a source close to Hezbollah, when they were attacked by a pair of missile-firing Israeli U.A.V.s just north of Quneitra. The I.R.G.C. general and six Hezbollah men, including two senior cadres, were killed in the attack.

Israel is aware of Iranian and Hezbollah ambitions for the Golan and has declared their presence on the strategic heights as a "red line." The subject has repeatedly topped talks between Israel and Russia. Presently, Iranian and Hezbollah forces are said to be observing a 10-15 kilometer buffer zone in the

Golan, but Russia has rejected Israeli demands that the zone be expanded to 40 kilometers.[8] However, in the longer term, it is unclear whether Russia will — or can — persuade or pressure Iran to back away from its Golan agenda. If the conflict in Syria begins to fade, the Golan could become the next theater of confrontation between Hezbollah and Israel.

A second potential role for Hezbollah in a future Syria is to use its training skills to help rebuild the Syrian army and security forces in the post-war era. The Syrian army traditionally was schooled in Soviet military doctrine with an emphasis on swift mass armored assaults. Given that Israel remains Syria's greatest external enemy, Damascus lacks the resources to build a conventional army that poses a serious threat to the I.D.F. Furthermore, the Syrian army proved ill-suited to confront the challenge posed by rebel groups when the street protests morphed into armed conflict in late 2011. What may transpire instead in Syria is a leaner and more mobile army that adopts some of Hezbollah's hybrid-warfare doctrine with more emphasis on anti-tank missiles, air defense systems, and surface-to-surface rockets than on tanks and aircraft. Such a development could potentially pose more of a challenge to the I.D.F. than would a restored conventional force. The level of influence Russia would bring to bear in the creation of a new Syrian military is unclear, although Moscow's main priority could be ensuring it secures lucrative deals to arm and equip the new force. If Syria chooses to adopt this path, Hezbollah will be well-placed to help train the new Syrian army.

ROLES IN IRAQ AND YEMEN

While Syria remains Hezbollah's largest battlefield deployment outside the traditional theater with Israel, it also fields cadres in two other conflicts roiling the region — Iraq and Yemen. Hezbollah dispatched some 250 specialist cadres to Iraq in June 2014 in the wake of the seizure of Mosul by ISIS and subsequent advance toward Baghdad. The original team was composed of seasoned veterans and was responsible for advising, training, and coordinating the Hashd Shaabi, the 130,000-strong coalition of government-sanctioned, Iran-backed Shi'a militias. Hezbollah continues to maintain a limited presence in Iraq of perhaps no more than 500 personnel. Its operational activity does not appear to have changed significantly since 2014 and is focused on the anti-ISIS campaign.

In Yemen, Hezbollah runs a covert training and support mission to assist Houthi militiamen battling a Saudi-led military coalition. Saudi Arabia launched Operation Decisive Storm in March 2015 in an attempt to restore to office the deposed Yemeni president, Abd Rabbu Mansour Hadi, and to defeat the Houthi forces that had overrun Sanaa six months earlier.

The scale of Iranian (and therefore Hezbollah) support for the Houthis is disputed, although it is evident that there is some military assistance. Hezbollah's presence in Yemen has not been publicly acknowledged by the party leadership, although the relationship between the organization and Ansarallah, the Houthi militia, is well known and dates from long before the current conflict. Ansarallah officials live and work in Beirut's southern suburbs where Hezbollah is headquartered. Ansarallah fighters have received training at Hezbollah camps in the Bekaa Valley and Yemeni casualties are treated at Hezbollah-run hospitals in Beirut, according to several sources close to Hezbollah and Ansarallah officials.

Risk of Confrontation with Israel

The new U.S. administration of President Donald Trump has signaled a tougher stance against Iran and a determination to roll back the Islamic Republic's influence across the Middle East. On October 13, Trump refused to re-certify Iranian compliance with the J.C.P.O.A. agreement, handing Congress a 60-day window to decide whether to maintain or abandon the 2015 deal. Two weeks later, Congress voted for new sanctions on Iran's ballistic missile program. On October 10, the United States slapped ransoms totaling $12 million on two top Hezbollah commanders, and Congress is widely expected before the end of the year to tighten existing restrictions on fundraising for Hezbollah.

The heightened moves against Iran and Hezbollah, coupled with repeated threats from Israel, have sent jitters running through Lebanon that a new war between Hezbollah and Israel could be imminent. In February, shortly after Trump took office, Nasrallah sought to bolster his party's deterrence posture by warning Israel that there would be no "red lines" in the next war, and threatened to strike Israel's nuclear reactor in Dimona and the ammonia plants in Haifa if Israel attacks Lebanon. On June 23, Nasrallah additionally warned that a war with Israel could "open the way for thousands, even hundreds of thousands, of fighters from all over the Arab and Islamic world to participate — from Iraq, Yemen, Iran, Afghanistan, and Pakistan."

The choice of countries used to illustrate his warning was deliberate. Shi'a volunteers from all five countries are fighting, or have fought, in Syria under the aegis of the I.R.G.C. to uphold the Assad regime.

The inconclusive end to the 2006 war has long fueled expectations of a "second round." However, the " balance of terror" that exists between Hezbollah and Israel is still fundamentally strong. Both parties know that the next war will be of an order of magnitude that will completely dwarf the 2006 conflict, a grim reality that has helped ensure a mutual deterrence. Both sides repeatedly say that they do not want a war and the deterrence factor remains strong, but there remains the risk of miscalculation by one side or the other. Israel has been the more assertive party in recent years, staging assassinations of Hezbollah personnel and airstrikes against the group's suspected arms depots or convoys located in Syria. When Hezbollah has felt compelled to respond to an Israeli action, it has been careful to tailor its reprisal to deliver a slap to Israel, but not so hard as to upset the "balance of terror." Until recently, Israel's airstrikes against Hezbollah armaments in Syria have either been protested verbally by Damascus or ignored. But on March 16, when Israeli jets targeted a Hezbollah arms convoy near Palmyra in central Syria, several SA-5 anti-aircraft missiles were fired at the departing aircraft. It was the first time that Syria has reacted militarily to the airstrikes. Israel promises it will continue to attack "game-changing" weapons when it identifies them, while a Syrian official said that the March 16 attack had "changed the rules of the game" and that Israel would "think a million times from now on" before staging more airstrikes.[9] Syria fired another SA-5 missile at Israeli aircraft flying over Lebanon in October. The missile missed its target and Israel bombed the air defense facility in reprisal. If another war does break out, it is likely to be the result of a miscalculation that quickly spirals out of control faster than either side can dial it back, rather than a planned unilateral and unprovoked attack by one side against the other.

IMPACTING STATE STABILITY IN LEBANON, SYRIA, IRAQ, AND YEMEN

With the exception of Lebanon, Hezbollah is participating to a greater or lesser degree in conflicts in Syria, Iraq, and Yemen, where stability is practically non-existent. In these conflicts, Hezbollah is simply one of many moving parts and its impact on stability in each of these countries is negligible.

In Lebanon, Hezbollah's armed status lies at the root of the political divide of the past decade. Hezbollah's determination to maintain its armed status and its opponents' once equally determined efforts to see it disarmed have caused multiple political disputes that have stifled the legislative process, undermined the economy, aggravated sectarian tensions, and provoked sporadic violence. Lebanon also continues to live under the shadow of a devastating war with Israel due in part to Hezbollah's military strength, and the threat it poses to the Jewish state. However, Hezbollah has emerged from this struggle as the victor, having witnessed the gradual dissolution of the March 14 parliamentary coalition, secured the election of its ally, Michel Aoun, as president, and compelled its chief opponent, Saad Hariri, into a compromise that saw him return as prime minister. From a domestic political perspective, Hezbollah faces little threat in the near to medium term that could alter the status quo.

IMPACT ON REGIONAL SECURITY

The multiple conflicts in the Middle East in which Iran has influence have allowed Hezbollah to expand from the relatively limited purview of the Arab-Israeli conflict to become a regional actor. Its military assistance missions in Syria, Iraq, and Yemen present another component of Hezbollah's utility beyond direct combat, demonstrating its value as a force multiplier for Iran-backed or -allied groups across the region in service of Tehran's regional ambitions. For Hezbollah, the struggle against Israel remains paramount and at the heart of its "resistance" narrative and priority. But the confrontation between Iran and Saudi Arabia and their respective allies, which has only intensified in the past decade, has created a new expanded regional role for the organization as an enabler of Iranian power projection across the Middle East.

IMPACT ON THE RISE OF OTHER ARMED NON-STATE ACTORS

Hezbollah's existence in itself has not triggered the emergence of other radical groups either supportive of Hezbollah, such as some Palestinian factions and Iraqi Shi'a militias, or opposed to Hezbollah, such as al-Qaeda and ISIS. However, as a powerful Shi'a organization that is deeply engaged in Lebanese politics, the war in Syria, and conflicts in Iraq and Yemen, Hezbollah is considered an implacable enemy of radical Sunni Islamist groups.

In Lebanon, there have been few serious efforts among domestic Sunni Islamist actors to form militant cells or groups to directly tackle Hezbollah. Even the short-lived movement of Sheikh Ahmad Assir, a firebrand Salafist cleric from Sidon, posed no real threat to Hezbollah. Assir's movement was crushed in a two-day battle with Lebanese troops and local Hezbollah elements at his mosque complex in Abra, on the eastern outskirts of Sidon, in June 2013.[10] The fighting resulted in the deaths of 18 soldiers and between 25 and 40 of Assir's followers.

Sunni reticence in Lebanon to tackle Hezbollah militarily is in part due to Hezbollah's military and political dominance, which serves as a deterrent, and in part due to the pervasive nature of Lebanon's intelligence and security services that have acted effectively to monitor and arrest radical Sunni individuals. Furthermore, Lebanon's Sunni community is generally passive in nature with a mercantile, rather than militant, tradition.

Where Hezbollah has played a more direct role in the emergence of armed groups across the region is through the training of Iran-backed militias in Syria, Iraq, and Yemen.

IMPACT ON FUELING SHIITE-SUNNI SECTARIANISM AND VIOLENT EXTREMISM

Lebanon's sectarian schism historically was between Christians and Muslims, but in the past decade it has shifted to an intra-Muslim split between Sunnis and Shiites with Christians navigating a path between the two.

Hezbollah's intervention in Syria has only enflamed those sectarian tensions further, alienating not just Lebanese Sunnis, but Sunnis across the region. The intervention triggered a backlash in Lebanon with dozens of rockets fired by Syrian militant groups into the Bekaa Valley from early 2013 and a wave of vehicle-borne improvised explosive device (V.B.I.E.D.) attacks and suicide V.B.I.E.D.s between July 2013 and the end of June 2014, which left nearly 100 people dead and nearly 900 wounded. A twin suicide bomb blast in the Shiite-populated Bourj Barajneh neighborhood of southern Beirut in November 2015 killed 43 people and wounded 239, the largest loss of life in a single domestic bomb attack since the end of the Lebanese Civil War in 1990.

Most of the suicide V.B.I.E.D.s were claimed by extremist Sunni factions such as the then-al-Qaeda-linked Jabhat al-Nusra and the Lebanon-based Abdullah al-Azzam Brigades. They made it clear in their statements that the attacks were a response to Hezbollah's intervention in Syria.

COUNTERING THIS VIOLENT TRANSNATIONAL MOVEMENT: RESPONSES AND SCENARIOS

HOW CAN THE EXTERNAL INFLUENCE EXERTED BY IRAN ON HEZBOLLAH BE WEAKENED OR INFLUENCED IN A LESS DESTRUCTIVE DIRECTION?

There are no simple solutions to breaking the tight ideological, financial, and material links between Hezbollah and Iran. Hezbollah is Iran's greatest success in exporting the Islamic Revolution, and the Lebanese organization has proven itself a dependable and efficient partner in helping Tehran exert influence into the Middle East. There are few realistic options that can be pursued by the United States in the short to medium term that will break that partnership without risking destabilization that could impact U.S. interests and those of its allies in the region.

Options include resorting to force to effect regime change in Iran. But that would plunge the Middle East into even greater turmoil with few guarantees of a successful outcome.

Washington could choose to abandon the J.C.P.O.A. agreement and re-impose crippling sanctions to compel Iran to break ties with Hezbollah and reverse its reach into the region. But the other parties to the J.C.P.O.A. deal have sent clear signals that they will continue to honor the agreement, which would leave the U.S. isolated among leading world powers in its anti-Iran stance. Furthermore, it could provoke a punishing backlash by Iran against U.S. interests in the Gulf and beyond.

WHAT CAN BE DONE TO MODERATE OR CONFRONT HEZBOLLAH'S MESSAGING AND APPEAL IN LEBANON AND OUTSIDE THE COUNTRY'S BORDERS?

The extent of Hezbollah's popularity currently is being shaped by its own actions in Lebanon and elsewhere, and any external influence on the organization's messaging and appeal is unlikely to have much impact. In Lebanon, few citizens have indifferent feelings toward Hezbollah — the Lebanese are split between supporters and opponents and their views are generally not susceptible to change.

Hezbollah's determination to maintain its "resistance priority" alienated a large segment of the Lebanese population from 2000 when Israel withdrew from south Lebanon. Across the Arab world, Hezbollah's popularity remained high, peaking in 2006 during the war with Israel, until its armed intervention in Syria was revealed in 2013. Since then, Hezbollah's popular standing in the MENA region has tumbled significantly and it is today reviled by most of the region's Sunnis. Even another war with Israel is unlikely to change that perception.

WHAT STEPS CAN BE TAKEN TO IMPACT THE GROUP'S FINANCIAL INFLOWS AND RESOURCES, AS WELL AS THE INFLOW OF ARMS AND WEAPONS?

In December 2015, the United States passed the Hezbollah International Financing Prevention Act (HIFPA), which targets financial institutions found to knowingly facilitate significant transactions on behalf of Hezbollah or anyone affiliated with or acting on its behalf.[11] HIFPA requires Lebanese banks to freeze the accounts of individuals and organizations named by the U.S. Treasury's Office of Foreign Assets Control. Failure to follow the order risks banks being sanctioned and cut off from accessing the U.S. financial system, not only in Lebanon but internationally.

Hezbollah has denied using the Lebanese banking system. But it is concerned that an overly aggressive enforcement of HIFPA by Lebanese banks could backfire on the party's popularity if its supporters, perhaps people with only marginal associations with the party, have their bank accounts frozen.

In June 2016, a small bomb exploded beside the head office of BLOM Bank, one of Lebanon's leading banks that reportedly had been among the most diligent in adhering to HIFPA. There was no claim of responsibility although it was widely believed to have been a message from Hezbollah to the banking sector.

As of October, Congress is debating expanding HIFPA's reach to impede Hezbollah's fundraising capabilities with high expectations that new legislation will be passed before the end of the year. There is even speculation that Hezbollah-controlled regions of Lebanon could be designated under Section 311 of the Patriot Act as areas of "primary money laundering concern."[12] The targeted areas would presumably include the southern suburbs of Beirut, south Lebanon, and the Bekaa Valley.

However, any tightening of financial measures against Hezbollah should be implemented in a manner that does not undermine Lebanon's fragile economy and the banking sector, which is the mainstay of Lebanon's financial stability. Hezbollah is deeply immersed within Lebanese political and commercial society, which greatly complicates creating a sanctions campaign that targets in isolation associations, companies, and individuals that may have dealings with the organization. For example, the Rassoul al-Azzam hospital in southern Beirut is a Hezbollah-run institution that provides health services, often discounted, to the local community. But the hospital, like any other in Lebanon, has dealings with non-Hezbollah entities, including the Lebanese government through the ministries of health and social affairs. Hezbollah's social-welfare services are vast and include hospitals, schools, clinics, social centers, and charitable institutions, all of which could potentially be threatened by a reinforced HIFPA or separate legislation, with consequent repercussions on employees and beneficiaries. Additional anti-Hezbollah financing legislation, if intensely enforced, could induce a lack of confidence in the Lebanese banking sector, precipitating both capital flight from banks and a reduction in overseas remittances — which amount to more than $7 billion a year — from expatriate Lebanese. Furthermore, correspondent banks overseas may come to view the Lebanese banking sector as too exposed and vulnerable to warrant the risk of maintaining a fiscal relationship. If correspondent banks choose to de-risk by ending their relationships with Lebanese financial institutions, the banking sector could find itself shut off from international money markets.

Lebanon's mountainous and porous eastern border traditionally has been the main conduit for Hezbollah to receive its armaments from neighboring Syria via smuggling trails. In theory, the L.A.F. has the capacity to block the smuggling routes with physical obstacles and to monitor any breaches of the border. However, in reality no Lebanese government would take such a decision and risk a repetition of the May 2008 events. Another suspected route for the transfer of weapons to Hezbollah is by sea. The United Nations Interim Force in Lebanon (UNIFIL), which patrols the southern border with Israel, has had a maritime component since 2006 tasked with supporting the Lebanese navy in securing the Lebanese coastline. Part of the Maritime Task Force's (M.T.F.) duties are to prevent the smuggling of weapons or related materials into Lebanon. To that end, between October 2006 when the M.T.F. first deployed and June 2017, more than 77,000 vessels have been hailed by the peacekeepers and over 10,500 referred to the Lebanese navy for inspection.[13] So far, no weapons destined for Hezbollah have been discovered.

WHAT ARE THE WEAK LINKS IN HEZBOLLAH'S RECRUITMENT PIPELINE AND HOW CAN RECRUITMENT BE IMPEDED?

Hezbollah's massive manpower expansion in the past decade and the war in Syria has resulted in the emergence of two tiers of new recruits. The first and most significant tier is the traditional recruit who subscribes to the *wilayat al-faqih*, passes through the extensive religious and military training programs, and is a loyal and committed cadre. The second, and smaller, tier has emerged in the past year or two and consists of young Shi'a conscripts whose adherence to the party's ideology initially is minimal, but have been drawn to join mainly for financial reward as well as benefitting from Hezbollah's social welfare services. This second tier is recruited specifically with the Syrian theater in mind. They receive basic training lasting a month at camps in the Bekaa Valley before being deployed to various battlefronts in Syria. Despite being motivated primarily by money, these new recruits are also given intensive religious lessons in order that, in time, they can assimilate more fully into Hezbollah's ideological core, which many of them do.

A monthly salary of $600 is not an inconsiderable sum in Lebanon, especially for unemployed youths. Many of them live in poor regions of the country, such as the central and northern Bekaa Valley, where there are few job opportunities. One means of diminishing the attraction of joining Hezbollah is to improve the economic health of Hezbollah's recruitment catchment areas. In the rural Bekaa, investments in the agro-industrial sector could provide livelihoods for local residents, reducing the attraction of fighting with Hezbollah.

Scenarios: What are the scenarios in which Hezbollah can walk-back from deployments in Syria, and involvements in Iraq and Yemen?

The Lebanese and Arab media have speculated that Hezbollah is on the verge of withdrawing its forces from Syria for almost as long as the cadres have been there. However, there never has been any real indication that Hezbollah would return to Lebanon before either victory or defeat against the anti-Assad rebels. Sheikh Naim Qassem, Hezbollah's deputy secretary-general, said at the end of October that a withdrawal of Hezbollah personnel "is linked to the political solution in Syria and to the eradication of terrorism."[14] Although the tide of the war is turning in favor of the Assad regime, the fighting continues and given the chronic manpower shortage within the ranks of the Syrian army, Hezbollah's battle-hardened fighters are still required. Iran has invested billions of dollars in propping up the Assad regime and is unlikely to weaken its investment by allowing Hezbollah to return to Lebanon prematurely. As discussed above, there is a likelihood of a post-war role for Hezbollah in Syria even if most of the expeditionary force eventually returns home.

While fighting continues, Russia and Iran will have a shared interest in cooperating with each other, even if those interests could begin to diverge in the post-conflict era. Russia needs Iranian-supported forces on the ground as President Vladimir Putin is unwilling to commit sizeable ground forces of his own. Iran also requires Russian air support, which has been so critical in swinging the conflict in Assad's favor. Therefore, Russia has little leverage at this time against Iran, even if Moscow views with unease a prolonged presence of Hezbollah in Syria and the implications it could have in terms of a future war with Israel over the Golan Heights.

Hezbollah's presence in Iraq and Yemen is more tactical than strategic. Once ISIS is defeated in Iraq, Hezbollah is likely to withdraw its forces back to Lebanon, possibly leaving a few personnel for liaison and training. Similarly, if the Saudi-led coalition in Yemen either abandons its offensive or succeeds in defeating its Houthi opponents, Hezbollah may pull out.

What are the scenarios in which Hezbollah's Deployments Widen in the Region?

Setbacks in Syria, Iraq, or Yemen or the emergence of new theaters of conflict in which Iran has a key stake could lead to an expansion of Hezbollah's regional presence. In the unlikely event that Syrian rebel groups are able to reverse Assad's gains over the past 18 months and once again threaten the durability of the regime, it is possible that Hezbollah would increase its manpower commitment in Syria.

Hezbollah's regional role is more closely linked to Iran's ambitions than to the organization's parochial interests. Therefore, a key requirement to keep Hezbollah confined to Lebanon is to reduce the number of conflicts involving Iran in the region. De-confliction between Iran and Saudi Arabia and its Gulf partners would lessen the need for the Islamic Republic to seek the martial expertise of its Lebanese proxy.

WHAT ARE THE SCENARIOS FOR HEZBOLLAH'S FUTURE IN LEBANON?

The shape of Hezbollah's immediate future will be guided very much by developments in Syria. If, in the next year, the Assad regime regains sufficient control of the country so that the armed threat it faces is reduced to a low-level insurgency that indigenous forces can handle, Hezbollah could withdraw the bulk of its forces back to Lebanon. The party leadership would declare victory and note that Hezbollah's sacrifices had spared Lebanon the possibility of Sunni radicals taking over Damascus, and the horrors of a potential invasion by ISIS. An end to hostilities in Syria could revive Hezbollah's popularity among its support base, especially if party funds that had been spent on the war effort are diverted to the constituency in terms of higher salaries and benefits. Success in Syria would allow Hezbollah to refocus efforts on the Israel front, and with it a possible military deployment on the Golan Heights, which in turn would raise the risk of a fresh confrontation with a Jewish state alarmed by an Assad-Iran-Hezbollah victory in Syria.

If, on the other hand, the war drags on in Syria with Syrian government forces and their allies unable to decisively defeat the armed opposition, and no progress is made on a negotiated settlement, it could negatively impact Hezbollah's popularity within its Shi'a constituency. While Hezbollah still retains the overwhelming support of Lebanon's Shi'a population, the war in Syria has caused cracks in that consensus. War fatigue has set in among some cadres and supporters alike. In the past two years, numerous anecdotal examples have emerged of fighters refusing to serve further tours in Syria with some even quitting the party altogether. While most supporters accept the rationale given by the party leadership for the Syria intervention, the justifications are challenged each day by the return of brothers, sons, husbands, and fathers killed in Syria's far-flung battlefields.

Hezbollah seems ill-prepared to handle the growing restlessness of its supporters who are beginning to chafe at the party's omnipresence and heavy-handed interference in people's daily lives. While victories in Syria such as the seizure of eastern Aleppo in December 2016 help revive flagging spirits, the long-term trend among Hezbollah's support base is one of growing impatience and unhappiness with the war in Syria.

In the years following Israel's troop withdrawal from south Lebanon in 2000, as opponents to Hezbollah's armed status grew more vocal, one of the more persistent ideas of reaching a solution was to weave the Islamic Resistance into the L.A.F., perhaps as a southern border force, thus bringing Hezbollah's arms under state control. The idea never went beyond public debate because Hezbollah rejected such a move, and was backed in its opposition by Damascus, which then controlled the political process in Lebanon. Blending the Islamic Resistance with the L.A.F. would be tantamount to the end of Hezbollah as a military force. It is also difficult to see how the Islamic Resistance, which has its own military doctrine, let alone strict religio-ideological purview, could operate within the de-confessionalized L.A.F., even as an adjunct force. Israeli withdrawals from the Shebaa Farms area on Lebanon's south east border with the Golan Heights, and from the northern end of the village of Ghajar would go some way toward undermining Hezbollah's rationale for maintaining its arms to liberate occupied Lebanese territory, but it would not be enough. Hezbollah long ago moved beyond predicating the future of its armed status on the withdrawal of Israeli forces from Lebanese territory. In June 2006, Ali Ammar, a Hezbollah parliamentarian, said that "the extent of the resistance is not the Shebaa Farms ... nor the return of the prisoners [from Israel], but its extent is when it becomes impossible for Israel to violate Lebanon's sovereignty even with a paper kite."

Challenges Ahead

Twenty years ago, Hezbollah was a relatively small organization that carried little political weight in Lebanon, and was committed fully to the resistance campaign to oust Israeli forces from south Lebanon. It generally eschewed daily parochial politics beyond a parliamentary presence, and won broad consensus across the sectarian divide for its military prowess in south Lebanon. The range of its largest rocket was a mere 12 miles, and its military wing numbered no more than 3,000 fighters, both full- and part-time. It maintained air-tight internal secrecy, and had a laudable reputation for financial integrity.

The Hezbollah of today, however, is very different. It dominates the political and military landscape of Lebanon, has tens of thousands of trained fighters at its disposal, and an array of sophisticated armaments and technical equipment. It has reached into almost every facet of Lebanon's political, administrative, military, and social structures, and has a de facto veto on any government decision and appointments covering all sectors.

But for all its weight and influence in Lebanon, Hezbollah also faces a series of stresses and strains that threaten its long-term cohesion, and are in some respects symptoms of its own success.

Corruption has taken root within Hezbollah in the past few years in marked contrast to its earlier reputation for financial probity. When the phenomenon began to appear in 2008, the party's leadership tried to stamp it out. But Hezbollah today in some respects resembles a massive bureaucracy and once corruption emerges it is difficult to eradicate. Corruption is eroding Hezbollah's internal moral fabric, breeding resentment and disrespect from cadres and supporters alike, which weakens the party's strong sense of discipline and obedience, the glue that binds its constituent parts into an effective whole.

It is also suffering from an internal cash flow problem. The Iran nuclear deal in 2015 and subsequent lifting of sanctions was expected to revive Hezbollah's flagging financial fortunes. Although there appeared to be an initial uptick in the revenue flow from Iran, it has since either dwindled or remains insufficient to cover the party's operating costs, along with Hezbollah's other revenue sources. In early 2017, there were indications that Hezbollah appeared to have ceased paying monthly salaries to new recruits joining specifically to serve in Syria. Instead, they now receive only the social welfare benefits the organization offers, such as discounted medical treatment and school fees, according to numerous sources close to Hezbollah. Given the fact that the incentive of most of these second tier recruits to join Hezbollah is to win monthly salaries, the cessation of income payments underlines the seriousness of the financial squeeze. Furthermore, the organization has also launched a fundraising drive entitled "Equip a Mujahid campaign" for public donations to arm, equip, and train Hezbollah fighters.

Hezbollah also faces a challenge in keeping its support base on its side, especially given the casualty toll of the war in Syria. As mentioned above, if the war in Syria drags on, Hezbollah may face difficulties in maintaining morale within its constituency which could undermine its popular standing. Retaining the support of Lebanon's Shi'a community is absolutely fundamental to Hezbollah's existence. Without popular support, Hezbollah's leverage in Lebanon declines. Without influence in Lebanon, Hezbollah cannot act as Iran's most reliable regional enabler to project influence across the region.

Given the party's deep immersion within Lebanon's political, economic, and social milieu, the number of realistic options for external powers to weaken Hezbollah or persuade it to forsake its military role for one solely limited to domestic politics are minimal without creating spin-off effects that could destabilize Lebanon. The military option will merely invite massive destruction on Lebanon and Israel with no guarantees that Hezbollah would be decisively defeated. Imposing tighter sanctions might help further choke Hezbollah's revenue flows but could have unwanted consequences for Lebanon's already fragile economy and fiscal stability, which in turn could create civil strife and political unrest.

Ultimately, change may come from the gradual unraveling of the social contract between Hezbollah and its support base rather than from external initiatives. Hezbollah has worked hard since the Israeli withdrawal from south Lebanon in 2000 to reconcile its resistance priority with the needs and interests of its supporters. But Hezbollah's determination to maintain its resistance narrative and its newfound role as an enabler of Iranian power across the region increasingly lie at odds with its other role as protector and champion of Lebanon's Shi'a community. Those conflicting agendas are growing more pronounced and it is unclear if Hezbollah will — or can — reconcile the two in the long term.

ENDNOTES

1. Ayatollah Ruhollah Khomeini, "Manhajiat al-Thawra al-Islamiah" as quoted in Naim Qassem, *Hizbullah: The Story from Within* (Saqi Books, 2005).

2. Yonah Jeremy Bob, "Massive Iranian Funding for Anti-Israel Terror Groups Revealed," *The Jerusalem Post*, June 23, 2017.

3. Matthew Levitt, "Hezbollah Finances: Funding the Party of God," *The Washington Institute for Near East Policy*, February 2005.

4. Scott Wilson, "Lebanese wary of a rising Hezbollah," *The Washington Post*, December 20, 2004.

5. Beirut "A Strategy session with Prime Minister Siniora and his friends," Wikileaks Cable: 06BEIRUT2291_a, dated July 7, 2006.

6. Nicholas Blanford, "Look who's training: Hezbollah prepares for war," *The Christian Science Monitor*, December 4, 2013.

7. Shapir, Yiftah S. "Hezbollah as an army", *Institute for National Security Studies Strategic Assessment* 19, no. 4 (January 2017).

8. Ahronheim, Anna. "Russia agrees to keep Iran, Hezbollah forces away from Israeli border," *The Jerusalem Post*, October 18, 2017.

9. Eichner Itamar and Roi Keis, "Syria's UN envoy: Retaliation against Israel 'changed rules of the game'," *Ynet*, March 20, 2017.

10. Nicholas Blanford, "Sunni cleric incites gun battle with Lebanese army and Hezbollah," *The Christian Science Monitor*, June 24, 2013.

11. Hizballah International Financing Prevention Act of 2015, U. S. C. § 2297 (2015).

12. Johnathan Schanze, Orde Kittrie, and Alex Entz, "How Washington can counter the rise of Hezbollah," *Foreign Affairs*, September 29, 2017.

13. Information supplied by UNIFIL.

14. "Qassem: No withdrawal from Syria before political solution." *Naharnet*, October 28, 2017.

CHAPTER TEN

IRAQ'S FIFTH COLUMN:
IRAN'S PROXY NETWORK

NICHOLAS A. HERAS

INTRODUCTION

Iraq is again becoming a critical site of contestation for influence in the Middle East between the United States and Iran, as the Trump administration and its regional partners seek to confront Iran's destabilizing activities in the region. Iran's Islamic Revolutionary Guard Corps (I.R.G.C.), and its expeditionary branch, the Quds Force, are utilizing the campaign against the Islamic State (ISIS) in Iraq to expand Iran's proxy network of predominately Shi'a militias, based on the model of Hezbollah, across the Middle East.[2] The Quds Force's growing network of loyal Iraqi Shi'a militias is being integrated, particularly via the Syrian civil war, into a larger, multi-national force that can be activated and used around the Middle East to support Iranian national security policy goals.

An important recruitment pool for the Quds Force's proxy network is Iraq's Popular Mobilization Units (P.M.U.s), a network of militias that is officially part of the Iraqi government's security apparatus and under the prime minister's authority. The P.M.U.s are shaped by the policy decisions made by their Deputy Commissioner Jamal Ja'far Muhammad Ali Ibrahimi — a.k.a. Abu Mahdi al-Muhandis — one of the most important Iraqi Quds Force operatives. With the support of Muhandis and other Iraqi Shi'a veterans of the Islamic Resistance Movement that was established to overthrow Saddam Hussein's government in the 1980s and 1990s, the Quds Force is building powerful networks of influence within the country that will have a strong impact on Iraq's future.

As the conflict against ISIS shifts to the stabilization phase in Iraq, the militias within the state that are backed by the Quds Force will continue to position themselves as powerbrokers within the Iraqi Shi'a community. The transition from the P.M.U.s being a force for the mobilization of militias to being participants in mass politics will be highly important in defining the future dynamics of politicking within the Iraqi Shi'a community. This transition will also test the Quds Force's ability to utilize Iraq as a talent incubator for its trans-national network. This paper analyzes the historical process through which the Quds Force has shaped Iraqi Shi'a militant networks, and the impact that these shaping efforts are having on the development of the P.M.U.s.

THE P.M.U.s — A SECURITY STRUCTURE BEING BUILT TO LAST

Since July 2014, it is estimated that 67 constituent militias have been raised under the P.M.U. umbrella, of which 40 militias are believed to be closely tied to the Quds Force.[2] Analysts believe that most of the P.M.U. constituent militias and fighters come from Iraq's Shi'a community, although P.M.U. militias have also been raised from Iraq's Sunni, Christian, Yazidi, and Turkmen communities during the counter-ISIS campaign.[3]

The Iraqi government estimates that there are 110,000-122,000 P.M.U. fighters, a figure that it arrives at due to the government's obligation to pay the salaries of their members.[4] Despite this large mobilization, it is estimated that 70,000-90,000 P.M.U. fighters have been deployed, ranging from checkpoint duty to actual combat, in Iraq or Syria.[5] Of this total, an estimated 50,000 P.M.U. fighters are mobilized in organizations that are under the influence of the Quds Force, particularly within the three largest I.R.G.C.-backed organizations — Asa'ib Ahl al-Haq, Kata'ib Hezbollah, and Faylaq al-Badr.[6]

Although the role of the P.M.U. network is now formalized within Iraq's national security architecture, the long-term impact of the P.M.U.s on the mass politics of Iraq, particularly in the Shi'a community, is unclear.[7] Formally, the law that made the P.M.U.s an official Iraqi government organization states that the P.M.U.s are to be apolitical, non-sectarian, and separate from nongovernmental militia forces.[8] However, the most powerful of the P.M.U. groups are still linked to armed movements that support powerful Iraqi political actors, such as Moqtada al-Sadr or Ammar al-Hakim, are proxies for the Quds Force and support the institution of the *wilayat al-faqih* — rule of the jurisprudent — in Iraq.[9] *Wilayat al-faqih* governs Iran's Islamic Republic.[10]

It remains an open question whether the militia mobilization that has occurred through the P.M.U. system will also serve as a vehicle for mass politics, particularly within the Shi'a community, in Iraq's upcoming provincial elections and parliamentary elections, currently scheduled for April 2018.

A History of Quds Force Proxy-Shaping in Iraq

The Quds Force is fundamentally an organization that conducts irregular warfare, often combining asymmetric warfare and foreign internal defense (F.I.D.). Not dissimilar to the U.S. Army's Special Forces, the Quds Force operates in foreign countries and seeks to follow a "whole country" strategy that blends socio-politics and warfare.[11] Iraq and, since 2011, Syria are important arenas for the Quds Force to maintain friendly regime partners. The Quds Force upholds positive relationships through its F.I.D. operations, which facilitate the Quds Force's mission to spread Ayatollah Ruhollah Khomeini's Islamic Revolution across the Middle East.

In Iraq, the P.M.U.s represent a contemporary growth opportunity for the Quds Force, which allow it to identify, mobilize, and when necessary, cultivate a future generation of operatives for its regional proxy network. Qassem Soleimani, the leader of the Quds Force, minced few words in describing his and his organization's view on the importance of their proxy network to protect Iran from its enemies.

"No force or country except for Iran is capable of leading the Muslim world today due to Iran's support for revolutionary and Islamic movements and fighters as well as its defense of Muslims against aggressors."[12]

I.R.G.C. investment in the Iraqi Shi'a population as a recruitment ground for the battle to spread Ayatollah Khomeini's vision across the region dates back to the early 1980s. Saddam Hussein invaded Iran in September 1980, and Khomeini called for a pan-Islamic revolution to defeat Saddam Hussein and the regional and international governments that backed him. To achieve this national security objective, the I.R.G.C. created and empowered the Quds Force to build a strong organizational network between Iranian elite Shi'a clerics, the I.R.G.C., and a nascent, external proxy militia network.[13]

At that time, the young Islamic Republic sought opportunities to subvert the Saddam regime. The I.R.G.C. was empowered by Khomeini to spread the Islamic Revolution throughout the Middle East, starting with Iraq and Lebanon, and the I.R.G.C. established an "Office of Liberation Movements" to achieve this goal. Eventually falling under the mandate of the Quds Force, the Office of Liberation Movements sought to provide military, ideological, and political training (shaping operations) to build a loyal proxy network — Lebanon's Hezbollah being the prime example, and now serving as the model for replication elsewhere.

Therefore, the Quds Force's interest in Iraq is not new, and the country has been a long-time proving ground for the I.R.G.C. effort to establish its proxy network. Since the early 1980s, Iraqi Shi'a operatives have supported Khomeini's message to spread the Islamic Revolution, both inside and outside of Iraq. The first generation of non-ethnic Iranian, Arab leadership of the proxy network was nurtured within the Iraqi Shiite, "Islamic Resistance" armed opposition movement against Saddam during the 1980-88 Iran-Iraq War. The Islamic Resistance movement was a product of these shaping operations, and it was through this effort that the Quds Force was able to establish a deep network of influence within the security structures of the Iraqi state post-2003.[14]

The P.M.U. groups that currently have the closest relationship with the I.R.G.C. are led by commanders that began as fighters within the Islamic Resistance of the 1980s and 1990s, continued to be active in the Quds Force-supported armed opposition to the U.S. military presence in Iraq from 2003-11, supported the Shi'a jihad in the Syrian civil war, and are now working to implement *wilayat al-faqih* in Iraq. The Islamic Resistance was a formative period for many of the prominent I.R.G.C.-backed P.M.U. commanders, most of whom were young men that were active in the armed opposition against Saddam Hussein in the 1980s and 1990s. These commanders include Shaykh Auws al-Khafaji (Quwat Abu Fadhil al-Abbas), Shaykh Akram al-Ka'abi (Harakat Hezbollah al-Nujaba'), and Ali al-Yasseri (Saraya al-Khorasani).[15]

Although the Islamic Resistance was ultimately unsuccessful in overthrowing Saddam Hussein or cutting short the Iran-Iraq War, it did provide the Quds Force with a legacy network of young, motivated Iraqi Shi'a operatives.[16]

The U.S. invasion of Iraq in March 2003 and the subsequent toppling of Iran's fiercest regional rival was considered a great opportunity for the Quds Force to expand its influence in Iraq and direct Iraq's politics to benefit Iran.[17]

According to former C.I.A. operative Robert Baer, shortly after Saddam was deposed, Iraqi Shi'a operatives that were mobilized during the Islamic Resistance movement in the 1980s and 1990s and had subsequently joined the Quds Force's network and worked with Lebanese Hezbollah began returning to Iraq. Baer states that the Iraqi operatives' objective was to continue to enact the I.R.G.C.'s strategy of controlling Iraq. In order to fulfill this mission, they sought to develop proxy militias, indoctrinate a new generation of Iraqi Shi'a operatives, and win revolutionary legitimacy by contesting the U.S. presence in the country though asymmetric warfare.[18]

The I.R.G.C. strategy to submerge Iraq under Iranian political control had reached such a point by 2004 that the Coalition Provisional Authority head, Paul Bremer, referred to it as a "concentrated long-term strategy." Bremer recommended to then-U.S. Secretary of Defense Donald Rumsfeld that Coalition forces act aggressively to capture Quds Force operatives in Iraq and close the Iranian embassy in Baghdad.[19] Quds Force operatives frequently utilized the homes of powerful Iraqi Shi'a politicians such as Abdul Aziz al-Hakim to coordinate the Quds Force's Iraqi proxy militias and plan attacks against U.S.-led forces.[20] The success of the Quds Force's Iraqi Shi'a proxy militias motivated the U.S. Department of Treasury to designate the Quds Force as a Special Designated Global Terrorist on October 25, 2007 and its liaison in Iraq, Abdul Reza Shalai, as an individual supporting terrorism on September 16, 2008.[21]

The I.R.G.C. was not in complete control of the Iraqi Shi'a armed opposition to the U.S.-led Coalition, and has been forced to compete with a range of local Iraqi clerical and political actors for influence within that community. However, the Quds Force's current success in infiltrating the P.M.U.s rests on the power and influence that its Iraqi operatives, most important among them Muhandis, developed during the early 2000s. The success of the Quds Force in shaping operations and providing financial and military support for Shi'a armed opposition groups has enabled its Iraqi operatives to become powerbrokers, despite the efforts of U.S. military forces. Demonstrating the reach and effectiveness of the I.R.G.C. in Iraq, Soleimani is reported to have sent U.S. General David Petraeus a text message in 2007 that read:

"General Petraeus, you should know that I, Qassem Soleimani, control policy for Iran with respect to Iraq, Lebanon, Gaza, and Afghanistan. The [Iranian] ambassador to Iraq is a Quds Force member. The individual who is going to replace him is a Quds Force member."[22]

Muhandis was the decisive agent in the Quds Force's Iraq operations, particularly in supporting the armed opposition campaign of the Special Groups from 2007-10.[23] During that period, U.S. officials asserted that Muhandis was Soleimani's envoy in Iraq, and that Soleimani used him to relay messages to Iraqi politicians, including all the way up the hierarchy to Nouri al-Maliki.[24] For his part, Muhandis, in an April 2017 interview on Iranian television, stated that he was, "a solder of Haj Qassem [Soleimani]." This statement demonstrated the lines of influence that the Quds Force has established at the highest levels of the Iraqi security infrastructure and the P.M.U.s.[25]

Iran's proxy network in Iraq, with the active support and encouragement of the I.R.G.C., was intimately involved in the development of the P.M.U.s prior to ISIS's conquest of Mosul in June 2014. This effort, which led to the formation of the "Sons of Iraq" organization in the winter of 2014, was spearheaded by then Prime Minister Nouri al-Maliki and Iranian proxy groups including Faylaq al-Badr, Asa'ib Ahl al-Haq, Kata'ib Hezbollah, and Jaysh al-Mukhtar.[26] The Sons of Iraq, whose existence was first reported in March 2014, was created to fight against the rising Sunni armed opposition, including ISIS, in western Iraq. Both the Sons of Iraq and its successor, the P.M.U.s, were designed by Maliki and the proxy militias to be Iranian, Islamic Republic-style *basij* militia networks inside of Iraq.[27]

The relationship between Muhandis and Soleimani actively shaped the P.M.U.s as they were being built up. In June 2014, Muhandis was appointed by Maliki as the deputy commissioner on the prime minister's Commission on the Popular Mobilization.[28] Muhandis states that shortly after the fall of Mosul, Soleimani was sent to Iraq and the two leaders liaised with Kurdish peshmerga commanders in Erbil, and received Lebanese Hezbollah trainers that were then sent to Iraq to support the P.M.U.s' counter-ISIS campaign.[29]

Following ISIS's capture of Mosul, and under the supervision of Soleimani, Quds Force operatives and highly experienced Iraqi senior militia operatives from Faylaq al-Badr, Asa'ib Ahl al-Haq, Kata'ib Hezbollah, and Jaysh al-Mukhtar trained and coordinated constituent militias in the nascent P.M.U.s.[30] Even groups that were not part of Iran's proxy network were subordinated to the Quds Force and its operatives. These groups included Sadr's Saraya al-Salam (Peace Brigades) and the P.M.U. militias organized in the shrine city of Karbala such as Liwa Ali al-Akbar (Ali al-Akbar Brigade, organized by the Imam Husayn Mosque) and Firqa al-Abbas al-Qataliyya (al-Abbas Fighting Division, organized by the Al-Abbas Mosque).[31] This training process was a continuation of the proxy network's strategy to infiltrate Iraq's internal security forces, including its SWAT forces, in order to solidify I.R.G.C. influence in Iraq, as Baghdad grappled with the immense challenge presented by ISIS.[32]

THE P.M.U.s, OR HEZBOLLAH 4.0, WALKING ON THE PATH OF THE *WILAYAT AL-FAQIH*

The history of the Quds Force's activities in Iraq sowed the seeds of support for the establishment of an Islamic Republic in Iraq, in close connection with Iran, and in obedience to Iran's Supreme Leader Ali Khamenei.[33] Since the start of the Syrian civil war, and the threat to the important Shi'a shrines in the southern Damascus suburbs, obedience to the supreme leader has also come to mean jihad in protection of the broader Shi'a population, wherever it is located.

Proxy groups in Iraq such as Faylaq al-Badr, Asa'ib Ahl al-Haq, and Kata'ib Hezbollah, as well as their splinter groups, have been incorporated into this latest "sacred defense" mission. By encouraging the jihad in Syria, the Quds Force has been able to identify and build influence over a new generation of Iraqi Shi'a leaders, many of whom have joined the P.M.U.s. This progress will sustain the Quds Force's proxy network for its future, trans-national operations.[34]

However, a distinction should be made between the Shi'a P.M.U. militias that support the imposition of *wilayat al-faqih* in Iraq and those that do not. Shi'a P.M.U. militias can be Shi'a Islamist in their ideological outlook while simultaneously supporting the current Iraqi state and pan-sectarian peace in the country, such as is espoused by Sadr's Saraya al-Salam.[35] These two factors do not necessarily contradict one another. Regardless of whether groups support the imposition of *wilayat al-faqih* or not, a narrative of resistance is widespread and important in the intra-Shi'a politics of Iraq, and is woven into the ideology that motivates all P.M.U. militias. This resistance narrative does not necessarily imply support for "Khomeinism." Nevertheless, constituent groups within the P.M.U.s that are led by commanders who support the institution of the *wilayat al-faqih* or that have significant numbers of pro-*wilayat al-faqih* rank-and-file represent a growth pool of recruitment for the Quds Force's proxy network.

These groups that are controlled or significantly influenced by the I.R.G.C. categorically support the institution of the *wilayat al-faqih* in Iraq. At this point, the Quds Force has developed the fourth generation of its proxy network in Iraq and is currently nurturing the forces to support the imposition of the *wilayat al-faqih* in Iraq. The first and second generations of this network consisted of the Shi'a armed opposition organizations that were organized inside the Islamic Resistance and emerged from the Dawa Party and the Badr Organization in the 1980s and 1990s. The third generation of the Quds Force Iraq network were composed of Shi'a Iraqi "Special Groups," the majority of which splintered off of Sadr's Jaysh al-Mahdi between 2007 and 2010, such as Asa'ib Ahl al-Haq, Kata'ib Hezbollah, and Jaysh al-Mukhtar.

The fourth generation is made up of organizations that developed from Asa'ib Ahl al-Haq and Kata'ib Hezbollah to wage jihad in Syria and groups formed by veteran Islamic Resistance leaders who were motivated to contribute to the defense of Iraq against ISIS after June 2014. A significant number of Iraq's fourth generation network groups were first mobilized to protect the Shi'a shrines in Syria. These groups included Quwat Abu al-Fadhal al-Abbas (Abu al-Fadhal al-Abbas Force), Harakat Hezbollah al-Nujaba' (Movement of the Outstanding Ones of the Party of God), Saraya al-Khorasani (Khorasani Brigade), Kata'ib Sayyid al-Shuhada' (Lord of the Martyrs Brigade), Liwa' Zulfiqar (Zulfiqar Brigade), Liwa' Ammar Ibn Yassir (Ammar Ibn Yassir Brigade), and Liwa' al-Yum al-Mawud (Brigade of the Promised Day).[36] Most of these groups also currently participate in the P.M.U.s' structure, while maintaining an expeditionary arm that fights alongside Bashar al-Assad's forces in Syria. Other pro-Iranian network groups in Iraq such as Kata'ib al-Imam Ali (Imam Ali Brigades) and Liwa Jund al-Imam (Soldiers of the Imam Brigade) were raised after the fall of Mosul to ISIS in June 2014, and are now starting to develop expeditionary forces to send to Syria.

Currently, the three most prominent proxy network groups in Hashd Shaab are Harakat Hezbollah al-Nujaba', Saraya al-Khorasani, and Quwat Abu Fadhil al-Abbas, all of which are led by commanders who were operatives for the Quds Force's Islamic Resistance in the 1980s and 1990s. Harakat Hezbollah al-Nujaba', led by Akram al-Ka'abi with an estimated 4,000 fighters, began as a Special Group that developed from the larger Kata'ib Hezbollah organization. It is now used as an expeditionary force that is frequently deployed to Syria. Saraya al-Khorasani, led by Ali al-Yasseri with an estimated 3,500 fighters, is associated with the political movement, Hizb al-Tal'ia al-Islamiyya (Islamic Vanguard Party), which works toward the implementation of the *wilayat al-faqih* through the Iraqi political process. Hizb al-Tali'a al-Islamiyya is closely associated with Saraya al-Khorasani and is aligned with the objectives of the Quds Force. The party is gaining power in the southern Iraqi provinces of Dhi Qar and Karbala. Quwat Abu Fadhil al-Abbas, led by Auws al-Khafaji with an estimated 2,000 fighters, has an expeditionary force that is also frequently deployed to Syria. The group is aggressively seeking to participate in the counter-ISIS campaign in Iraq's Ninewah province with a focus on seizing territory on the Iraqi-Syrian border.[37]

Other independent P.M.U. groups are also targets for influence and recruitment by the I.R.G.C., particularly Saraya al-Jihad (Jihad Brigade) and Kata'ib al-Risali (Missionaries' Brigades), led by Members of the Iraqi Parliament Hassan al-Sari and Adnan al-Shahmani, respectively. With a combined estimated strength of 10,000 fighters — 5,000 in each group — Sarayah al-Jihad and Kata'ib al-Risali are among the most powerful non-Iranian proxy network, non-Sadrist groups in the P.M.U.s.[38] Kata'ib al-Risali has absorbed a large component of Liwa al-Sayyida Shuhada, a pro-Iranian group, so as to benefit from the fighting expertise that estimated hundreds of Liwa al-Sayyida Shuhada members earned in combat in Syria.

Both led by Iraqi M.P.s, Sarayah al-Jihad and Kata'ib al-Risali are examples of how Iraqi Shi'a politicians have also used the P.M.U.s to mobilize militias to advance their socio-political power. The leaders of these two groups do not support the imposition of *wilayat al-faqih* in Iraq, but both leaders maintain a good working relationship with Muhandis. Both groups also have constituent militias that are favorable to *wilayat al-faqih* and follow Khomeini as their *marja' al-taqlid*, or source of emulation. It is therefore possible for the Quds Force, through the role of individuals such as Muhandis as deputy commissioner of the P.M.U.s, to build networks among the rank-and-file of individual P.M.U. groups including Saraya al-Jihad and Kata'ib al-Risali. As result network development is possible, even when the leaders of those groups do not actively promote *wilayat al-faqih*. Because of its absorption of the pro-Iranian network group, Liwa al-Sayyida Shuhada, Saraya al-Jihad is a particularly inviting target for I.R.G.C. cooptation.[39]

IMPLICATIONS FOR THE FUTURE OF IRAQ

Iraq is a key focus in the Quds Force's mission to protect the Iranian homeland. Strong I.R.G.C. influence over Iraq also provides an opportunity for Iran to achieve several important foreign policy objectives. Fundamentally, the I.R.G.C.'s purpose since its founding has been to achieve Khomeini's vision of Iran as leader of the Islamic world. Iraq was the young Islamic Republic's first target in its effort to spread a pan-sectarian Islamic Revolution beyond the borders of Iran.[40]

Due to regional geopolitics, for the time being Iran is limited to seeking control over the politics of Shiite-majority areas; in years to come it will focus on the larger mission of becoming the leader of the Islamic world. The P.M.U.s provide the I.R.G.C. with the capability to prevent a repeat of the June 2014 security debacle in Mosul, which threatened the Iranian homeland. Quds Force influence over the P.M.U.s also provides the I.R.G.C. with the ability to shape the power dynamics of Iraqi Shi'a politics, and thereby influence the socio-politics of the largest ethnically Arab Shi'a population.

However, the Quds Force's ability to control the P.M.U.s, and therefore major security structures of the Iraqi state, will not be uncontested, particularly from within the Shi'a community. Grand Ayatollah Ali al-Sistani, who opposes the implementation of the *wilayat al-faqih* in Iraq, will also be a constraining factor on the ability of the I.R.G.C. to assert its dominance over intra-Iraqi Shi'a politics. Sistani's personal authority as the popular source of emulation for many Iraqi Shiites, combined with his heretofore resistance against the concept of *wilayat al-faqih*, presents a social and political challenge to P.M.U. groups backed by the Quds Force. Sistani's position could stunt the efforts of these P.M.U.s to use their participation in the counter-ISIS campaign to build the social capital needed to establish themselves as political movements within the Shi'a community in Iraq, in the manner of Hezbollah in Lebanon.

Further, the I.R.G.C. may decide not to actively support the political efforts of the P.M.U. groups that are seeking to implement *wilayat al-faqih*, so as to avoid stoking greater tension within the Shi'a community and between Shi'a and Sunni communities. Iraq's stability and territorial integrity is a national security objective for policymakers in Tehran. To prevent communal violence in Iraq that would benefit ISIS or a successor organization, the I.R.G.C. could demand the cessation of controversial political activities of its proxy P.M.U. groups. This would include requiring the P.M.U. groups to stand down from participating in municipal elections, and to refrain from running candidates in parliamentary elections. The I.R.G.C. is seeking to build stability in Iraq by alleviating Iraqi Sunni grievances. In an attempt to accomplish that objective, the I.R.G.C. could decide to support inter-communal dialogues as a process of national reconciliation, through the initiative of Sistani and the clerical establishment in Najaf and Karbala.[41]

The Quds Force-backed P.M.U. groups are also challenged in their objective to establish *wilayat al-faqih* in Iraq by Moqtada al-Sadr's Saraya al-Salam and groups such as Liwa Ali al-Akbar and Firqa al-Abbas al-Qataliyya. These groups are mobilized and funded by organizations tied to the prominent Shi'a shrines in Najaf and Karbala, and are closer socially and politically to Sistani and his allies than the Quds Force. These shrine-backed groups have sought independence from the P.M.U. chain-of-command, and have even attempted to receive support and funding from the defense ministry rather than from the Badr Organization-dominated interior ministry.[42] Prime Minister Haider al-Abadi has the opportunity, through the shrine-backed groups and Saraya al-Salam, to reduce the strength of the Quds Force-backed groups in the P.M.U.s.

Saraya al-Salam, under the command of Sadr's deputy, Kazim Hassan al-Issawi, supports Sadr's policy of a pan-sectarian, Iraqi nationalist political platform that is meant to serve as a counterweight to the I.R.G.C.[43] Sadr's vision of a pan-sectarian, Iraqi nationalist political platform will be highly consequential to this simmering dispute, as his vision also aims to oppose the Quds Force's promotion of *wilayat al-faqih*. This dynamic demonstrates the complexity of socio-politics of identity within the P.M.U.s. It also points to the looming and potentially violent competition between two main P.M.U. camps: Groups that are close to the Quds Force and want to impose *wilayat al-faqih*, and groups that oppose that end state. The outcome of this intra-Shi'a conflict is likely to have a decisive effect on the socio-politics of the Iraqi Shi'a community and the future of Iraqi national politics, particularly regarding inter-communal harmony and the country's territorial integrity.

Since 2003, and particularly in the post-June 2014 period, the Quds Force has taken a "let a thousand flowers bloom" approach to shaping the socio-political development of Iraqi Shi'a militia groups that are now incorporated into the state-sponsored P.M.U.s. As in the period between 2007 and 2010, when the Quds Force actively supported Special Groups operations while shaping their ideological development, the I.R.G.C. now has an officially Baghdad-sponsored opportunity to continue to seed its Iraqi operatives in the P.M.U.s. The overarching objective of the Quds Force strategy is to continually develop networks of influence, so as to identify, recruit, and mobilize future fighters for a regional proxy network, while making it difficult to root out the Islamic Resistance from Iraqi state security structures.

ENDNOTES

1. This a process that the analyst Phillip Smyth refers to as building the Quds Force's "Foreign Legion of Sorts." Smyth, Phillip. "Testimony of Phillip Smyth, Research Analyst at the University of Maryland-Laboratory for Computational Cultural Dynamics-House Foreign Affairs Committee-Subcommittee on Terrorism, Nonproliferation, and Trade-Hearing on Terrorist Groups in Syria." November 20, 2013.

2. This total derived from analysis of the most update, comprehensive list of the P.M.U. groups provided by the Rawabet Center.

3. Author's review of the media production of the P.M.U. groups on Twitter, Facebook, and the Iraqi media.

4. Kalin, Stephen. "Iraq's Shi'ite Militias Could Prove Bigger Test than Mosul," Reuters, December 1, 2016; al-Kadhimi, Mustafa. "Will Sistani be Able to Control Popular Mobilization Forces?", *Al-Monitor*, March 12, 2015.

5. Author's discussions with U.S. military officials with knowledge of the P.M.U. force structure. Discussions occurred between March 1, 2016 and September 20, 2017.

6. Author's discussions with U.S. military officials with knowledge of the P.M.U. force structure. Discussions occurred between March 1, 2016 and September 20, 2017.

7. "Al-'Abadi min New York: Al-Hashd al-Sha'abi huwwa ahad tashkeelat al-dawlat al-rasmiyya [Al-'Abadi from New York: The P.M.U.s are one of the Official State Formations]," *Al-Qurat News*, October 1, 2015.

8. Sattar, Omar. "How Iraq's PMU Law is Disrupting National Unity Efforts," *Al-Monitor*, December 14, 2016; Aziz, Jean. "What are Iraq's Popular Mobilization Units Doing in Beirut?" *Al-Monitor*, August 18, 2016.

9. Author's review of the media production of the P.M.U. groups on Twitter, Facebook, and the Iraqi media, and the author's discussions with U.S. military officials with knowledge of the P.M.U. force structure. Discussions occurred between March 1, 2016 and September 20, 2017.

10. Author's review of the media production of Hashd Shaabithe P.M.U. groups on Twitter, Facebook, and the Iraqi media, and the author's discussions with U.S. military officials with knowledge of the Hashd Shaabi P.M.U. force structure. Discussions occurred between March 1, 2016 to September 20, 2017.

11. The comparison between the I.R.G.C.-Q.F. and the U.S. Army "Green Berets" was made by noted U.S. government historian, Navy SEAL officer, and the son of the former head of U.S. Central Command, David Crist. See: Crist, David. *The Twilight War: The Secret History of America's Thirty-Year Conflict with Iran*. New York, NY: Penguin, 2012, pg. 123.

12. "Qassem Soleimani: Iran's Near Invisible Quds Force Commander." *Agence France Presse*. July 2, 2014.

13. Rahimi, Babak. "Contentious Legacies of the Ayatollah." *A Critical Introduction to Khomeini*. Edited by Arshin Adib-Moghaddam. New York, N.Y.: Cambridge University Press, 2014, pg. 301; Takeyh, Ray. *Hidden Iran: Paradox and Power in the Islamic Republic*. New York, NY: Henry Holt and Company, 2007, pg. 34.

14. Alfoneh, Ali. *Iran Unveiled: How the Revolutionary Guards is Turning Theocracy into Military Dictatorship*. Washington, DC: The American Enterprise Institute Press, 2013, pg. 222; Baer, Robert. *The Devil We Know: Dealing with the New Iranian Superpower*. New York, NY: Crown Publishers, 2008, pg. 35.

15. Research and analysis provided in the following articles written by the author:

16. I.R.G.C. Major General Hossein Hamdani, in a May 2014 interview with the I.R.G.C.-leaning Fars News Agency, made a direct comparison between the Sacred Duty of the Iran-Iraq War and the current conflict in Syria. The Syrian civil war was the proving ground for Iraqi Shi'a militant organizations close to the Quds Force that would later mobilize Hashd Shaabi militias. See: Karami, Arash. "Former I.R.G.C. Commander's on Syria Censored." *Al-Monitor Iran Pulse*. May 6, 2014.

17. Crist, David. *The Twilight War: The Secret History of America's Thirty-Year Conflict with Iran*. New York, NY: Penguin Books, 2012, pgs. 460, 513.

18. Baer, Robert. *The Devil We Know: Dealing With the New Iranian Superpower*. New York, NY: Crown Publishers, 2008, pg. 21.

19. Crist, David. *The Twilight War: The Secret History of America's Thirty-Year Conflict with Iran*. New York, NY: Penguin Books, 2012, pg. 471.

20. Ricks, Thomas E. *The Gamble: General David Petraeus and the American Military Adventure in Iraq, 2006-2008*. New York, NY: Penguin Press, 2009, pg. 51.

21. "Treasury Designates Individuals and Entities Fueling Violence in Iraq." U.S. Department of the Treasury. September 16, 2008.

22. Black, Ian and Dehgan, Saeed Kamali. "Qassim Suleimani: Commander of Quds Force, Puppeteer of the Middle East." *The Guardian*. June 16, 2014.

23. "Abu Mahdi and Iran's Web in Iraq," *UPI*, October 20, 2010.

24. Rayburn, Joel. *Iraq After America: Strongmen, Sectarians, Resistance*. Palo Alto, CA: Stanford University Press, 2014, pg. 200.

25. Hamid, Salih. "Qa'id al-Hashd al-Shaabi: Afkhar Bikuni Jundiaan ladaa Solemani [the P.M.U.'s Leader: I Am Proud to be Soleimani's Soldier]," *Al-Arabiyya*, April 4, 2017.

26. Parker, Ned, Rasheed, Ahmed, and Salman, Raheem. "Before Iraq Election, Shi'ite Militias Unleashed in War on Sunni Insurgents," *Reuters*, April 27, 2016.

27. "Iraq's al-Hashd al-Shaabi Forces Inspired by Iran's Basij/Saudi Regime is the Root of All Evil," *Ahlul Bayt News Agency*, August 17, 2015.

28. Knights, Michael. "Iraq's Popular Demobilisation,"*Al-Jazeera*, February 26, 2016. Zana K. "A Short Profile of Iraq's Shi'a Militias," *Jamestown Foundation Terrorism Monitor*, Volume 13, Issue 8, April 17, 2015.

29. "Press TV's Interview with Abu Mahdi al-Muhandis," *Press TV*, May 31, 2016; Dehghanpisheh, Babak. "Special Report: The Fighters of Iraq who Answer to Iran," Reuters, November 12, 2014.

30. Esfandiari, Golnaz. "Explainer: How Iran Could Help Iraq Fight ISIL." *Radio Free Europe/ Radio Liberty*. July 4, 2014; Black, Ian and Dehgan, Saeed Kamali. "Qassim Suleimani: Commander of Quds Force, Puppeteer of the Middle East." *The Guardian*. June 16, 2014; Cockburn, Patrick. "Iraq Crisis: Iran to Step in to Defend Baghdad from Sunni Extremists and Prevent Collapse of Iraqi State." *The Independent*. June 13, 2014; Fassihi, Farnaz. "Iran Deploys Forces to Fight Al-Qaeda Inspired Militants in Iraq." *The Wall Street Journal*. June 12, 2014.

31. Siegel, Jacob. "Baghdad's Shi'a Militia Plans for War on ISIS." *The Daily Beast*. July 16, 2014; Brown, Jeremy. "The Fearsome Iraqi Militia Vowing to Vanquish ISIS." *BBC*. July 7, 2014; Freeman, Colin. "Iraq Crisis: Baghdad's Shi'a Militia in Defiant 50,000-Strong Rally as ISIS Makes Further Gains." *The Telegraph*. June 21, 2014.

32. Siegel, Jacob. "The Brewing Battle for Baghdad." *The Daily Beast*. August 3, 2014; Heras, Nicholas A. "Iraqi Shi'a Militia Asa'ib Ahl al-Haq Expands Operations to Syria." *Jamestown Foundation Terrorism Monitor*. May 15, 2014; Morris, Loveday. "Shi'a Militias in Iraq Begin to Remobilize." *The Washington Post*. February 9, 2014.

33. Smyth, Phillip. "Testimony of Phillip Smyth, Research Analyst at the University of Maryland-Laboratory for Computational Cultural Dynamics-House Foreign Affairs Committee-Subcommittee on Terrorism, Nonproliferation, and Trade-Hearing on Terrorist Groups in Syria." November 20, 2013.

34. Al-Sarhan, Saud. "From Qusair to Yabrud: Shi'a Foreign Fighters in Syria." *Al-Monitor*. March 6, 2014; Al-Salhy, Suad. "Syria War Widens Rift Between Shi'ite Clergy in Iraq, Iran." *Reuters*. July 20, 2013; Mahmoud, Mona and Chulov, Martin. "Syrian War Widens Sunni-Shi'a Schism as Foreign Jihadis Join Fight for Shrines." *The Guardian*. June 4, 2013.

35. Heras, Nicholas A. "Shi'a Popular Mobilization Units in a Post-Islamic State Iraq: A Look at Peace Brigade Commander Shaykh Kazim al-Issawi," *Jamestown Foundation Militant Leadership Monitor*, May 2, 2017.

36. The Quds Force's battle-hardened, expanding, and expeditionary Hezbollah network would not be possible without the large number of veteran, Iraqi Shi'a fighters inside of it. According to the analyst Phillip Smyth, the

Quds Force's growing Hezbollah network represents a "foreign legion of sorts that can be used as a rapid reaction force." Smyth, Phillip. *The Shi'ite Jihad and Its Regional Effects*, (Washington Institute for Near East Policy), February 2015; "Testimony of Phillip Smyth, Research Analyst at the University of Maryland-Laboratory for Computational Cultural Dynamics-House Foreign Affairs Committee-Subcommittee on Terrorism, Nonproliferation, and Trade-Hearing on Terrorist Groups in Syria." November 20, 2013; Smyth, Phillip. "From Karbala to Sayyida Zaynab: Iraqi Fighters in Syria's Shi'a Militias." *CTC Sentinel*. August 27, 2013.

37. Research and analysis provided in the following articles written by the author: "A Look at Iraq's Battlefield Parliamentarians: The P.M.U. Commanders Leading the Fight Against Mosul," *Jamestown Foundation Militant Leadership Monitor*, November 1, 2016; "To the Gates of Mosul: A Snapshot of Sayyid Ali al-Yasseri & Sayyid Hamid al-Jazaeri, Co-Leaders of the Khorasani Brigades Shi'a Militias," *Jamestown Foundation Militant Leadership Monitor*, July 31, 2016; "The I.R.G.C.'S Iraqi Point Men in Syria: Shaykh Auws al-Khafaji and Shaykh Ammar al-Lami," *Jamestown Foundation Militant Leadership Monitor*, October 31, 2015; "Akram al-Ka'abi and Harakat al-Nujaba: Iraqi Shi'a Militia Takes on the Islamic State," *Jamestown Foundation Militant Leadership Monitor*, August 31, 2014.

38. Heras, Nicholas A. "A Look at Iraq's Battlefield Parliamentarians: The P.M.U. Commanders Leading the Fight Against Mosul," *Jamestown Foundation Militant Leadership Monitor*, November 1, 2016.

39. Heras, Nicholas A. "A Look at Iraq's Battlefield Parliamentarians: The P.M.U. Commanders Leading the Fight Against Mosul," *Jamestown Foundation Militant Leadership Monitor*, November 1, 2016.

40. Reda, L.A. "Khatt-e Imam: The Followers of Khomeini's Line." A Critical Introduction to Khomeini. Edited by Arshin Adib-Moghaddam. New York, NY: Cambridge University Press, 2014, pg. 133.

41. This paragraph is based on the author's interviews in Europe with Iranian national security experts based in Tehran, July 9-12, 2017 and February 13-15, 2017.

42. Author's discussions with U.S. military officials with knowledge of the P.M.U.s' force structure. Discussions occurred between March 1, 2016 and September 20, 2017.

43. Heras, Nicholas A. "Shi'a Popular Mobilization Units in a Post-Islamic State Iraq: A Look at Peace Brigade Commander Shaykh Kazim al-Issawi," *Jamestown Foundation Militant Leadership Monitor*, May 2, 2017.

Chapter Eleven

The Fatemiyoun Division:

Afghan Fighters in the Syrian Civil War

Tobias Schneider

Introduction

In the late fall of 2012, one year into the Syrian civil war, opposition activists appeared to be steadily losing their grip on reality. As they battled loyalists across the country, their explanations for why they still hadn't managed to dislodge the recalcitrant regime of Bashar al-Assad grew ever more outlandish. Rebels reported seeing among their enemies all sorts of "mercenaries" including Egyptians, Yemenis, and — incredibly — Afghans. Eventually, one rebel group managed to capture a confused and disheveled-looking Afghan fighter who identified himself to opposition cameras as Mortada Hussein. Since then, Liwa al-Fatemiyoun, or the Fatemiyoun Division, an Iranian Islamic Revolutionary Guards Corps (IRGC) affiliate composed almost entirely of Shi'i Afghans, has become a fixture on the Syrian battlefield. The group holds some of the most dangerous front lines, leading some of the most well-publicized war campaigns on behalf the Assad regime. They operate under orders of the Iranian leadership, represented by General Qassem Soleimani on the battlefield.

ORIGIN STORY

The conservative Iranian daily *Kayhan* published a semi-official history of the Fatemiyoun Division based on what it claims are interviews with veterans of the group.[1] The daily traces the division's origins to a small and fluctuating number of volunteers organized as the Muhammad Corps. The group first fought against the Soviet occupation of Afghanistan, and later responded to the late Imam Khomeini's popular mass mobilization for the Iran-Iraq War, known as "The Imposed War" in Iranian regime parlance. Already then, *Kayhan* notes, at least one fighter received Iranian citizenship for his devotion to the Islamic Republic. The group returned to Afghanistan in the 1990s to fight the budding Taliban movement, but according to *Kayhan*, it was later forced to dissolve. Its fighters fled their homeland yet again following the 2001 invasion for fear of persecution by the new Afghan government and its American-led coalition backers.

According to the paper, when the Syrian conflict erupted, the group's commander Ali-Reza Tavassoli, known as Abu Hamed, and senior cleric Mohammad Baqir Alaoui petitioned the Iranian government for his then 22-25 fighters based around Mashhad to be sent to Syria to defend the shrine of Sayyeda Zaynab. The request was swiftly approved in Tehran under the new umbrella of the "Fatemiyoun."

In its earlier days, the group was said to have collaborated closely with the Iraqi militia Kata'ib Sayyid al-Shuhada, a splinter faction of Kataeb Hezbollah active in Syria since the summer of 2013,[2] and other formations including Lebanese Hezbollah. According to the history, Tavassoli's leadership and the sacrifices committed by his group managed to quickly mobilize thousands of Afghans. Some Afghans already resided in Damascus and others lived in Iran. Two other groups of 15 and 22 members each, all with similar personal backgrounds, quickly joined the fight. While still closely cooperating with other IRGC groups, the Kayhan article notes, the Fatemiyoun grew in size to the point where they constituted their own formal militia, brigade, and eventually division.

SEPARATING FACT FROM FICTION

While obviously highly embellished for propaganda purposes, *Kayhan's* historical account appears to correspond to the individual biographies of senior Fatemiyoun commanders who were killed in battle and whose exploits could be recounted. According to his biography, for example, the formation's founder and first leader, Ali Reza Tavassoli,[3] moved from Afghanistan to Iran in the 1980s. He joined the Abouzar Brigade, an early subdivision of the IRGC composed predominantly of Afghan Shi'i fighters dedicated to the Islamic Revolution proclaimed by Imam Khomeini. The Abouzar Brigade was based in the Ramazan Garrison in Iranian Kurdistan and was engaged in confronting Saddam Hussein's invasion as well as Kurdish separatists. According to reports, official Iranian figures account for 2,000 members of the brigade who perished over the course of the conflict with Iraq.[4] In the 1990s, Tavassoli reportedly returned to Afghanistan to fight the Taliban movement. Other Fatemiyoun commanders of his generation, such as Sayyed Hakim, Hossein Fadaei Abdarchaya,[5] Reza Khavari, Seyyed Ibrahim, and others share similar biographies of early service in the "Sacred Defense," as the Islamic Republic refers to the Iran-Iraq War, as well as battles against the Taliban in 1990s.[6] According to Iranian Defa Press, Sayyed Hakim, killed in Syria in 2016, was the last surviving veteran Fatemiyoun commander of that generation[7]

However, beyond the personal motivations and backgrounds of individuals, narrative and history quickly begin to diverge. The IRGC began to cultivate a narrative of "indigenous resistance" in Syria in an early attempt to legitimize the presence of foreign fighters and to deflect attention from its increasingly heavy-handed recruitment methods. In the IRGC narrative, Afghans volunteered not only to defend the Shi'i shrines in Damascus but also to protect the small community of Hazara refugees that had settled around the holy Sayyeda Zaynab mosque since the 1990s after assault by radical Sunni groups. In this version of events, Iran, which continues to insist its mission in Syria is purely advisory, was merely assisting dedicated Afghan volunteers in their efforts to reach Damascus until the organization would be large enough to manage its own affairs and logistics.

In reality, the Afghan community of Sayyeda Zaynab had been very minor prior to the outbreak of conflict in Syria, numbering no more than 2,000 individuals, many of whom had been displaced again or attempted to flee Syria by 2013.[8] It also did not provide any significant contribution to the early or later versions of the Fatemiyoun Division, which swiftly emerged as an ideological and institutional appendage of the IRGC. Indeed, as Ahmad Shuja points out, Fatemiyoun members were usually allowed only scheduled visits to the shrine at the bookends of their deployments to Syria.[9] Members were also prohibited from interacting with Afghan residents. While some recruitment efforts coordinated by official Iranian representatives reached into Afghanistan, the majority of recruits were drawn from the large Afghan migrant and refugee underclass within Iran itself. Thus, when Tavassoli died in battle in Syria's southern Daraa governorate in early 2015, his body was returned and interred in Iran, not Afghanistan — just like the other nearly 900 confirmed dead Fatemiyoun fighters documented by researcher Ali Alfoneh.[10]

[11] Indeed, Tavassoli's deputy Reza Bakhshi, who perished just ten days before his commander, had been born and raised entirely in Iran.[12] After both were killed in Syria, the Fatemiyoun formation was reportedly placed entirely under the direct command of IRGC officers.

ESTIMATING NUMBERS

The initial handful of veterans from battles with Iraq and with the Taliban in Afghanistan has grown today's Fatemiyoun movement. In his interview with Raja News, Hosseini Tavassoli said the first volunteer group was 22 people who arrived in Syria in late 2012. This was apparently followed by a second group of 15, and a third of another 22 volunteers, including himself. The fifth batch, according to Hosseini, was already five times the initial size — a hundred men. Within a span of three years, the formation would grow to several thousand.[13]

Estimates of the numerical strength of the Fatemiyoun throughout the conflict vary significantly. The most often-cited count of 20,000 appears to originate with a report by the IRGC-affiliated Mashregh News. Al Jazeera English deemed the same number credible, after confirming with other military officials and speaking to retired IRGC Colonel Hussain Kanani Moghdam, a centrist member of Parliament.[14] He estimated Fatemiyoun strength to be "in the tens of thousands," though he also misattributed the group's origins to Afghanistan proper. The aforementioned fallen Fatemiyoun commander Mohammad Hassan Hosseini put the total count at a more realistic peak of 12,000-14,000, acknowledging fluctuations due to rotations, availability of logistics, and need for specific skills in-theater.[15] The reported 2015 elevation of the Fatemiyoun from brigade to division status is similarly said by Iran's Alef News Agency to suggest a minimum strength of 10,000 men.[16]

Such estimates can be considered credible if Iranian and Fatemiyoun sources include within their count individuals off rotation or those busy in the formation's cultural and support units. Opposition officials are prone to inflating the Iranian-sponsored threat and generally speak of much lower numbers ranging from 4,000-8,000 fighters deployed at any given time.[17] Such estimates match reports by defectors and captives, such as Hamid Ali, who told Human Rights Watch (HRW) that between its military bases in Aleppo, Hama, Latakia, Damascus, and Homs, the Fatemiyoun fielded 3,000-4,000 fighters. Ali's description of roughly 400 fighters per sector also matches propaganda releases by the Fatemiyoun's media offices, which usually show no more than one or two IRGC companies, roughly 200-250 men each, in a single frame. Even larger battles, such as the capture of Palmyra from Islamic State forces in 2015, were fought at similar manpower levels.

RECRUITMENT

In their testimonies to journalists and human rights activists, survivors and deserters of the Fatemiyoun paint a disturbing picture of recruitment, as well as of life and service in the purported volunteer division. These individuals consistently and independently from one another reported being coerced or bribed into joining; being funneled onto battlefields with little or no preparation; not understanding the context of the war they were fighting; and finally, being expended as cannon fodder in some of the most intense battles of the Syrian war.[18 19]

The approximately 3 million Afghan refugees and migrants residing in Iran from which the Fatemiyoun draws its manpower face extraordinary economic hardship as well as xenophobic and bureaucratic discrimination. Witnessing Iran's ethnically and religiously persecuted Shi'i Hazara minority, Afghan refugees are fearful of potentially being delivered back across the border into the arms of the Taliban or other Sunni extremist movements rampant in their war-ravaged home country. Caught between a rock and a hard place,[20] they live in regular fear of Iranian authorities[21] and struggle to make a living, often operating on the margins of Iranian society as builders, domestic staff or street vendors.[22] After Syrians, Afghan Hazaras from Iran and Afghanistan make up a disproportionate share of refugee arrivals on European shores[23]

A number of former fighters interviewed in international media report being arrested by Iranian security forces — generally for residency or drug-related charges — and offered the stark choice of prison, deportation, or service in Syria.[24] In an extensive report from January 2016, HRW corroborated these accounts after speaking with two dozen former Fatemiyoun fighters.[25] Next to regularizing their residency status, other interviewees note the appeal of monthly salaries of $450[26] to $800[27,28] being offered by recruiters. Such an amount is a veritable fortune for many Afghans scraping by at the bottom of an economy that struggles to provide sufficient opportunity for its own nationals.

BBC Persia visited a Fatemiyoun recruitment office in Mashhad and spoke to migrants in Europe who reported that promises of amnesty or financial rewards were not always honored. One refugee arrived in Mytilene, Greece and signed up to avoid a lengthy prison sentence or deportation. He said he served 12 months in Syria only to be offered a 30-day temporary residency card upon his return to Iran. Disappointed, he decided to escape to Europe.[29]

In a separate report, HRW found evidence of child recruitment, forbidden under the Optional Protocol of the Rome Statute. HRW identified at least 14 individual Afghan minors, aged 14-17 years old, who had fought and died in Syria under Fatemiyoun command.[30]

In recent years, as word of the fighters' fates travelled back to Iran, the Islamic

Republic has begun pushing back against such reports. State authorities allege that former fighters embellished horror stories in the hope of receiving asylum in Europe, or in the case of those captured and interviewed by Syrian rebel groups, were coerced into making derogatory statements. Following a prisoner exchange in 2016, the IRGC put on a press conference with two survivors who recanted the statements they had made to opposition TV stations,[31] and who instead professed their religious devotion to defending the Shrine of Zaynab.

A COMMUNITY CAUGHT BETWEEN STARK CHOICES

In a more free-flowing interview with the ultra-conservative Raja News,[32] now-deceased Fatemiyoun commander Mohammad Hassan Hosseini, known as Sayyed Hakim, tackled some of these issues, acknowledging the hardships of refugee life, the difficulties of obtaining residency status, and the many who have crossed to Europe. At the same time, he sold jihad in Syria not merely as a means of achieving residency, but as a pursuit of dignity, self-reliance, and salvation. The vanguard status of the Fatemiyoun to him was a point of pride. At one point he even suggested that the Fatemiyoun had attracted returnees from the West.

Indeed, the motivations of fighters are impossible to understand outside the political and socioeconomic context of the Hazara community of Iran. All forced impressment, especially of minors, is reprehensible. Due to the stark choices at their disposal, Iran-based Afghan refugees may see fighting in Syria, whether coerced or voluntary, as an opportunity to find religious, personal, or financial fulfillment. Motivations for joining the Fatemiyoun could be complex and multi-layered. On a research trip across Iran in early 2016, this author interviewed a number of young Afghan men in Tehran, Qom, and Mashhad who related their personal dilemmas. Many spoke of choosing between paying smugglers to take them on the perilous road to Europe or being paid by the IRGC to go to Syria. They hoped for a more dignified existence for themselves and their families in this life or the next.

RISING PROFILE

In a wide-ranging interview with the IRGC-affiliated Tasnim News Agency, the purportedly retired Iranian Brigadier General Mohammad Ali Falaki, who led Fatemiyoun forces in Syria, acknowledges these tensions as well.[33] He extolled the extraordinary sacrifice and bemoaning prejudice against Afghan migrants in Iran, stating: "We in Iran have sometimes looked at [Afghans] as drug-dealing criminals, trouble-makers, or construction workers. ... Their blood has proven to us that there are 2.5 million Afghans in [Iran] and we must have a positive view towards them."

Framing the issue in ideological and historical terms, Falaki noted the significance of the Fatemiyoun next to other foreign Shi'i fighting groups in Syria. He highlighted the Iraqi division (Hayderiyoun) and the Pakistani division (Zaynabiyoun) as part of a combined Khomeinist vanguard force that transcends national and tribal identities. He related his experience of the Iran-Iraq war, when, under pressure by Iraq, they had to quickly organize various groups for the fight, even Sunnis. Included in this effort was the Abouzar Brigade, in which many of the original Fatemiyoun had served.

Indeed, as the Fatemiyoun Division has grown in size and importance so too has its public outreach campaign.[34] Through the Fatemiyoun, the IRGC has recognized an opportunity to bridge the ethnic and socioeconomic divides that Hazaras face in Iran. The rise of the division led the IRGC to construct a more inclusive transnational jihadi ideology that ties the vulnerable and defensive minority community to the Islamic Republic's own state ideology. It also channels budding notions of Shi'i Hazara emancipation and self-defense into Iran's own established framework of resistance, thereby expanding this framework's reach and softening the sense of Tehran as simply a rising geopolitical hegemon.

The IRGC has made a concerted effort to raise the profile of the Fatemiyoun as a vanguard unit for both the Hazara community and transnational Shi'ism — both at home and abroad. In collaboration with the official Fatemiyoun media office, which operates its own social media channels and public outreach, Iranian film director Mortaza Fallahfar produced a series of short films introducing and extolling the division to a wider audience over the course of two years.[35] [36] The films blend personal stories of martial courage, religious exultation, and individual resilience with fast-paced, high-resolution footage filmed during embeds in some of the pivotal battles fought by the division. For example, one film centers around a Fatemiyoun fighter who spent 14 months in rebel captivity. The films were screened at IRGC-affiliated theaters and events throughout the country and shared widely via Telegram and other social media channels with tens of thousands of subscribers. They are meant to instill pride, devotion, and potential curiosity among Afghan youth to enlist themselves.

Next to visual and social media, more traditionally Shi'i modes to express reverence have also been used. A memorial service held for three Fatemiyoun fighters killed in August 2017 in the holy shrine city of Mashhad was attended by thousands of mourners.[37] Traditional lamentation and eulogy songs have been written and distributed. Supreme Leader Ali Khamenei has repeatedly commended the sacrifice of Afghans sent to the Levant under his authority. He has visited the gravesites of Afghan martyrs and issued regular proclamations to those still fighting in the field. In a March 2016 audience, for example, he expressed pride for the relatives of Fatemiyoun fighters killed in the war, proclaiming that their "children have created a shield with their lives to protect the holy shrines from these evil [forces]."[38]

Training and Material

After joining, Afghan recruits receive between two and four weeks of rudimentary infantry training administered by IRGC cadres in at least nine camps identified by U.S. intelligence inside Iran.[39] One has been identified as Padegan-e Shahid Pazouki near Qarchak outside Tehran,[40,41] and another two reportedly near Shiraz and Yazd.[42] Scarce visual evidence of these training camps show basic facilities and no more than a few hundred recruits, including Pakistanis and Arabs, present at any time.[43] Additional open source information suggests that once inside Syria, certain units may then receive additional training at IRGC bases scattered throughout the country. For example, propaganda material and social media posts released by the division and its affiliates show specialized combat units, such as reconnaissance and sniper formations, trained by what are claimed to be Lebanese Hezbollah instructors.[44] The training infrastructure is shared with other nationality-based groups, such as Iraqis and Pakistanis.

The division also operates a wide array of heavy weapons and tanks. As per an arrangement between the IRGC and the Syrian Arab Army, on top of their own imports, Iranian proxy forces have liberal access to the manpower-depleted Syrian Army's overflowing depots and facilities[45] and have outfitted themselves accordingly. As a result, Fatemiyoun fighters have been observed operating a wide array of Soviet-era heavy weapons, including field artillery pieces, armored personnel carriers, anti-tank missiles, and tanks. Most notably, Fatemiyoun have at multiple times been observed operating a Russian-delivered sophisticated T-90 model tank,[46] the most advanced main battle tank (MBT) operating in the Syrian theater. An entire series of the tank has apparently been transferred to — or fallen into the hands of — IRGC-backed groups. While the Fatemiyoun's connection with Syrian and Shi'i forces is relatively transparent, there remains some speculation regarding the precise relationship between IRGC formations and Russian supply chains and fighters. Afghan researcher Ahmad Shuja found one Fatemiyoun fighter apparently bragging about having received training on a BMP armored infantry fighting vehicle from Russian nationals.[47] Most likely, IRGC units have built working relationships with Russian Special Forces and Wagner mercenary units operating in their sectors.

OPERATIONS

Despite high access to training and materiel, former fighters have suggested that no other group has been as mentally and tactically unprepared for combat or kept in positions of social isolation as the Fatemiyoun. Many allege that, due to prejudice and a lack of local constituency, they have been unduly used as "cannon fodder." Despite the fact that the group has developed nominally advanced capabilities for the Syrian battlefield, it continues to suffer extraordinary rates of attrition.

The Fatemiyoun are among the only formations in Syria whose absolute and relative casualty numbers have increased over the course of the conflict, even when compared to Iraqi and Lebanese sister formations under the IRGC umbrella. Data based on funerals shows a steady rise in Afghan combat fatalities, beginning with initial reports in 2013 to unprecedented heights throughout 2016 and 2017, when the Fatemiyoun suffered especially heavy attrition — as many as 45 per month — in battles against rebels in Aleppo and multiple campaigns against ISIS across Syria's vast eastern regions.[48]

Since their initial arrival on the Syrian battlefield, the Fatemiyoun have fought on every front of the war: Latakia, Hama, Idlib, Aleppo, Homs, Deir Ezzor, Damascus, and Daraa. Culturally and linguistically isolated and unaware of the context of any given battle, loyalist commanders concerned about issues like defection or corruption have instead relied on disoriented Fatemiyoun units to hold positions that Syrian forces might otherwise abandon. While most contemporary Syrian forces are locally raised and largely bound to their respective areas, the Fatemiyoun also offer flexibility.

RETURN TO AFGHANISTAN

In Afghanistan itself, the relationship between these Fatemiyoun fighters and the native Hazara community remains a highly contentious issue. In the majority conservative Sunni country, many consider the Fatemiyoun's participation in jihad against Sunnis abroad both a national and sectarian affront.[49] The Afghan government outlawed the group and worked to suppress it, largely in order to avoid further sectarian strife and proxy warfare in the war-ravaged country.[50] A number of individuals accused of association or recruitment on its behalf, including the representative of Iran's supreme leader in Kabul, Qurban Ghalambor, have been arrested by Afghan authorities.[51] One Afghan official caused a stir in late 2017, when he participated in a Fatemiyoun gathering in Iran, praising the brigade and its leaders.[52]

Nonetheless, journalists who pursued the story found that while IRGC recruitment for Syria may have gone underground, it has by no means disappeared and is still coordinated out of the Iranian embassy in Kabul.[53] Both the Afghan capital and Herat (the regional city closest to Iran) are reported to host active Fatemiyoun recruitment offices.[54,55]

Similar reports also continue to emerge about recruitment and mobilization efforts among Shi'i communities based along Pakistan's western frontier. The area is a principal recruitment ground for the Fatemiyoun's Urdu-speaking sister unit, the aforementioned Zeinabiyoun.

As the IRGC's outreach efforts continue inside Afghanistan, observers are rightly worried that Iran may eventually chose to reverse the flow of militancy and shift thousands of now battle-hardened Fatemiyoun from Syria back to Afghanistan. Indeed, some outside observers claim to have identified active Fatemiyoun returnee networks operating inside Afghanistan. In a brief for IHS Jane's Terrorism & Insurgency Monitor from July 2017, well-respected Afghanistan researcher Antonio Giustozzi reported on an active Shi'i Hazara militant network of up to 4,000 individuals led by returnees from Syria and funded by the IRGC with active branches in Hazarajat, Kabul, and Mazar-i Sharif. The author cited both Fatemiyoun and Afghan intelligence sources and suggested that the groups had already engaged in limited armed operations against anti-Hazara and anti-Iranian groups in Wardak province.[56]

While on the face credible, there has been no independent corroboration of such reports. While many veterans of the Syrian fight have returned to Afghanistan, there is little evidence that they pose any direct threat to the country. In a recent report for *The Washington Post*, Pamela Constable meets a number of demobilized returnees in Herat trying to adjust to normal civilian lives in Afghanistan — others re-enlisting over and over again due to economic necessity.[57]

Identification of Afghan ethnic and religious communities with sectarian warfare in the Levant has the potential to further destabilize a fraught situation along the Hindukush. Already, radical Sunni groups on both sides of the border have targeted Shi'i communities in retribution for their supposed support for Iranian-backed militant activity in Syria and Iraq. After a bloody 2016 attack on Hazaras in Kabul that left 80 people dead, a local ISIS militant leader told Reuters that "unless [the Hazaras] stop going to Syria and stop being slaves of Iran, we will definitely continue such attacks." A similar justification was given for a December 2017 suicide bombing on the Shi'i Tabayan cultural center in Kabul, which ISIS claimed recruited young Afghans to fight in Syria that killed at least 40 people.[58]

Afghan and coalition officials, therefore, remain rightly worried about the potential blowback from its citizens participating and returning from both the Shi'i and Sunni jihad in the Levant.[59]

OUTLOOK

On Nov. 21, 2017, Iran's President Hassan Rouhani declared that "with God's guidance and the resistance of people in the region, we can say that this evil has either been lifted from the head of the people or has been reduced" and that the so-called caliphate had been destroyed.[60] Following months of operations across wide-open desert terrain, hundreds of miles from the shrines it was sworn to protect, the Fatemiyoun Division, as part of a multinational IRGC-led force consisting primarily of Iraqi, Syrian, Lebanese, Afghan, and Pakistani Shi'i fighters, had zig-zagged across the border from Syria to Iraq and back towards al-Bukamal,[61] threatening ISIS's last territorial holdings and establishing an overland connection from Iran to Syria and Lebanon.

While Fatemiyoun fighters continue to fight and die on Syrian soil, especially in restive Deir Ezzor in the east, their principal mission has come to an end. Assad has been retained in power and fighting around the country is winding down, as rebel pocket after rebel pocket surrenders or evacuates.

Contrary to fears voiced by the opposition, there is no evidence that Afghans affiliated with the Fatemiyoun Division are made to — or even allowed to — settle in Syria as part of a sectarian re-engineering scheme. There are also no signs of an imminent redeployment to Yemen, the Golan, or any other tense conflict zone in which the IRGC has meddled in the past. While some officials, such as Deputy Commander of the Quds Force Ismail Ghani have reaffirmed the Fatemiyoun's dedication to the transnational militant cause, the next battle does not appear to have been chosen.

Instead, most early signals suggest that the IRGC has at least temporarily frozen recruitment, suggesting it plans to either maintain or slowly decrease troop levels. Meanwhile, senior officials and propaganda outlets affiliated with the groups have shifted in tone from military to ideological battle. As Ahmad Shuja noted, the division's cultural deputy, Hojjat Ganabadinejad, announced via Telegram the end of military operations and the beginning of a "cultural, ideological and social front." As the IRGC consolidates its military gains in Syria, it will seek to translate them into ideological and political currency at home, as well as across its non-Persian constituencies — including the many thousands who have come to identify with the Syrian jihad of the Fatemiyoun.

In the course of no more than three years, the IRGC was able to set up and mobilize a powerful militia, many thousand strong, drawing on a dedicated but long-dormant core of militants for leadership and large vulnerable social strata for recruits. Even if it chooses to demobilize the Fatemiyoun, the emergence of a single, largely cohesive military and ideological web from the Hindu Kush to the Mediterranean, anchored in Qom and Mashhad, means that if Iran ever again feels similarly threatened, it could likely re-create the experiment.

ENDNOTES

1. "لشكر «فاطميون» چگونه شكل گرفت؟" (How was the Fatemiyoun Division formed?), *Kayhan*, May 30, 2015.

2. "Appendix 2: Understanding the Organizations Deployed to Syria," *The Washington Institute*, February 2015.

3. شهید علیرضا توسلی فرمانده افغانی تیپ فاطمیون(س)/ سرداری كه به بیس دیدار یار رفت (Martyr Alireza Tvassoli, Afghan Fatemiyoun Commander), *DSRC*, Mar. 4, 2015.

4. "تیپ فاطميون «لشكر» شد", *Defa Press*, May 20, 2015.

5. "آبادرچايی كه «قوماندان» لشكر بود/ به نام «كيش» به ماك «حلب» (Abdarchaya—the commander of the "Keesh" Division in Aleppo), *Fars News Agency*, May 5, 2016.

6. "سید حكيم" تنها بازمانده هسته اوليه فاطميون به شهادت رسید (Sayyed Hakim was the last survivor of the original Fatemiyoun), *Defa Press*, Jun. 6, 2016.

7. Ibid.

8. Ahmad Shuja, "Syria's Afghan refugees trapped in a double crisis," *UN Dispatch*, Jan. 28, 2013.

9. Ahmad Shuja, "Mission accomplished? What's next for Iran's Afghan fighters in Syria," *War on the Rocks*, Feb. 13, 2018.

10. Ali Afoneh, "Shi'a Afghan Fighters in Syria," *SyriaSource*, Apr. 19, 2017.

11. Ali Afoneh, Twitter post, May 7, 2018, 3:43 a.m.

12. زاغ كی تغییری: نیروی انتظامی ایران برای شهدای مهاجر افغانستان شرم نظامی میزند (Beginning of change: Iran's police forces march for Afghan refugee martyrs), *Tasnim News Agency*, Apr. 11, 2015.

13. "تشكيلات فعلی فاطميون ابتدا كی ئيئت خانگی مشهد بود/ تعدادی از افغانها به اروپا رفتند و شهيد شدند/ چیزی برای «پنهان كردن» نداریم (Interview with the martyr Mohammad Hassan Hosseini [Sayyed Hakim]), *Raja News*, Jun. 17, 2016.

14. Hashmatallah Moslih, "Iran 'foreign legion' leans on Afghan Shi'a in Syria war," *Al Jazeera*, Jan. 22, 2016.

15. Interview with the martyr Mohammad Hassan Hosseini [Sayyed Hakim]), *Raja News*, Jun. 17, 2016.

16. "تیپ فاطميون، لشكر شد / 200 شهيد افغان در سوریه" (The Fatemiyoun Brigade: 200 Afghan martyrs in Syria), *Alef*, May 20, 2015.

17. Sune Engel Rasmussen and Zahra Nader, "Iran covertly recruits Afghan Shi'as to fight in Syria," *The Guardian*, Jun. 30, 2016

18. Fariba Sahraei, "Syria war: The Afghans sent by Iran to fight for Assad," *BBC*, Apr. 15, 2016.

19. Christoph Reuter, "Murad's War: An Afghan face to the Syrian conflict," *Afghanistan Analysts Network*, Jun. 26, 2016.

20. Patrick Strickland, "Why are Afghan refugees leaving Iran?" *Al Jazeera*, May 17, 2016.

21. Noor Zahid and Mehdi Jedinia, "Iran Continues Deporting Undocumented Afghan Refugees," *VOA*, May 21, 2017.

22. "Afghan Refugees in Iran & Pakistan," *European Resettlement Network*, 2013.

23. Peter Bouckaert, "Europe's Refugee Crisis Isn't Only About Syria," *Foreign Policy*, Sept. 18, 2015.

24. Ali Latifi, "How Iran Recruited Afghan Refugees to Fight Assad's War," *New York Times*, Jun. 30, 2017.

25. "Iran Sending Thousands of Afghans to Fight in Syria," *Human Rights Watch*, Jan. 29, 2016.

26. "تشكيلات فعلی فاطميون ابتدا كی ئيئت خانگی بود/ تعدادی از افغانها به اروپا آمدند و شهيد شدند" (A number of fighters came to the Fatemiyoun from Europe), *Tasnim News Agency*, Jun. 18, 2016.

27. Amir Toumaj, "IRGC commander discusses Afghan militia, 'Shi'a liberation army,' and Syria," *Long War Journal*, Aug. 24, 2016.

28. Ramin Mostaghim and Nabih Bulos, "Members of this Afghan minority flee to Iran to escape persecution — and get sent to fight in Syria," *Los Angeles Times*, Aug. 18, 2016.

29. "مستند گنج جنگجویان خارجی ایران" لشكر گنج برای اسد: لشكر خارجیان ایران (For Assad: The Foreign Army of Iran), *BBC Persian*, Apr. 21, 2016.

30. "Iran: Afghan Children Recruited to Fight in Syria," *Human Rights Watch*, Oct. 1, 2017.

31. "Released Afghan Fighters Rebut BBC's Story on 'Forced' Recruitment to Syria," *Tasnim News Agency*, Jul. 25, 2016.

32. Interview with the martyr Mohammad Hassan Hosseini [Sayyed Hakim]), *Raja News*, Jun. 17, 2016.

33. "Fatemiyoun were on the forefront of the Syrian battle," *Tasnim News Agency*, Aug. 18, 2016.

34. Frud Bezhan, "Iran Aims To Boost Prestige Of Beleaguered Afghan Proxy Force In Syria," *Radio Free Europe/Radio Liberty*, Jul. 16, 2017.

35. "مستند «نقاشی یک رویا»" (Documentary: "Drawing a Dream"), *Basij News Agency*, Aug. 26, 2017.

36. Ibid.

37. Tobias Schneider, Twitter post, Aug. 31, 2017, 1:45 p.m.

38. Golnaz Esfandiari, "Iran's Leader Tells Families of Afghans Killed In Syria: 'I'm Proud of You,'" *Radio Free Europe/Radio Liberty*, May 13, 2016.

39. Bill Gertz, "U.S. Identifies Nine Training Camps in Iran for Afghans," *The Washington Free Beacon*, Jul. 1, 2016.

40. "Iran Sending Thousands of Afghans to Fight in Syria," *Human Rights Watch*, Jan. 29, 2016.

41. Fariba Sahraei, "Syria war: The Afghans sent by Iran to fight for Assad," BBC, Apr. 15, 2016.

42. "راوی یک مهاجر افغان که به جنگ سوریه رفت" (The Story of an Afghan refugee who went to Syria), 8 am, Aug. 17, 2016.

43. Tobias Schneider, Twitter post, Aug. 27, 2017, 2:09 p.m.

44. Barbara Opall-Rome, "Iran Deploys Hezbollah-Trained Afghan Sniper Brigade in Syria," *Defense News*, Jul. 18, 2016.

45. Aymenn Jawad Al-Tamimi, "Administrative Decisions on Local Defence Forces Personnel: Translation & Analysis," Aymenn Jawad Al-Tamimi's Blog, May 3, 2017.

46. Lost Weapons, Twitter post, Feb. 7, 2018, 8:04 p.m.

47. "Russia trains Iran-sponsored Shi'a militias in Syria," *Afghanistan Analysis*, Dec. 1, 2017.

48. Ali Alfoneh, Twitter post, May 7, 2018, 3:34 a.m.

49. "ورز از فتنه‌های دولتهای منطقه" (Avoiding the temptations of regional states), 8 am, Nov. 29, 2017.

50. Ahmad Majidyar, "Afghan Official in Deep Water after Praising Role of Soleimani and Shi'a Militias in Syria," *Middle East Institute*, Nov. 29, 2017.

51. Ibid.

52. "Afghan govt leader spotted in Fatemiyoun brigade gathering sparks concerns," *Khaama Press*, Nov. 26, 2017.

53. Tom Coghlan, Aimal Yaqubi, and Sara Elizabeth Williams, "Assad recruits Afghan mercenaries to fight Isis," *The Times*, Jun. 2, 2015.

54. Naomi Conrad, "Iran recruits Afghan teenagers to fight war in Syria," *Deutsche Welle*, May 5, 2018.

55. Scott Peterson, "Iran steps up recruitment of Shi'a mercenaries for Syrian war," *Christian Science Monitor*, Jun. 12, 2016.

56. "Presence of Shi'a Muslim militia in Afghanistan becomes more overt," *Jane's Terrorism & Insurgency Monitor*, July 2017.

57. "Recruited by Iran to fight for Syrian regime, young Afghans bring home cash and scars," *Washington Post*, Jul. 29, 2018.

58. Thomas Joscelyn, "Islamic State's Khorasan 'province' claims responsibility for attack on cultural center in Kabul," *Long War Journal*, Dec. 28, 2017.

59. Ahmad Majidyar, "Iran Recruits and Trains Large Numbers of Afghan and Pakistani Shiites," *Middle East Institute*, Jan. 18, 2017.

60. "Iran Declares End of ISIS," *The Iran Primer*, Nov. 21, 2017.

61. Amir Toumaj, "Iraqi militia publicizes Iranian Qods Force chief by Syrian border town," *Long War Journal*, Nov. 18, 2017.

CHAPTER TWELVE

TERRORISM AND HUMAN RIGHTS:

THE PERSPECTIVE OF INTERNATIONAL LAW

DAVID P. STEWART

INTRODUCTION

Law (including international law) necessarily reflects the community it serves. It mirrors the community's values and structure and should serve the interests of the community in resolving disputes among its members in accordance with their expressed values. Law provides only one way of defining and dealing with communal problems, but without clear legal principles and effective legal processes, the community lacks a critical stabilizing force.

Human rights and terrorism are broad phenomena, not just legal problems, and the legal perspective is surely not the only one relevant to an analysis of their role in contemporary international relations. But law can contribute to viable solutions, and an awareness of the legal perspective is just as important for policy makers as other perspectives are for international lawyers.

WHAT ARE "HUMAN RIGHTS"?

Internationally-recognized human rights are commonly understood to encompass those rights to which all persons are entitled without discrimination by the mere fact of being human — that is, rights that cannot be denied or restricted on the basis of culture, tradition, nationality, political orientation, social standing or other factors, but must be protected in fact and given effect by law.

Broadly speaking, these rights include the most fundamental preconditions for a dignified human existence. They are primarily asserted against government authorities (i.e., must be respected, protected, and given effect by the government) but in some instances are also capable of assertion against other individuals in their private capacities (e.g. discrimination).

INTERNATIONAL HUMAN RIGHTS LAW

The main articulation of international human rights law is found in various human rights treaties and other international instruments.[1] The core documents are the 1948 Universal Declaration of Human Rights (UDHR) and two multilateral treaties, the 1966 International Covenant on Civil and Political Rights (ICCPR) and the International Covenant on Economic, Social and Cultural Rights (ICESCR) (sometimes referred to collectively as the "International Bill of Rights"). As a General Assembly resolution, the UDHR is technically non-binding under international law but is generally accepted as articulating the obligations undertaken by UN Member States under the UN Charter. The two Covenants are legally binding on States that have ratified them, and they are in fact widely ratified (if not equally widely respected in practice).[2]

Other core universal human rights treaties include the 1965 International Convention on the Elimination of All Forms of Racial Discrimination,[3] the 1980 Convention on the Elimination of All Forms of Discrimination against Women,[4] the 1984 Convention against Torture and other Cruel, Inhuman or Degrading Treatment or Punishment,[5] the 1989 Convention on the Rights of the Child,[6] the 1990 International Convention on the Protection of the Rights of All Migrant Workers and Members of Their Families,[7] the 2006 International Convention for the Protection of All Persons from Enforced Disappearance, and the 2006 Convention on the Rights of Persons with Disabilities.

In addition to these "universal" conventions, several regional human rights systems are founded on their own treaties and feature regional enforcement mechanisms (e.g., commissions and courts), specifically in Europe (under the Council of Europe), Africa (within the African Union), and the Americas

(OAS). No such agreements or mechanisms exist for the Middle East (or Asia).

Categories of Rights

With the proliferation of international human rights instruments, it has become common to differentiate between

> Civil and political rights, sometimes called "first generation" rights,
> Economic, social, and cultural rights ("second generation" rights), and
> Group or collective rights, often denominated "third generation" rights.

These are not precise categorizations but nonetheless serve to highlight some helpful distinctions. By way of example, "first generation" rights relate primarily to personal freedom and liberty from governmental interference. They encompass many of the basic individual rights protected by the U.S. Constitution and related legislation, including (i) such "physical integrity rights" as the rights to life, liberty, and security of the person, protection from physical violence including torture and inhuman treatment, exile, slavery, and servitude; (ii) "due process" rights such as protection against arbitrary arrest and detention, the right to a public hearing by an independent and impartial tribunal, the presumption of innocence, freedom from double jeopardy, the right to equal treatment and protection in law; and (iii) "personal freedom" rights such as protection of one's privacy and rights of ownership, freedom of expression, thought, conscience and religion, association, assembly, movement, etc. They also include "political participation rights" common to democratic governance, including the right to take part in the government of one's country, to vote, to stand for election at genuine periodic elections held by secret ballot, etc.

By contrast, the "second generation" of human rights addresses the broader societal conditions necessary for well-being and prosperity, including, for example, the rights to property, work (which one freely chooses or accepts), a fair wage, a reasonable limitation of working hours, safe working conditions, and trade union rights. Notably this category extends to elements considered necessary for an adequate standard of living, including inter alia rights to health, shelter, food, water, social care, education, to participate freely in the cultural life of the community, to share in scientific advancement, and to the protection of the moral and material interests resulting from any scientific, literary or artistic production of which one is the author.

"Third generation" rights include both "solidarity rights" deemed necessary to protect specific groups in need of particular protection (women, children, migrants, the disabled, the indigenous, etc.) and rights owing to the "global community" in general, for example the rights to development, peace or a clean global environment. Perhaps the most fundamental "collective" human right is the right to self-determination, which is textually vested in "peoples" rather than in individuals. (A vibrant debate has emerged over whether this right applies outside the context of a struggle for post-colonial independence, e.g., to the "people" in Quebec, Catalonia, California or Corsica.) It is generally accepted that collective rights may not infringe on universally-accepted individual rights, such as the right to life and freedom from torture.

These categories reflect different concepts of the nature of "rights" and the role of government in their protection and promotion. Broadly speaking, "first generation" rights can be thought of as limitations on governmental action (freedoms) while "second generation" rights function as demands on government (entitlements). To illustrate, freedom of speech, press, assembly, and religion are largely respected when the government does not interfere, while rights to work, education, and health care likely require affirmative governmental action. The distinction is not perfect, but in its origins it reflected the differing approaches of the liberal/Western democracies on the one hand and the socialist/communist approach on the other (thus, the decision taken in the United Nations during the Cold War to separate the rights described in the Universal Declaration into two separate "human right covenants").

In their legal formulations, civil and political rights are sometimes said to reflect "negative obligations" capable of immediate implementation and are therefore expressed in precise language, while economic, social, and cultural rights are viewed as imposing "positive obligations" which are often conditional on the existence of available resources and therefore require "progressive realization" and can consequently be expressed in less precise terms.

In consequence, civil and political rights are often said to be "justiciable," i.e., legal rights capable of being asserted against governmental authority in court, while economic, social, and cultural rights are by nature "non-justiciable" and instead matters for governmental decision (such as legislative enactment) since they involve commitment of resources and funding. While that may reflect the situation in many traditional democratic systems, it is not true of many countries today (such as South Africa, which specifically vests its courts with powers to instruct the government on the necessary allocation of funds to satisfy legally-recognized economic and social rights).

The "human rights revolution" has also opened up new opportunities for international examination of how governments give effect to their human rights obligations at the domestic level. Once considered an intrusion into "domestic affairs" to criticize how a government dealt with its own citizens, that discussion has now been legitimized for example through the "universal periodic review" of every State's human rights performance by the UN Human Rights Council, as well as the examinations undertaken by other human rights entities such as the "treaty bodies" established by the various human rights conventions (e.g., the Human Rights Committee under the ICCPR and the Committee on Economic, Social, and Cultural Rights under the ICESCR), both of which can receive and consider individual and collective complaints alleging violations of rights protected under their respective treaties.

What is "Terrorism"?

At its most general level, the term "terrorism" denotes the (generally criminal) use of politically-motivated violence. It is typically used to refer to "a special form or tactic of fear-generating, coercive political violence" as well as "a conspiratorial practice of calculated, demonstrative, direct violent action without legal or moral restraints, targeting mainly civilians and non-combatants, performed for its propagandistic and psychological effects on various audiences and conflict parties."[8]

However, no single or agreed legal definition exists at the international level. The term is frequently employed to describe a wide range of acts committed in response to varying circumstances and phenomena at both the domestic and international levels. Its use is often politically-charged.

Domestic U.S. Definitions

Most acts of terrorism violate "ordinary" domestic criminal law (assault, malicious wounding, manslaughter, murder, property destruction, etc.). The "terrorist" distinction arises from the purpose or intent behind the acts.

As a matter of U.S. law, the U.S. Department of Defense defines terrorism as "[t]he unlawful use of violence or threat of violence, often motivated by religious, political, or other ideological beliefs, to instill fear and coerce governments or societies in pursuit of goals that are usually political."[9]

The Department of State's definition is broader. As applied to the preparation of the annual country reports on terrorism, the term "terrorism" means "premeditated, politically motivated violence perpetrated against noncombatant targets by subnational groups or clandestine agents."[10]

For the specific purposes of U.S. federal criminal law, the term "international terrorism" means activities that involve violent acts or acts dangerous to human life that are a violation of the criminal laws of the United States or of any State, or that would be a criminal violation if committed within the jurisdiction of the United States or of any State; appear to be intended (i) to intimidate or coerce a civilian population; (ii) to influence the policy of a government by intimidation or coercion; or (iii) to affect the conduct of a government by mass destruction, assassination, or kidnapping; and occur primarily outside the territorial jurisdiction of the United States, or transcend national boundaries in terms of the means by which they are accomplished, the persons they appear intended to intimidate or coerce, or the locale in which their perpetrators operate or seek asylum.[11]

INTERNATIONAL APPROACHES

Despite repeated condemnation of "terrorism" in the United Nations,[12] it has to date proven impossible for the international community to agree on a single definition of terrorism. In consequence, no international criminal tribunal currently has jurisdiction over a distinct crime of terrorism.

Perhaps the most debated definition of terrorism, as an international crime, was adopted by the Appeals Chamber of the Special Tribunal for Lebanon (STL), which stated that:

The international crime of terrorism … requires the following three key elements: (i) The perpetration of a criminal act (such as murder, kidnapping, hostage-taking, arson, and so on), or threatening such an act; (ii) the intent to spread fear among the population (which would generally entail the creation of public danger) or directly or indirectly coerce a national or international authority to take some action, or to refrain from taking it; (iii) when the act involves a transnational element.[13]

Numerous efforts have been made since the 1920s to achieve an international agreement on the definition of the crime of "terrorism" as such, but without success. For instance, a concerted effort has been since 2000 in the UN General Assembly to draft a comprehensive convention on international terrorism but remains frustrated by sharp disagreement over the definition, in particular the insistence by some delegations on drawing a clear distinction between illegal "terrorism" and the use of force and violence in the exercise of the legitimate right of peoples to seek self-determination and resist foreign occupation.

The 1998 Arab Convention on the Suppression of Terrorism, adopted by the League of Arab States, defined the term "terrorism" to include "[a]ny act or threat of violence, whatever its motives or purposes, that occurs in the advancement of an individual or collective criminal agenda and seeking to sow panic among people, causing fear by harming them, or placing their lives, liberty or security in danger, or seeking to cause damage to the environment or to public or private installations or property or to occupying or seizing them, or seeking to jeopardize a national resources [sic]." Art. 1(2). However, Article 2(a) then narrowed that definition by providing that "[a]ll cases of struggle by whatever means, including armed struggle, against foreign occupation and aggression for liberation and self-determination, in accordance with the principles of international law, shall not be regarded as an offence."

To much the same effect, the 1999 Convention of the Organization of the

Islamic Conference on Combating International Terrorism defined "terrorism" to include "any act of violence or threat thereof notwithstanding its motives or intentions perpetrated to carry out an individual or collective criminal plan with the aim of terrorizing people or threatening to harm them or imperiling their lives, honor, freedoms, security or rights or exposing the environment or any facility or public or private property to hazards or occupying or seizing them, or endangering a national resource, or international facilities, or threatening the stability, territorial integrity, political unity or sovereignty of independent States."[14]

But the Convention then excluded a series of acts (including "aggression" against heads of state, ambassadors, acts of sabotage, etc.) even when "politically motivated."[15]

The most productive approach at the international level has therefore been to condemn specific terrorist acts in focused multilateral "counter-terrorism" conventions addressing particular, narrowly defined acts deemed criminal (typically in response to international incidents). For instance, Article 2(1) of the 1999 International Convention for the Suppression of the Financing of Terrorism (the most widely ratified anti-terrorism convention)[16], provides that:

(1) Any person commits an offence within the meaning of this Convention if that person by any means, directly or indirectly, unlawfully and willfully, provides or collects funds with the intention that they should be used or in the knowledge that they are to be used, in full or in part, in order to carry out:

(a) An act which constitutes an offence within the scope of and as defined in one of the treaties listed in the annex; (emphasis added) or

(b) Any other act intended to cause death or serious bodily injury to a civilian, or to any other person not taking an active part in the hostilities in a situation of armed conflict, when the purpose of such act, by its nature or context, is to intimidate a population, or to compel a government or an international organization to do or to abstain from doing any act.

This same "list" approach was followed in the 2002 Inter-American Convention against Terrorism[17] as well as the 2005 Council of Europe Convention on the Prevention of Terrorism.[18]

Under this approach, the specific crimes defined in the following "counter-terrorism" conventions are generally considered terrorist crimes, at least with respect to the States that have ratified or acceded to these conventions:

1. 1963 Tokyo Convention on Offences and Other Acts Committed on Board of Aircrafts
2. 1970 Hague Convention for the Suppression of Unlawful Seizure of Aircraft, of December 16, 1970

3. 1971 Montreal Convention on Suppression of Unlawful Acts Against the Safety of Civil Aviation, its 1988 Protocol for the Suppression of Unlawful Acts of Violence at Airports, and its 2010 supplement
4. 1973 New York Convention on the "Prevention and Punishment of Crimes Against Persons Enjoying International Immunity, Including Diplomatic Agents"
5. 1979 International Convention against the Taking of Hostages (New York, 1979)
6. 1979 Convention on the Physical Protection of Nuclear Material and its 2005 amendment
7. 1988 Rome Convention for the Suppression of Unlawful Acts Against the Safety of Maritime Navigation, its 1988 protocol relating to unlawful acts against the safety of fixed platforms located on the continental shelf, and the 2005 Protocol thereto
8. 1991 Montreal Convention on the Marking of Plastic Explosives for the Purposes of Detection
9. 1997 International Convention for the Suppression of Terrorist Bombings
10. 1999 International Convention for the Suppression of the Financing of Terrorism
11. 2005 International Convention for the Suppression of Acts of Nuclear Terrorism
12. 1982 United Nations Convention on the Law of the Sea (provisions relating to piracy on the high seas)

While adherence to these counter-terrorism conventions varies among "Middle Eastern" States (as does compliance with their treaty obligations), the overall regional record of ratification is quite respectable.[19]

Terrorism and Human Rights

How do these separate but related bodies of international law interact with each other?[20]

Terrorism as a Violation of Human Rights

If one accepts that terrorism involves the use of politically-motivated, fear-generating violence to commit criminal acts aimed at harming innocent individuals for the purpose of coercing governments or societies to take or refrain from action, then it clearly violates — indeed, is precisely intended to violate — fundamental human rights (and, more generally, the very concept of rule of law).

By committing acts of terror, terrorists by definition attack the values at the heart of the Universal Declaration of Human Rights, the two Covenants, and other international instruments, in particular many "first generation" rights (such as the rights to life, liberty, and physical integrity) but also second and third generation rights.

Moreover, terrorist acts can be distinguished from "ordinary" crimes precisely because they are aimed at destabilizing governments, undermining civil society, jeopardizing peace and security, and threatening social and economic development, all outside "normal" political and legal channels and in defiance of the law.

The destructive impact of terrorism on human rights and security has repeatedly been recognized by the United Nations. Consider, for instance, the preamble to UN Security Council Resolution 2396 (adopted Dec. 21, 2017):

> *Reaffirming that terrorism in all forms and manifestations constitutes one of the most serious threats to international peace and security and that any acts of terrorism are criminal and unjustifiable regardless of their motivations, whenever, wherever and by whomsoever committed, and remaining determined to contribute further to enhancing the effectiveness of the overall effort to fight this scourge on a global level,*
>
> *Reaffirming that terrorism poses a threat to international peace and security and that countering this threat requires collective efforts on national, regional and international levels on the basis of respect for international law and the Charter of the United Nations,*
>
> *Emphasizing that terrorism and violent extremism conducive to terrorism cannot and should not be associated with any religion, nationality, or civilization....*[21]

As a matter of contemporary international law, States have an affirmative duty to protect individuals under their jurisdiction against interference in the enjoyment of their human rights, in particular the right to life and the right to security. These rights have been described as "preeminent" rights because without them all the other rights would effectively be meaningless. In many respects, terrorism aims to undermine the ability of governments and governmental entities — and perhaps more importantly, the confidence of the population in that ability — to safeguard society in precisely this fundamental respect. Perhaps more directly, acts of terrorism violate the rights of individual victims, who suffer an attack on their most basic right to live in peace and security.

Increasingly, support for the victims of terrorism has become an important aspect of international focus. In the 2005 World Summit Outcome (General

Assembly Resolution 60/1), for example, Member States stressed "the importance of assisting victims of terrorism and of providing them and their families with support to cope with their loss and their grief." Similarly, the United Nations Global Counter-Terrorism Strategy reflects the pledge by Member States to "promote international solidarity in support of victims and foster the involvement of civil society in a global campaign against terrorism and for its condemnation." In one sense, the failure of governments to provide assistance and relief to victims of terrorism may well be described as a human rights violation itself.

TERRORISM AS A CONSEQUENCE OF HUMAN RIGHTS VIOLATIONS

Terrorism is not a single phenomenon. It comes in many varieties. Nor is it generated by a single "cause" but can arise from a variety of circumstances and motivations which differ (in nature, impact, and extent) from situation to situation. In many instances, those circumstances and motivations involve real or perceived human rights violations.

Among the commonly-cited conditions that make terrorism possible or likely ("precursors") are extreme poverty, social exclusion, and economic privation; religious and ethnic prejudice and discrimination; political repression and denials of due process; communal alienation; and lack of education, employment opportunities, and social services. Without question, political objectives and ideological orientation have frequently played important roles (i.e., desire to end foreign occupation or outside interference, to overthrow or promote a particular form of governance), as have religious factors (belief in the superiority of one's faith or in commandments from the Deity).

Yet it seems clear that in many if not most circumstances the conditions that create susceptibility to radicalization, that make terrorist violence against innocent civilians appear to be a reasonable, justifiable, and even necessary option, themselves reflect human rights violations. It is not simply that people choose terrorism when they are just trying to correct what they perceive to be social, political or historical injustices, but perhaps more likely when they have (or perceive they have) no other options, when they feel excluded from other ways of achieving their desired changes. Terrorism appeals to individuals and groups denied fundamental human rights (for example, those subjected to oppressive and authoritarian regimes) because they have no alternatives. Deprivation of human rights unquestionably fuels that sense of alienation and exclusion that is often used to justify terrorist acts.

Of course, more personal factors — marital difficulties, broken relationships, recent loss of employment, mental health problems, etc. — can all be "triggers" in specific instances. It is also surely the case that some individuals who become terrorists have certain predispositions or psychological traits conducive to violent or anti-social behavior. Many are drawn to emulate what they see as the heroic feats of others. It may also be true that a "tyrannical mindset" does exist in some segment of every population, and perhaps it does take "monstrous people to produce atrocious deeds."[22] Without question, violent crime occurs even in the most human-rights-compliant societies. Compliance with international human rights obligations cannot prevent all acts of violence or terrorism.

Yet it also seems true that recruitment by international terrorist groups is aided by deeply-felt grievances nurtured by poverty, foreign occupation, and the absence of human rights and fundamental freedoms, as well as the lack of means of redress "within the system." Democracy may be neither a necessary nor sufficient bulwark against terrorism (even from within) but it certainly seems that the social and political communities that are most compliant with human rights norms tend to suffer the least from domestic ("home grown") terrorism. It also appears that improvements in domestic human rights conditions tends to reduce the level of terrorist violence.

HUMAN RIGHTS IMPLICATIONS OF COUNTER-TERRORISM

At the same time, some measures to counter or prevent terrorist acts can themselves pose serious challenges to the protection and promotion of human rights — both for the perpetrators and for the population at large. The declaration of the "Global War on Terror" in the wake of the 9/11 attacks, which led to the use of torture and other "enhanced interrogation techniques" and to such practices as "irregular rendition" and prolonged incommunicado detention at Guantanamo, put this aspect of the relationship between human rights and terrorism squarely before the international community. It has since become a dominant theme in the international consideration of terrorism.

The UN General Assembly has repeatedly emphasized that the rights of the alleged perpetrators of terrorist attacks must be respected in the course of their apprehension and prosecution, including their rights to public trial, to be presumed innocent until proven guilty, and not to be subject to torture or other degrading treatment. For example, in adopting its fundamental "Global Counter-Terrorism Strategy" in 2006, the UNGA reaffirmed that "the promotion and protection of human rights for all and the rule of law is essential to all components of the Strategy, recognizing that effective counter-terrorism measures and the protection of human rights are not conflicting goals, but complementary and mutually reinforcing, and stressing the need to promote and protect the rights of victims of terrorism."[23]

To the same effect, the 2009 UNGA resolution on the "protection of human rights and fundamental freedoms while countering terrorism" stressed "the fundamental importance, including in response to terrorism and the fear of terrorism, of respecting all human rights and fundamental freedoms and the rule of law." It emphasized that "Member States must ensure that any measures taken to counter terrorism comply with all their obligations under international law, in particular international human rights law, international refugee law, and international humanitarian law" and underscored that "respect for human rights, fundamental freedoms, and the rule of law are complementary and mutually reinforcing with effective counter-terrorism measures, and are an essential part of a successful counter-terrorism effort" and notes the importance of respect for the rule of law so as to effectively prevent and combat terrorism." Finally, it noted that "failure to comply with these and other international obligations, including under the Charter of the United Nations, is one of the factors contributing to increased radicalization to violence and fosters a sense of impunity."[24]

The UN Security Council echoed these principles in a recent anti-terrorism resolution, reaffirming that "Member States must ensure that any measures taken to counter terrorism comply with all their obligations under international law, in particular international human rights law, international refugee law, and international humanitarian law." It also stressed that "[r]espect for human rights, fundamental freedoms, and the rule of law are complementary and mutually reinforcing with effective counter-terrorism measures, and are an essential part of a successful counter-terrorism effort," noted "the importance of respect for the rule of law so as to effectively prevent and combat terrorism," and said "failure to comply with these and other international obligations, including under the Charter of the United Nations, is one of the factors contributing to increased radicalization to violence and fosters a sense of impunity."[25]

These principles have become embedded in the expanding UN structures for dealing with terrorism and counter-terrorism. The Security Council's Counter-Terrorism Committee, established in 2001, emphasizes that States must ensure that any measures taken to combat terrorism comply with all their obligations under international law and should adopt such measures in accordance with international law, in particular international human rights, refugee, and humanitarian law, including coordination with the Office of the UN High Commissioner for Human Rights.[26]

Within the UN Secretariat, an Office of Counter-Terrorism headed by an Under-Secretary General was recently established[27] to assist Member States in implementing the UN Global Counter-Terrorism Strategy. It will evidently combine the functions of the pre-existing UN Counter-Terrorism Implementation Task Force and the UN Counter-Terrorism Centre. Among its mandates is preventing violent extremism in accordance with the 2006 Global

Counter-Terrorism Strategy (thus ensuring emphasis on compliance with human rights norms).

The newly-appointed Special Rapporteur of the UN Human Rights Council on "the promotion and protection of human rights and fundamental freedoms while countering terrorism," Fionnuala Ní Aoláin, indicated in her recent report to the UN General Assembly that she will focus on four substantive areas: (1) The proliferation of permanent states of emergency and the normalization of exceptional national security powers within ordinary legal systems; (2) the need for greater clarity in respect to the legal relationships between national security regimes and international legal regimes (human rights, international humanitarian law, and international criminal law) as well as the relationship of human rights to the emergence of stand-alone international security regimes regulating terrorism and counter-terrorism; (3) the advancement of greater normative attention to the gendered dimensions of terrorism and counterterrorism; and (4) advancing the rights and protection of civil society in the fight against terrorism.[28]

The same themes are being given attention in other international bodies. On July 6, 2017, the European Parliament set up a special 12-month committee on the impact of EU anti-terror laws on fundamental rights.[29] Within the OSCE's "human dimension" component, attention has long been paid to the relationship between the need for security in response to terrorism and the risks that counter-measures can pose for fundamental rights and freedoms, including the rights to a fair trial, to privacy, and the freedoms of association and of religion or belief. Participating States have pledged under a "Plan of Action" to fully respect international law, including the international law of human rights, in the development and implementation of their counter-terrorism initiatives. A very useful discussion of the issues can be found in the OCSE's Manual on Countering Terrorism, Protecting Human Rights.[30]

TERRORISM AND OTHER ASPECTS OF INTERNATIONAL LAW

TERRORISM AND INTERNATIONAL REFUGEE LAW

Alongside the specific obligations of human rights law, international refugee law provides a set of principles that have increasingly become relevant to the effort to combat international terrorism, particularly with respect to crimes committed in European and other states of refuge for persons fleeing the conflicts in the Middle East.

The basic international instruments are the 1951 Convention Relating to the Status of Refugees and its 1967 Protocol, which taken together define the term refugee to denote an individual who is outside his or her country of nationality or habitual residence and is unable or unwilling to return due to a "well-founded fear of persecution based on his or her race, religion, nationality, political opinion, or membership in a particular social group." As a technical legal matter, the definition excludes those who are economic migrants or victims of natural disasters or violent conflict (but not personally subject to discrimination amounting to persecution) as well as the "internally displaced."[31]

The definition also excludes persons who would otherwise meet the refugee definition when there are "serious reasons" for considering that he or she (a) has committed a crime against peace, a war crime, or a crime against humanity, as defined in the international instruments drawn up to make provision in respect of such crimes, (b) has committed a serious non-political crime outside the country of refuge prior to admission to that country as a refugee, or (c) has been guilty of acts contrary to the purposes and principles of the United Nations.[32] Acts which bear the characteristics of terrorism will almost invariably amount to serious non-political crimes.[33]

The basic principle of refugee law is the obligation of States not to return (refouler) a refugee to "the frontiers of territories where his life or freedom would be threatened on account of his race, religion, nationality, membership of a particular social group or political opinion."[34] This "non-refoulement" obligation is generally acknowledged as a human right and has been expressly incorporated into a number of human rights treaties (including the UN Convention against Torture, the American Convention on Human Rights, and the African [Banjul] Charter on Human and Peoples' Rights).

As a strictly legal matter, however, the obligation only precludes the "return" of individuals who have been "admitted" into a State's territory; it does not obligate States to grant admission to individuals seeking entry as refugees. In other words, it does not mandate automatic acceptance or "open borders" even for those who might eventually be adjudicated to have the necessary "well-founded fear." Nor does it prohibit requiring an individual to leave for a third country where he or she would not face persecution on one of the prohibited bases.

Immediately following the 9/11 attacks, the UN Security Council called upon Member States inter alia to "take appropriate measures in conformity with the relevant provisions of national and international law, including international standards of human rights, before granting refugee status, for the purpose of ensuring that the asylum-seeker has not planned, facilitated or participated in the commission of terrorist acts" and to "ensure, in conformity with international law, that refugee status is not abused by the perpetrators, organizers or facilitators of terrorist acts, and that claims of political motivation are not recognized as grounds for refusing requests for the extradition of alleged terrorists."[35]

TERRORISM AND INTERNATIONAL CRIMINAL LAW

As indicated above (Part I), the main emphasis in the international community's legally-oriented counter-terrorism efforts over the past several decades has been to develop a body of binding international conventions aimed at coordinating and strengthening domestic criminal law responses to specific terrorist acts that span different national jurisdictions or otherwise have an international element. These treaties have typically been negotiated in reaction to egregious terrorist events (such as the hijacking of aircraft, the killing of diplomats, the taking of hostages, the use of plastic explosives, the hijacking of the Italian cruise ship Achille Lauro, acts of terrorist financing, etc.) to provide a consensual framework for international cooperation.

In general, they follow a common approach: They define the particular "terrorist" acts in question and require States Party to criminalize those acts under their respective domestic laws, to prosecute the perpetrators in certain situations (for instance, when the offense is committed in their territory or by their nationals), and to cooperate with other States Party in preventing such acts.

Importantly, most of the treaties also obligate States Party to extradite an accused individual to other States Party if they find that person in their territory but lack one of the required jurisdictional elements to prosecute — for example, because the crime was not committed in their territory or the accused is not their national. But if for some reason they cannot accomplish the requested extradition, the treaties require them to proceed with a domestic prosecution. In other words, the treaty provides an internationally-agreed jurisdictional basis for prosecution. This *aut dedere aut judicare* ("extradite or prosecute") principle was intended to eliminate safe havens for terrorists.

Deterrence is obviously among the broader policy objectives of this approach, by eliminating terrorists' refuges and fostering a coordinated international approach to criminal prosecution of specific types of terrorism. Encouraging States to pursue terrorists through criminal prosecution also serves, to some extent, to prevent summary or extra-legal punishment and to protect the "first generation" due process rights of the defendants.

Domestic legal systems vary, of course, in their effectiveness and consistency. To date, no international criminal tribunal has been given jurisdiction over the specific crime of international terrorism (or most of the treaty-based counter-terrorism crimes). One decision of an international tribunal specifically involving terrorism came in the case against General Stanislav Galić before the

International Criminal Tribunal for the Former Yugoslavia (ICTY). In 2003, the Tribunal convicted General Galić of terrorism as a war crime and a crime against humanity for directing acts of violence "with the primary aim to spread terror among the civilian population of Sarajevo" between 1992 and 1994. While convicting him for those crimes, the ICTY trial chamber considered the campaign of shelling and sniping of civilians in Sarajevo (for which it found Galić responsible) to be "an act of terrorizing the civilian population."[36]

An effort was made to include "terrorism" as a distinct crime during the negotiation of the Rome Statute creating the International Criminal Court (ICC) but failed because of disagreement over the definition. Conceivably, following the Galić precedent, certain types of terrorist conduct might be encompassed by various other offences within the ICC's mandate, depending on the facts — as a war crime, for example, or a crime against humanity if the acts included certain acts committed as "part of a widespread or systematic attack directed against any civilian population, with knowledge of the attack" or even as an act of genocide if the requisite "specific intent" could be proven.

Additionally, proposals have occasionally been made for the creation of a specialized stand-alone court for the prosecution of acts of international terrorism.[37] For self-evident reasons, such proposals seem unlikely (in the foreseeable future) to garner the necessary international support for adoption.

TERRORISM AND INTERNATIONAL HUMANITARIAN LAW

International humanitarian law ("IHL" for short), often considered part of the law of armed conflict, sets forth rules on the protection of persons in "armed conflict" and more generally for the conduct of "hostilities." These rules are reflected in a number of treaties, including the four Geneva Conventions and their two Additional Protocols, as well as other international instruments aimed at reducing human suffering in armed conflict. Generally, they apply to armed conflict between States and are designed to prevent the unnecessary or disproportionate use of force during military operations as well as the infliction of unnecessary suffering and to protect certain categories of non-combatants (including, for example, civilians, the wounded, the shipwrecked, and prisoners of war).

In recent years considerable debate has arisen about whether these IHL rules do or should apply to "terrorist" situations, specifically with respect to acts by or against terrorists that are significant enough to amount to the use of "armed conflict" (consider, for example, the 9/11 attacks). The latter view draws some support from such actions by the UN Security Council as the adoption of a resolution shortly after the 9/11 attacks, under Chapter VII of the Charter of the United Nations, stating explicitly that every act of terrorism constitutes a "threat to international peace and security" (thus permitting invocation of the right of self-defense) and that the "acts, methods, and practices of terrorism are contrary to the purposes and principles of the United Nations" (potentially justifying collective action by States against the terrorists and their supporters).[38]

The question is whether (or when) the acts in question are more properly considered crimes committed by private individuals (non-state actors), to be dealt with judicially, or amount to the conduct of armed hostilities justifying military responses to which IHL rules (permissive as well as restrictive) apply. IHL contains no explicit definition of "terrorism" as such, much less general rules regarding actions by or against terrorists. It does permit the use of armed force that would not be legitimate in a "civilian" criminal context not involving "hostilities," while at the same time prohibiting many acts during armed conflict that would be considered terrorist if committed in times of peace (such as deliberate acts of violence against civilians and civilian objects constitute war crimes under international law, for which individuals may be prosecuted).

By way of example, the proportionate use of lethal force is lawful during armed conflict, without regard to normal "civil and political rights," while disproportionate or indiscriminate attacks are strictly prohibited as are "measures" or "acts of terrorism" or "acts or threats of violence the primary purpose of which is to spread terror among the civilian population." The International Court of Justice has affirmed the applicability of fundamental human rights during armed conflicts, stating that "[in] principle, the right not arbitrarily to be deprived of one's life applies also in hostilities."[39]

This debate (about the rules governing use of armed force in the terrorism context) becomes particularly intense in relation to the terrorist activities of organized groups capable of operating across national boundaries and those claiming to have governmental or proto-governmental status. It is even sharper when the focus shifts to "state sponsored terrorism" and allegations that the actions of the terrorists have been supported, facilitated or financed by foreign governments.

RECOMMENDATIONS

Several important steps could be taken by the international community to address some of the issues identified above.

- ➤ Perhaps most important is the recognition that human rights violations are themselves among the main generators of terrorist violence. Consequently, respecting the rights of marginalized groups, strengthening the protections available to minorities and the disadvantaged, ensuring equal participation in political, economic, and social life — these can be the most effective counter-terrorism (or terrorism-preventive) strategies.
- ➤ Equally important is acknowledging that repressive counter-terrorism policies and practices are demonstrably counter-productive. This point has been made repeatedly, and forcibly, by the current U.N. Special Rapporteur on the Promotion and Protection of Human Rights and Fundamental Freedoms while Countering Terrorism, Fionnuala Ní Aoláin.
- ➤ Agreement on a global or comprehensive Convention on International Terrorism could be a significant step forward legally. This effort, centered in a UN Committee, remains deadlocked over how to define the term. Of course, by itself, agreement on the text of such a treaty would not be sufficient; it would need to be coupled with a broad commitment by States Parties to implement it effectively.
- ➤ Regarding deterrence, effective action is needed to hold terrorists accountable both for their own acts and for providing compensation for victims of terrorism. A proper regime would cover state sponsors as well as others who "aid and abet" or provide material support to the terrorists.
- ➤ Eventually one might contemplate a global human rights court (as an extension of the existing regional mechanisms) as well as a global terrorism court (perhaps as an outgrowth of the ICC), but those developments are highly unlikely to gain support for many years into the future.

ENDNOTES

1. One useful reference is Buergentahl, Shelton, Stewart and Vazquez, *International Human Rights in a Nutshell* (West, 5th ed. 2018).

2. Currently, 169 States are party to the ICCPR (six others have signed but not yet ratified, but not Oman, Qatar, Saudi Arabia or the UAE); 166 States are party to the ICESCR and four others (including the United States) have signed but not yet ratified (not Oman, Qatar, Saudi Arabia or the UAE).

3. In the region, only Iran has not ratified the Racial Discrimination Convention.

4. CEDAW has 189 States Party, not including Somalia.

5. The Torture Convention has 162 States Parties, not including Iran or Oman.

6. The United States is the only State not to have ratified the Rights of the Child Convention.

7. Algeria, Egypt, Libya, Morocco, and Syria are among the 51 States Parties to the Migrant Workers Convention.

8. "At the origin of terrorism stands terror — instilled fear, dread, panic or mere anxiety — spread among those identifying, or sharing similarities, with the direct victims, generated by some of the modalities of the terrorist act — its shocking brutality, lack of discrimination, dramatic or symbolic quality and disregard of the rules of warfare and the rules of punishment…. [T]errorist violence is predominantly political — usually in its motivation but nearly always in its societal repercussions [and] [t]he immediate intent of acts of terrorism is to terrorize, intimidate, antagonize, disorientate, destabilize, coerce, compel, demoralize or provoke a target population or conflict partly in the hope of achieving from the resulting insecurity a favourable power outcome, e.g. obtaining publicity, extorting ransom money, submission to terrorist demands and/or mobilizing or immobilizing sectors of the public." A.P. Schmid (ed.), *Handbook of Terrorism Research* (Routledge 2011) at 86-87.

9. *Joint Publication 1-02: Department of Defense Dictionary of Military and Associated Terms* (amended through 15 June 2015), available at https://www.hsdl.org/?view&did=750658. See also NATO defines terrorism in the AAP-06 NATO Glossary of Terms and Definitions, Edition 2014 as "The unlawful use or threatened use of force or violence against individuals or property in an attempt to coerce or intimidate governments or societies to achieve political, religious or ideological objectives."

10. 22 U.S.C. § 2656f(d).

11. 18 U.S.C. § 1331(1).

12. See, e.g., para. 3, UNGA Res. 49/60 (Measures to eliminate international terrorism), Dec. 8, 1994), which referred to "[c]riminal acts intended or calculated to provoke a state of terror in the general public, a group of persons or particular persons for political purposes are in any circumstance unjustifiable, whatever the considerations of a political, philosophical, ideological, racial, ethnic, religious or any other nature that may be invoked to justify them"; see also para. 3 of UNSC Res 1566 (2004), recalling that "criminal acts, including against civilians, committed with the intent to cause death or serious bodily injury, or taking of hostages, with the purpose to provoke a state of terror in the general public or in a group of persons or particular persons, intimidate a population or compel a government or an international organization to do or to abstain from doing any act, which constitute offences within the scope of and as defined in the international conventions and protocols relating to terrorism, are under no circumstances justifiable by considerations of a political, philosophical, ideological, racial, ethnic, religious or other similar nature, and calls upon all States to prevent such acts and, if not prevented, to ensure that such acts are punished by penalties consistent with their grave nature."

13. *Interlocutory Decision on the Applicable Law: Terrorism, Conspiracy, Homicide, Perpetration, Cumulative Charging, Case No. STL-11-01/I* (Feb. 16, 2011), para. 85, available at https://www.stl-tsl.org/en/the-cases/stl-11-01/main/filings/orders-and-decisions/appeals-chamber/534-f0936.

14. Article 2(c).

15. Organization of the Islamic Conference, Convention of the Organization of the Islamic Conference on Combating International Terrorism, 1 July 1999, Annex to Resolution No: 59/26-P], art. 3: "In the implementation of the provisions of this Convention the following crimes shall not be considered political crimes even when politically motivated: (1) Aggression against kings and heads of state of Contracting States or against their spouses, their ascendants

or descendants. (2). Aggression against crown princes or vice-presidents or deputy heads of government or ministers in any of the Contracting States. (3). Aggression against persons enjoying international immunity including Ambassadors and diplomats in Contracting States or in countries of accreditation (4). Murder or robbery by force against individuals or authorities or means of transport and communications. (5). Acts of sabotage and destruction of public properties and properties geared for public services, even if belonging to another Contracting State. (6). Crimes of manufacturing, smuggling or possessing arms and ammunition or explosives or other materials prepared for committing terrorist crimes.

16. Among "Middle Eastern" States, only three have not ratified this treaty: Lebanon, Iran and Somalia (although Somalia has signed it).

17. AG/RES. 1840 (XXXII-O/02).

18. ETS 196, Warsaw, May 16, 2005.

19. Consider, for example, the Tokyo Aircraft Convention (186 States Party but not Somalia); the 1989 Hostages Convention (176 States Parties but not Somalia or Syria); the 1991 Plastic Explosives Convention (155 States Party, but not Comoros, Iran or Syria); the 1997 Terrorist Bombing Convention (170 States Party, but not Iran, Jordan, Lebanon, Oman, Somalia or Syria); the 2005 Nuclear Terrorism Convention (112 States Parties but not Iran, Oman or Syria — Egypt, Mauritius and Syria have signed but not ratified).

20. A thorough and thoughtful examination of these issues can be found in Manfred Nowak and Anne Crawford, *Using Human Rights to Counter Terrorism* (Elgar April 2018); see also *Human Rights, Terrorism and Counter-Terrorism: Fact Sheet No. 32*, Office of the UN High Commissioner for Human Rights (July 2008).

21. UNSC Res. 2396, preamb. paras 2-4 (Dec. 21, 2017).

22. Albert Bandura, "Selective Moral Disengagement In the Exercise of Moral Agency," *Journal of Moral Education*, Vol. 31, No. 2, 2002, cited in Coffee, "What Motivates Terrorists," *The Atlantic*, June 9, 2015, available at https://www.theatlantic.com/international/archive/2015/06/terrorism-isis-motive/395351.

23. Annexed Plan of Action, Part IV, UNGA Res 60/288 (Sept. 20, 2006) ("The United Nations Global Counter-Terrorism Strategy).

24. UNGA Res 63/185, preamb. paras. 2 and 7 (March 3, 2009) ("Protection of human rights and fundamental freedoms while countering terrorism")

25. UNSC Res. 2396, preamb. paras. 7 and 8 (Dec. 21, 2017).

26. See http://www.un.org/en/sc/ctc/rights.html.

27. UNGA Res. 71/291 (June 15, 2017) ("Strengthening the capability of the United Nations system").

28. See Promotion and protection of human rights and fundamental freedoms while countering terrorism, UN General Assembly Seventy-second session Item 73 (b) of the provisional agenda, September 27, 2017, A/72/43280.

29. European Parliament decision of July 6, 2017, on setting up a special committee on terrorism, its responsibilities, numerical strength and term of office. 2017/2758(RSO), P8_TA-PROV-(2017)0307.

30. Available at www.osce.org/odihr/29103?download=true.

31. Technically, a refugee is not the same as an "asylum-seeker," i.e., someone whose claim has not yet been definitively evaluated. In the case of mass refugee movements (usually a result of conflict), the reasons for fleeing are evident and there is no capacity to conduct individual interviews, such groups are often declared prima facie refugees. In U.S. law, the same legal standard is applied to those outside the country who seek admission to the U.S. as "refugees" and those in the country who seek to remain under the "asylum" provisions of our immigration law.

32. Art. 1F, 1951 Convention.

33. If a person has already been granted refugee status under the 1951 Convention, such status may be cancelled if there are grounds for considering that the person should not have been recognized as a refugee in the first place. This is the case where there are indications that, at the time of the initial decision, the applicant did not meet the inclusion criteria of the 1951 Convention, or that an exclusion clause of that Convention should have been applied to him or her (i.e., if the individual committed terrorist acts).

34. Art. 33(1). The Convention does, however, contemplates the possibility of expulsion to a third country on national security grounds under article 32.

35. UNSC Res. 1373 (Sept. 28, 2001), paras 3(f) and (g).

36. See Summary of Judgment, Prosecutor v. General Stanislav Galić. Dec. 5, 2003, available at http://www.icty.org/x/cases/galic/tjug/en/031205_Gali_summary_en.pdf, and the Judgement of the ICTY Trial Chamber, at http://www.icty.org/x/cases/galic/tjug/en/gal-tj031205e.pdf.

37. See, e.g., the report of a Spanish proposal, Apr. 14. 2015, at https://www.thelocal.es/20150414/spain-to-propose-that-un-set-up-terrorism-court, and a related Romanian initiative, Apr. 16, 2015, at http://www.mae.ro/en/node/31628.

38. UNSC Res. 1373 (Sept. 28 2001).

39. Legality of the Threat or Use of Nuclear Weapons, Advisory Opinion, July 8, 1996, ICJ Rep. 1996, para. 40.

Chapter Thirteen

Postscript

Charles Lister, Paul Salem

The scourge of terrorism looks set to be a persistent feature of 21st century reality. In a hyper-connected world and one in which alienation, information and misinformation, and the ability to disrupt abound, violent radical individuals and groups will continue to be a political and security challenge for societies and states. But in the Middle East, once fringe radicals have been able to build large-scale transnational armed movements, seize territories the size of nation states, and threaten the regional and international state order. This volume has tried to examine and understand the drivers and conditions that have enabled the rise of large terrorist groups in the Middle

East and to suggest ways forward.

The war on terror, launched after the events of September 11, 2001, has won many battles but the war itself is being lost. There are more terrorists in more countries today than when it started in 2001. Indeed, the dynamics of the war on terror, designed for short-term victories, have within them the generators for long-term failure. First, leading almost exclusively with the weapons of war escalates the general level of armed conflict and has broadened the arc of instability in the wider Middle East. The U.S. counter-terrorism mission has now spread to encompass operations in 80 countries around the world. Second, leaning on partner states to beef up their internal security structures, while necessary in finding and stopping terrorists, also encourages the creation of the conditions of political repression that generate radicalization and terrorists in the long run. The overall structure of the war on terror gives rise to more instability and creates fertile conditions for the growth and spread of terrorists and terrorist groups.

Terrorist groups use extreme violence to further their political ends; in that sense, terrorism, like war, is a continuation of politics by other means. In fact, the major terrorist challenges faced in recent years have presented themselves in the form of large-scale insurgent movements driven primarily by locally-rooted dynamics. Any long-term strategy to roll back terrorism must include an understanding of the global, regional, and local/national conditions that have created this extreme instability and protracted conflict, and a broad and sustained strategy — integrating the tools of diplomacy, politics, socioeconomics, and security — to create more stable conditions and de-escalate conflicts.

Indeed, the problem of large-scale Islamist terrorism is likely to be with us for the next 20 to 40 years; so it might behoove us to look beyond the immediate, military-driven, "whack-a-mole" strategy, to the broader political, diplomatic, and socioeconomic policies that might make a difference in the long run. There will be no full resolution to this problem in the short run; so while maintaining necessary short-term policies, we must also consider the long-term strategy. Currently, policy favors short-term kinetic approaches of finding and whacking terrorist groups, but steps back from large-scale diplomacy and steps away from policies that would contribute to robust stabilization, reconstruction, and state building.

THREE TIERS

What we might sketch out in this postscript is a three-tiered approach to thinking about countering these large-scale terrorist groups and the mobilization of a minority ideology into a greater threat: Short term, medium term, and long term.

In the short term, there might be no clear alternative to the kinetic, military-heavy, direct action strategy to engage and defeat terrorist groups where and when they emerge. This involves direct military engagement on the ground as well as various lines of accompanying effort that include (a) interdicting financial flows, (b) interdicting fighter flows, and (c) blocking and countering online messaging. This strategy pursued by the U.S. as well as partners and adversaries in the region has generally dealt very significant blows to both al-Qaeda and ISIS. And it might need to continue as long as these and similar groups pose a large-scale risk. But this strategy of trying to defeat the phenomenon of terrorism has done little to mitigate or improve the underlying conditions that enabled and fueled the rise of these groups — and in many cases it has made them worse. The conditions and drivers need to be part of the medium- and long-term approaches to addressing the challenge.

The medium-term component of this strategy would need to focus on de-escalating or ending the key civil wars that have provided an arena for these groups. Iraq is perhaps over its recent civil wars, and although it faces many challenges, has a reasonable pathway to avoiding another collapse; of course, it would need able leadership and robust support from the international community. The civil wars in Yemen and Libya are not unresolvable; indeed, peace talks at the end of 2018 showed progress in both cases, and robust international and regional effort in 2019 could help encourage parties in both countries to reach agreements to end the conflict; the challenge then would be to marshal regional and international political and economic support to these collapsed states so that they can move forward on the road to rebuilding state capacity. In Syria, the challenge is different; the Assad regime has survived and looks set to regain control over most of its territory, and rebuild its relations with the Arab states and a significant portion of the international community. On the one hand, a resurgent Assad state, with support from significant regional and international players, could regain fairly effective control over its territory and could prevent the re-emergence of major terrorist groups. On the other hand, because the Syrian war is ending without any political settlement, the risk of further rebellion and radicalization down the road will persist. The Afghan civil war is the one that seems to be on no pathway to ending. While the U.S. is likely to reduce its presence, it and other allies are not likely to abandon the Afghan government in the immediate future; neither side is able to win, nor are talks between the government and the Taliban likely to bear fruit. Of course, efforts to find a negotiated solution there need to continue, but the Afghan war might remain an open conflict for the foreseeable future.

The long-term component relates to creating a more stable and functional regional order in the Middle East. This has three aspects: The first is de-escalating regional proxy conflict and working toward an inclusive regional political and security architecture; the second is working with states to strengthen their national institutions and sovereignty capacities while at the same time encouraging them to grow domestic political and participation space; the third is enabling and investing in economic infrastructure and job creation to create the socioeconomic conditions that rising generations need. The long-term strategy might stretch out for many years, or a few decades, but the problem of terrorism is not going to go away in the short or medium terms, and hence having a long-term strategy is both necessary and possible. War is the continuation of politics by other means; and terrorism, as an extreme variant of war, is no different. Until the region moves toward a more functional and stable political order — both within nation states and as a regional order — the risk of radical armed insurgency will remain a large one.

Building a stable and inclusive regional order requires policy changes at both the global and regional levels. It was the Soviet Union's invasion of Afghanistan — and the American response — that helped create the conditions of today's Afghanistan in which terrorist groups have thrived. And it was the U.S.-led invasion of Iraq that helped create the conditions there. Building a more stable Middle East will require not only restraint from global powers, but ideally a common recognition among them that a stable Middle East is in their joint interest and to limit their competition to the political and economic spheres, while helping create and maintain a stable and inclusive regional order.

There are currently three main obstacles to establishing a stable and inclusive regional order in the Middle East. The first is the conflict system that dates back to 1979, between Iran on the one hand, and three sets of adversaries on the other: (a) Saudi Arabia and a number of Sunni Arab states; (b) Israel; and (c) the U.S. This broad conflict system drives Shi'a and Sunni armed radicalization, fuels conflict in Afghanistan, Iraq, Syria, Yemen, Lebanon, and Gaza, and is the single biggest contributor to the flows and conditions that enable and favor large-scale terrorist groups. Grappling with this Iranian challenge will not be easy; while it requires a robust push back that raises the costs for Iranian adventurism, it also requires a robust and forward-leaning diplomatic strategy that reaches out to Tehran, and to the Iranian public, and reassures them that the region and the world seek normal and positive relations and are ready to respect their legitimate national security defense concerns, in return for Iran changing its foreign policy of asymmetric intervention and accepting to play by the rules of interstate relations. Such a strategy has not yet been tried. The Arab states have felt too insecure to try it alone. President Barack Obama tried a sequential strategy, hoping that progress on nuclear issues would lay the groundwork for progress in other areas; but Iran ended up greatly escalating its military presence in the Arab region. Perhaps a Clinton presidency could have tested the way forward with Iran in this arena, but the Trump presidency sent the dynamic lurching in the opposite direction. Donald Trump has greatly escalated the conflict with Iran, which has intensified tensions in the region; and he has said that he seeks a wider agreement with Iran, but his confrontational and maximalist style — which might bear fruit with North Korea — has made talks with Tehran in the near term much less likely. In the meantime, the hardliners have gained ground in Tehran, playing off Trump, and have doubled down on their policy — not very popular in Iran — of consolidating their paramilitary presence in Iraq, Syria, Lebanon, and Yemen. Sooner or later a more proactive engagement with Iran — both tough and politically forward leaning — will have to be undertaken.

The second obstacle to a regional order is a recent split among the Sunni states. This has broken the only reasonably successful experiment in sub regional cooperation, the Gulf Cooperation Council, and has also pitted the two biggest Sunni states, Turkey and Egypt, against each other. It is the main regional driver preventing a negotiated end to the Libyan civil war. Stabilizing Libya and rebuilding state sovereignty there would be a great advance against terrorist groups in North Africa and help reduce their presence. This cold civil war within the Sunni world creates its own dynamics of radicalization and conflict; if resolved, it would help bring more stability to the region and less purchase for armed non-state actors.

The third obstacle relates to the Israel-Palestine conflict. Although Turkey and several Arab states have moved toward various forms of cooperation with Israel, the issues of Palestine and Jerusalem continue to animate radical groups around the region; and until there is a resolution to the Israel-Palestine issue that is accepted by the bulk of Palestinians, there can be no breakthrough to overall Israeli-Arab peace, and no integration of Israel into the region. And any long-term and stable regional security architecture will have to be inclusive not only of Iran and Turkey, but also of Israel.

Other regions, such as Europe and East Asia, have been able to find a pathway from long periods of ferocious intra-regional conflict to establishing regional co-existence and peace and building region-wide institutions, whether very ambitious such as the EU, or less restrictive such as ASEAN. It is not unrealistic — indeed, it is necessary — to find a pathway toward de-escalating the Middle East's intra-regional conflicts and working toward a stable and inclusive future regional order.

Building Middle Eastern states that are both strong in terms of security and sovereignty, and at the same time stable in the long term, in terms of allowing internal political expression and contestation, will be difficult. The current trend, both in terms of great power encouragement and local power preferences, is to prioritize security and top-down authority, at the expense of human rights, political participation, and possible pathways to democratization. With the recent illiberal turn in Europe and the US, and the rise of great authoritarian powers like Russia and China, it is hard to see how this tide will turn. But rebuilding more repressive autocracies in the Middle East is not a pathway to long-term stability, but rather to eventual violent eruptions. Whether this realization will dawn on at least some regional leaders, or whether there will be renewed pressure down the road from a recovering West, is hard to say. But a Middle East of refurbished national prisons is not a recipe for defeating radicalization and violent extremism in the long term.

In terms of the third component of socioeconomic development, this too is a longer-term goal. Until civil wars are ended and basic state authority restored, it is hard to make significant progress in region-wide socioeconomic development. The first task will be to address the urgent needs of civil war countries that have lost decades of economic development and have had their social and economic infrastructures devastated. This will require concerted and coordinated effort between wealthy regional players on the one hand, and wealthy global players from Asia and the West on the other. Reconstruction, repatriation of refugees, and just regaining lost decades in key Middle Eastern countries, will in itself create necessary economic momentum and millions of jobs for individuals who might otherwise drift toward the ideological and financial temptations of radical groups. But in the context of building a broader stable region, it is necessary that regional stabilization go hand in hand with regional economic integration. The wider Middle East is rich in capital, manpower, resources, and know-how; currently these various assets are locked up in warring nations or sub regions; a stable and integrated region could benefit from profound complementarity as well as significant economies of scale both in terms of production and consumption. An integrated Middle East would help create the millions of jobs that are needed — and not only in post-conflict reconstruction countries, but in other countries such as Egypt where large and young populations are crowding up against sluggish economies.

NEW THREATS, BUT THE SAME OLD TACTICS

Since the terrorist attacks that so spectacularly struck New York and Washington, DC on September 11, 2001, the terrorist threats faced by the United States and its allies have changed, but the tactics and strategies adopted to neutralize those threats have remained largely the same. Although substantial improvements have been made in the fields of countering terrorist finance (CTF); intelligence collection, sharing, and border security; data collection and online monitoring; and signals intelligence, electronic intelligence, and cybersecurity, efforts to counter terrorism remain heavily dependent on military means, the effects of which often undermine other methods and approaches.

On paper, actions taken under the guise of countering terrorism over the past two decades, whether in Afghanistan, Pakistan, Iraq, Yemen, Syria, North Africa and the Sahel, or elsewhere, have achieved the key desired objective: An immediate reduction in the terror threat emanating from the area in question. In practice however, most of these actions or responses have been tactical in nature; securing short-term military victories at the expense of, or in isolation from, any long-term effort to prevent the recurrence of the very same threats. What has resulted, therefore, is a dynamic of strategic stagnation in which counter-terrorist actors successively fail to "win the peace," and grant terrorists the potential opportunity to adapt and fight another day.

Perhaps most significantly, the onset of the so-called Arab Spring in 2010 and 2011 and the wave of instability that followed provided terrorist organizations with an opportunity to harness, embed within, or simply exploit a wave of change and chaos to become part of something bigger. The breakdown of states; the crumbling away of any semblance of good governance; the spread of dictatorial rule and repression of fundamental rights; and the proliferation of alternative political and religious visions all combined to provide an environment ripe for terrorist organizations seeking to grow and compete with regional regimes. Soon, terrorist groups that had previously operated largely in isolation from geopolitical dynamics surrounding them became an intrinsic part of those geopolitical dynamics. In some cases, they even defined them, and in most, these new platforms saw terrorist organizations transform into conventional insurgencies, thereby presenting their state adversaries with a qualitatively different challenge.

And yet despite this, the counter-terror response has been to continue to play "whack-a-mole," very effectively hitting threats and driving them back as they emerge, but failing almost entirely to address how and why they emerged in the first place. This state of affairs has been exacerbated further amid a political climate in the West in which sustaining a determined engagement to ameliorate the security crises of the Middle East has fallen deeply out of favor. Counter-terrorism policy in the U.S. had long been focused primarily on protecting the "homeland," but it has recently become even more so. Even despite gathering a multinational coalition of unprecedented size to counter ISIS in Iraq and Syria, the U.S. looks set to disengage from that fight prematurely and remains largely disinterested in the insurgency-focused and thus, locally-focused expansion of many other terrorist organizations across the region, despite the safe haven they inevitably offer to more globally interested terrorist actors.

This increasingly isolationist mindset that appears likely to shape foreign and security policy in regions like the Middle East also carries with it the risk of encouraging policymakers to consider more hasty, aggressive action to expedite "success." That appears to have been a factor in the Trump administration's early decision to delegate air strike targeting to the tactical level, thereby loosening — whether by design or not — the framework for limiting collateral damage. Civilian casualties caused by U.S.-led coalition airstrikes in Syria rose markedly after this decision, putting the durability of military gains made against ISIS at risk, post-U.S. withdrawal.

Amidst a proliferation of more complex terror threats, the 2018 U.S. National Security Strategy and National Defense Strategy both de-prioritized counter terrorism as a U.S. policy. One additional implication of this is an increasing emphasis on cost saving and burden sharing. Less capable, and in some cases, less interested allies are now expected to shoulder a heavier burden of responsibility to tackle terrorist threats at their origin, before they are given the chance to evolve into global threats or to prevent them from offering a safe haven to those plotting possible external attacks. Within this context of U.S. isolationism, the reliability of allies to achieve U.S. security interests remains unclear.

Although government resources remain a valuable commodity and political leaderships are understandably wary of making long-term commitments, launching multiple whack-a-mole campaigns, each operationally distinct from the other and detached almost entirely from any holistic strategy, appears certain to prove far more costly than a comprehensive strategy that combined short-, medium-, and long-term actions to seek more durable results. The expert community has long concluded that the terror threat is a multi-generational challenge, and successive political leaderships have acknowledged that fact, but the strategies developed to counter terrorism have consistently failed to embrace a sustainable design.

The chapters contained in this volume each make in their respective contexts the argument that it is primarily the underlying causes and drivers of instability that fuel the phenomenon of extremism and insurgency. While there is a clear need to develop tailor-made strategies for unique terror threats — to avoid embracing a one-size-fits-all philosophy — the core element missing is an underpinning framework that acknowledges that terrorism and terroristic insurgencies do not operate in a vacuum. Until their facilitating environments are more dealt with in a more determined and sustainable fashion, the international community will continue to play expensive games of whack-a-mole that ultimately risk justifying terrorist narratives more than they undermine them.

Going forward, the U.S. and its allies must better develop and sustain a counter-terrorism strategy that is both holistic in how it views threats and their causes and seeks to treat them by simultaneously employing short-, medium-, and long-term measures. Active or potential external plots should be neutralized upon detection, using means that limit as much as possible any collateral damage and insulate such targeted kinetic actions from their broader contexts. Terrorist safe havens should not merely be left alone, and local alternative realities should be presented to compete in their place. In some cases, militarily challenging such terrorist-controlled territories may in fact be counterproductive and a strategy of containment and "let them rot" may hold more potential value. Sometimes, locally-focused terrorist movements are most vulnerable when faced by local political dilemmas, not external military attack. Groups like the Taliban in Afghanistan and Hayat Tahrir al-Sham in Syria could in fact be more durably weakened, or their most dangerous extremist tendencies better eroded, by challenging them socially and politically, rather than with the butt of a gun. When faced by a challenge like that posed by ISIS in 2014, a strategic military response may well be required, but it should be underpinned by an even more significant effort focused on aid, development, reconstruction, reconciliation, good governance, and local de-radicalization initiatives.

As a constant, independent of the threat picture, the U.S. and its allies should sustain a more cohesive multilateral CTF effort. As terrorist groups increasingly seek to control territory and govern populations to compete with nation states, access to substantial financing and the ability to move money will prove existentially important and their most significant weakness. According to a 2015 study by the Financial Action Task Force, two-thirds of countries with developed CTF frameworks were in fact failing to properly implement them. Restricting terrorists' use of international financial networks is key, but so is acquiring and maintaining a detailed understanding of informal infrastructures, like the hawala system, exploiting human intelligence sources on the ground.

The U.S. and its allies also need to better grasp the value of countering violent extremism (CVE) efforts, specifically those that are locally-based, driven, and managed. Much thought and a great deal of money has been expended on CVE in recent years, but all too much of it has focused on the internet and in responding to extremist messaging rather than pre-empting or competing with it using genuine and credible alternative narratives. Terrorism would exist in a shadow of its current form if it were not for the largely unchallenged existence of potent ideologies, and yet U.S. budgetary allowances for CVE activities pale in comparison to resources devoted to counter terrorism — at roughly 0.01%. Moreover, the valuable work that is done on countering terrorists' use of the internet for propaganda purposes remains driven primarily by reaction. In most cases, we look to our adversaries like we are responding to events rather than running our own strategic counter-effort. In fact, the U.S. has not written an actual strategy to combat terrorists' use of the internet since 2007, years before the emergence of some of the most valuable platforms for spreading terrorist materials (like Telegram, for example).

Underpinning the need for improvements in specific aspects of counter-terrorism and CVE policy, the U.S. needs not only to more honestly acknowledge the generational challenges we face, but also to translate that acknowledgement into a truly strategic, holistic vision for how best to compete with extremist ideologies; to counter dangerous terrorists; and to more determinedly and sustainably remove the deep-seated underlying causes and drivers that look set to fuel extremism and terrorism for many years to come. It is not enough to pursue a containment strategy defined in large part by kinetic military action. Doing so means we are only kicking the can down the road, while that can grows in size over time. Each kick will require a little more effort and cost a little more. Kinetic and non-kinetic efforts must be better synthesized, each seeking to empower the other, rather than vice-versa.

Above all else, truly effective and sustainable counter-terrorism and CVE policies abroad should be composed of activities that many would not ordinarily associate with those labels. The unprecedented increase in terrorist activities in the Middle East in recent years has been directly correlated with the region's collapse into instability. The erosion of good governance; the rise of autocratic rule; rife corruption; geopolitical tensions and sectarian narratives; weak economies and widespread poverty; and high unemployment and resource mismanagement are just some of the root issues that require treatment. If the U.S. wants to avoid having to continue to successively step into crises to protect its security interests, political leaders must acknowledge that the root causes of the terrorism and extremism challenge in the region are deep seated and require a consistently implemented long-term strategy. Withdrawing from the region and falling back on unelected monarchies and dictatorial leaders to strong-arm their populations into subservience will not result in long-term stability. In fact, that scenario is precisely what terrorist organizations have long sought to create.

About the Middle East Institute

www.ingramcontent.com/pod-product-compliance
Lightning Source LLC
Chambersburg PA
CBHW051437250726
48655CB00001B/111